THEOLOGY AND C

M000219773

To

Joseph T. (1932–99) and Barbara Ann Sexton

Gary D. and Lynn Sexton

Paul J. and Wendy K. Dixon

who came out to work, have better lives, and found strange things in this

extraordinary place.

To my parents

Fred E. Sanders (1940–98) and Carol Lee Hedrick

who came out West, looked around for about 15 years, and went back home.

Theology and California

Theological Refractions on California's Culture

Edited by

FRED SANDERS
Biola University, California, USA

JASON S. SEXTON
California State University, Fullerton, USA

ASHGATE

Published by
Ashgate Publishing Limited
Wey Court East
Union Road
Farnham
Surrey, GU9 7PT
England

Ashgate Publishing Company
110 Cherry Street
Suite 3-1
Burlington, VT 05401-3818
USA

www.ashgate.com

British Library Cataloguing in Publication Data
A catalogue record for this book is available from the British Library

The Library of Congress has cataloged the printed edition as follows:
Theology and California : theological refractions on California's culture / edited by Fred Sanders and Jason S. Sexton.
    pages cm
Includes bibliographical references and index.
    ISBN 978-1-4724-0946-1 (hardcover : alk. paper) -- ISBN 978-1-4724-0947-8 (pbk. : alk. paper) -- ISBN 978-1-4724-0948-5 (ebook) -- ISBN 978-1-4724-0949-2 (epub) 1. Christianity and culture--California. 2. Theology--California. 3. California--Civilization--21st century. I. Sanders, Fred (Fred R.), editor.
    BR115.C8T4735 2014
    261.09794--dc23

                                                              2014006021

ISBN 978-1-4724-0946-1 (hbk)
ISBN 978-1-4724-0947-8 (pbk)
ISBN 978-1-4724-0948-5 (ebk – PDF)
ISBN 978-1-4724-0949-2 (ebk _ ePUB)

Printed in the United Kingdom by Henry Ling Limited,
at the Dorset Press, Dorchester, DT1 1HD

Providential thinking clearly shapes ideas about California. Does the opposite also take place? Does California shape religion and theology too? Is there perhaps a unique California theology, call it Californianity? In a state where religious adherence is increasing rather than declining—unlike the rest of the country— these questions have an unexpected purchase. And the theologians and scholars in this volume, following Josiah Royce's call for a "higher provincialism," bring welcome new light to the connections between place and faith.
Jon Christensen, Editor: *Boom: A Journal of California*

Theology is faith seeking understanding—yes, but of California? As a theologian and native Californian, I am delighted to recommend this collection of essays that seek to understand the spirit of the place that shaped my childhood (and millions of others), and how the Holy Spirit may be active in that place. The Church, after all, is always local, and a theology of California will undoubtedly serve Christ's body in California by fostering understanding and enabling her to continue her ongoing mission of witnessing both to the lordship of Jesus Christ over all things and to the renewal of all things in Christ.
Kevin J. Vanhoozer, Trinity Evangelical Divinity School, USA

This volume is an ambitious undertaking to bring theology into the conversation of California—what it was, what it is, and what it will become. To the degree that co-editors Sanders and Sexton have raised pertinent questions to interrogate our state's spiritual situation, as well as have offered clear examples of Californian theological reflection, they have succeeded admirably. Theology and California *is an excellent launching point for further theological work about California and the diversity of Californian experiences. It heads us in the right direction by asking the right questions.*
Russell M. Jeung, San Francisco State University

Arranged to encourage debate and discussion, their organization of the material drives their theme from the start with a series of poignant efforts to clarify the meaning of California as a theological subject, followed by a solid core of empirical contributions that extend from the historic role of the California missions to the theological efficacy of California's persisting surf culture and the theological implications of Silicon Valley's innovation proclivities. Ending with instructive speculations by a theologian, sociologist and historian on the book's overriding motifs, Theology and California *squarely puts its concerns on the academic and cultural map.*
Josef Chytry, University of California, Berkeley and California College of the Arts, USA

Contents

Notes on Contributors   ix
Foreword by Brian Brock   xiii
Preface   xv

Introduction   1
Jason S. Sexton

PART I   APPROACHING CALIFORNIA'S CULTURE
            THEOLOGICALLY

1   The Enigma of California: Reflections on a Theological Subject   9
       Richard J. Mouw

2   California, Localized Theology, and Theological Localism   19
       Fred Sanders

3   Can Theology Engage with California's Culture?   35
       Jason S. Sexton

PART II   CALIFORNIA'S CULTURE IN ECCLESIAL PERSPECTIVE

4   The Significance of the California Missions in
       Californian Theology and Culture   71
       Allen Yeh

5   "I Have Adonis DNA": Californian Entertainment,
       Celebrity Culture, and Evangelicalism   99
       Monica Ganas

6   In Pursuit of the Consumer Crown or the Crucified Crown?   113
       Matthew S. Farlow

PART III   CALIFORNIA'S CULTURE IN
            THEOLOGICAL PERSPECTIVE

7   From The Beach Boys to Surfer's Chapel: A Theology of
     California Surf Culture   139
     Robert S. Covolo

8   Silicon Valley and the Spirit of Innovation: How California's
     Entrepreneurial Ethos Bears Witness to Spiritual Reality   163
     Bruce Baker

9   Drive-By Evangelism, the Growth in Gang Violence and
     Community Development   189
     Paul Louis Metzger

PART IV   IS THERE A THEOLOGY OF CALIFORNIA?

10   Is There a Theology of California?   219
     Fred Sanders

11   Is There a Theology of California? A Sociologist's Response 229
     Richard Flory

12   Is There a Theology of California? An Historian's Response   239
     Richard Pointer

Selected Bibliography   *247*
Index   *255*

Notes on Contributors

Bruce Baker is Assistant Professor of Business Ethics at Seattle Pacific University's School of Business and Economics. Growing up in Los Angeles, he earned the BS in Physics from California Institute of Technology, and the MBA from Stanford. His research explores the intersection of the modern moral imaginary with today's business-driven culture. He was for many years in business management and scientific innovation: he co-founded Four Pi Systems Corporation in 1986; earned five patents for his inventions in X-ray physics, computer software, and machine vision; and was a general manager at Microsoft before earning the PhD in theology from the University of St Andrews.

Brian Brock has degrees in Medical Ethics (Loma Linda University), Christian Ethics (King's College, London) and Theology (Oxford University) and is Reader in Moral and Practical Theology at the University of Aberdeen. He is an advisor to the TECC Project and author of *Singing the Ethos of God: On the Place of Christian Ethics in Scripture* (Eerdmans, 2007) and *Christian Ethics in a Technological Age* (Eerdmans, 2010), and editor of *Theology, Disability and the New Genetics: Why Science Needs the Church* (T&T Clark, 2007) and *Disability in the Christian Tradition: A Reader* (Eerdmans, 2012), both with John Swinton.

Robert S. Covolo is a surfer, native Californian and dual doctoral candidate in Theology and Culture at Fuller Theological Seminary and the Vrije Universiteit Amsterdam, exploring the relationship between theology and the emerging discipline of fashion theory. He has contributed to a number of scholarly publications including *Cultural Encounters, European Journal of Theology, Journal of Reformed Theology* and *The International Journal of Public Theology*.

Matthew S. Farlow holds the BA from University of California, Davis in English and History, holds a California Professional Teaching Credential, and a PhD from the University of St Andrews. He has served as lecturer in Ethics at the University of St Andrews, and has taught adjunct at William Jessup University in Rocklin, California, while serving on pastoral staff at a megachurch in Folsom. He has recently become Associate Pastor of Grace Church of Mahomet (Illinois) where he serves as chaplain for the University of Illinois wrestling team.

Richard Flory is Research Scientist and and Director of Research in the Center for Religion and Civic Culture at the University of Southern California. He holds the PhD from the University of Chicago, is an advisor to the TECC Project and is author/editor of *Spirit and Power: The Growth and Global Impact of Pentecostalism* (Oxford University Press, 2013), *Growing up in America: The Power of Race in the Lives of Teens* (Stanford University Press, 2010), *Finding Faith: The Spiritual Quest of the Post-Boomer Generation* (Rutgers University Press, 2008) and *GenX Religion* (Routledge, 2000). His current research is focused on several projects that investigate the role of religion and religious institutions in Los Angeles, including an investigation of the civic role of faith-based organizations in Los Angeles since the 1992 civil unrest, an ethnographic study of the Los Angeles Dream Center, a large-scale Pentecostal social outreach ministry, and a project on religious competition in Southern California.

Monica Ganas is Professor of the Department of Theater, Film, and Television at Azusa Pacific University and a 30-year-veteran of the entertainment industry, performing principally in satirical comedy as an actor, writer, and occasional producer/director. Her primary interests are in popular culture, film, television, and other media, as well as theater, community development, and communication for social change. She serves on the organizational boards of the City of Angels Film Festival and Reel Spirituality. She graduated from San Francisco State University (BA, MA) and holds the PhD from the University of Kentucky, and has authored *Under the Influence: California's Intoxicating Spiritual and Cultural Impact on America* (Brazos Press, 2010).

Paul Louis Metzger is Professor of Christian Theology and Theology of Culture and Director of The Institute for the Theology of Culture: New Wine, New Wineskins, Multnomah Biblical Seminary of Multnomah University. He holds the PhD from King's College, London and has published *The Word of Christ and the World of Culture: Sacred and Secular through the Theology of Karl Barth* (Eerdmans, 2003); *Consuming Jesus: Beyond Race and Class Divisions in a Consumer Church* (Eerdmans, 2007); *New Wine Tastings: Theological Essays of Cultural Engagement* (Cascade, 2011); *A World for All? Global Civil Society in Political Theory and Trinitarian Theology* (co-edited with William F. Storrar and

Peter J. Casarella; Eerdmans, 2011), and *Connecting Christ: How to Discuss Jesus in a World of Diverse Paths* (Thomas Nelson, 2012). He has keen interest in the writings of John Steinbeck, and with his wife Mariko, a native of Japan, has been active in intercultural ministry in churches in the US, Japan, and England. He is an advisor to the TECC Project.

Richard J. Mouw was President of Fuller Theological Seminary (1993–2013). He holds the PhD in philosophy from the University of Chicago, served as editor of the *Reformed Journal* and is on the editorial board *Books and Culture*. He is the author of many books, including *He Shines in All That's Fair: Culture and Common Grace* (Eerdmans, 2002), *Calvinism in the Las Vegas Airport* (Zondervan, 2004), *Praying at Burger King* (Eerdmans, 2007), *Uncommon Decency: Christian Civility in an Uncivil World (rev., InterVarsity Press, 2010), Abraham Kuyper: A Short and Personal Introduction* (Eerdmans, 2011) and with Doug Sweeney, *The Suffering and Victorious Christ: Toward a More Compassionate Christology* (Baker, 2013). Mouw serves as a panelist in the online forum "On Faith," by the *Washington Post*. He has participated on many councils and boards, and recently served as president of the Association of Theological Schools (ATS).

Richard Pointer is Professor of History and holds the Fletcher Jones Foundation Chair in the Social Sciences at Westmont College. He earned the PhD at Johns Hopkins University. His research on colonial New York culminated in *Protestant Pluralism and the New York Experience: A Study of Eighteenth Century Religious Diversities* (Indiana University Press, 1988), and he also published *Encounters of the Spirit: Native Americans and European Colonial Religion* (Indiana University Press, 2007). He has published essays in *The New England Quarterly* and the *Pennsylvania Magazine of History and Biography*, along with an award-winning article in *New York History*. He has served as the president and vice-president of The Conference on Faith and History and as an associate editor for the *Christian Scholar's Review*, and is a core member of the TECC Project.

Fred Sanders is Professor of Theology in Biola University's great books program, the Torrey Honors Institute, and is a Faculty member for the Los Angeles Bible Training School. An evangelical Protestant theologian with a passion for the great tradition of Christian thought, he holds a degree in art from Murray State University, an MDiv from Asbury Theological Seminary (Kentucky), and upon moving back to California earned a PhD from the Graduate Theological Union

(Berkeley). He has published *The Image of the Immanent Trinity: Rahner's Rule and the Theological Interpretation of Scripture* (Peter Lang, 2005), *The Deep Things of God: How the Trinity Changes Everything* (Crossway, 2010), and *Wesley on the Christian Life: The Heart Renewed in Love* (Crossway, 2013), and is writing a book on the doctrine of the Trinity for Zondervan Academic. He is also the Co-Convener and a core member of the TECC Project.

Jason S. Sexton is a fourth generation Californian who taught theology in Cambridge while a visiting scholar at Ridley Hall. He is currently a Research Associate at USC's Center for Religion and Civic Culture, is a lecturer in the Honors Department at California State University, Fullerton, and is the Administrative Convener of the TECC Project. Ordained with the Evangelical Free Church of America, he has been a pastor and church planter in Central and Southern California. He earned a PhD in 2012 at the University of St Andrews and has published *The Trinitarian Theology of Stanley J. Grenz* (T&T Clark, 2013). He is editor of *Two Views on the Doctrine of the Trinity* (Zondervan, 2014), is reviews editor of the "mission & culture" section of *Themelios*, and a contributing editor of *Marginalia*, a *Los Angeles Review of Books* Channel (marginalia.lareviewofbooks.org).

Allen Yeh graduated from Yale and earned the DPhil at the University of Oxford. He is a missiologist who specializes in Latin America and China. He also has other academic interests in history, classical music, homiletics, social justice, the California missions, the Maya, Jonathan Edwards (America's greatest theologian) and Adoniram Judson (America's first intercontinental missionary). He serves on the Board of Directors for American Baptist International Ministries. He has been to over 50 countries in every continent, to study, do missions work, and experience the culture. He has contributed to the books, *Missions in Polycentric Dimensions: Essays in Global Theology in Honor of Tite Tienou, Routes and Radishes: and Other Things to Talk About at the Evangelical Crossroads* (Zondervan, 2010), and "Contextualization and the Chinese Term Controversy," in Kenneth R. Ross (ed.), *Edinburgh 2010: Fresh Perspectives on Christian Mission* (Pasadena: William Carey International University Press, 2010).

Foreword

Brian Brock

This book heralds an exciting new development in contemporary theology, theological ethics and cultural engagement. Its originality is thrown into stark relief when we notice what it is not. It is not one of the versions of theological engagement in which an attempt is made to apply theological truths to local contexts. Instead, it approaches theology explicitly and in a critically self-aware manner from within, and in engagement with, a local context. Though theology is always written within some local context, academic theology, ethics and cultural criticism have all too often proceeded as if it was best to hide the influence of local questions on the theology being written.

Nor do the authors of this volume engage with local contexts as occasions to promote some supposedly universal linkage of theology and social scientific study. Such a "mining" of local contexts to make academic points all too often characterizes not only social scientific studies of churches, but also attempts of academic theologians to find plausible methods for hitching theology and the social sciences as we see, for instance, in contemporary disputes about ecclesiology and ethnography.

We have here theology which begins from the refreshing admission that theology must be done by a living church, and must be done out of and as an address to living people. People, theologians have been slow to notice, live in places, and are not well addressed if the role of their place in their self-understanding is ignored. In this case the place in question is California, almost certainly the region of the United States that has the most cultural influence over developments in American popular culture(s). This is not to suggest that the authors in this volume have come to agreement yet on some crucial methodological questions. But they have embarked on a sustained inquiry into the difference it might make to do theology *in* California, or a theology *of* California, versus perhaps a theology which engages or speaks in the *voice* or *voices* of *Californians* (as Fred Sanders nicely puts it in this volume).

It is an inquiry that raises questions worthy of a Christianity which seriously asks, "To whom am I a neighbor?" In it we can see the coming of age of contemporary American Protestant evangelical Christianity which, having seen the futility of reducing its understanding of the mission of the church to apologetics and cultural naysaying, is returning with renewed confidence and vigor to try to show more explicitly how Christianity matters today in the lives of believers and non-believers alike. We see theologians doing so here not by refuting other "world views" but by displaying the critical insight and socially generative vision that can be expected from Christians who, out of love of people in specific places, ask what light the creating and redeeming work of the trinitarian God sheds on lives in one concrete culture—one which, ironically, is especially marked by the yearning to transcend mere locality. It is a promising place to begin once again where theology always must: trying to understand its confession before God and the neighbors God has given us to love.

Preface

The northern part of the state has an expansive river system formed by the convergence of the Sacramento River (flowing from Mt Shasta) with the San Joaquin River (flowing from the Sierra Nevada mountains) in the northern Central Valley just before the river enters Suisun Bay. As the fan-shaped area of this delta converges downstream the two rivers are forced to exit the Central Valley through the California coastal hill range and through the narrow channel known as the Carquinez Strait leading into the San Francisco Bay.

This book is like that Sacramento-San Joaquin River Delta, with two theologians, one senior and one junior, converging to form the expansive interdisciplinary, interinstitutional, international TECC Project, from which sprang a few meetings, a number of other collaborators, and finally this initial volume as the first published outing of the TECC Project efforts. But the TECC Project wouldn't be the same without the early assistance from a number of people, including David Bebbington for his idea of its interdisciplinary structure, Steve Holmes, Luke Bretherton, Michael Lindsay, Doug Sweeney, Rebecca Kim, Sarah Sumner, as well as the strong support from Rick Pointer, Barb Kennedy, Gayle Beebe, and Mark Sargent.

We are grateful for the enthusiastic support from Rich Mouw and the immense encouragement we received from Kevin and Sheila Starr. We owe a debt of thanks also to Howard Ahmanson, Steve Ferguson, and Fieldstead and Co. for their support of our 2013 workshop. Mike and Amy Shane have also provided helpful support for the work, as have Eric Miller, David Garza, Andy Fossett, Ted and Lorraine Bloemhof, The Foundation for the Advancement of Evangelical Theology in California, Bob and Muriel Hodel, and Grant and Cathy Olewiler. Joy Moore, Brian Brock, Oliver Crisp, David Nystrom, and especially Paul Metzger have been incredibly supportive.

We're grateful to the number of attendees of the 2011 event in San Francisco at the ETS meeting and those who participated in the more intimate 2013 workshop at the Berkeley City Club: Scot Sherman, Michael Barram, Jonathan St Clair, Jorge Mendoza, Russell Jeung, Charlie Farhadian, John Shouse, Bruce Baker, Matthew Farlow, Telford Work, and Po-Wei Chen. We are grateful to

Po-Wei Chen for his excellent work on this book's index, and also to Terry Scott Taylor and Mike Roe for helping us place some of our reflections on California and theology to music: it all seemed to make sense when we saw papa dancing on Olvera Street, the swallows flying over Capistrano Beach, and the Dodgers breaking the hearts of the Brooklyners. Monica Ganas and Bob Covolo lent courage and support by giving papers at our first gathering, and Justin Wilford read through portions of this manuscript.

Richard Flory has also been tremendously supportive, as have Don Miller, Brie Loskota, and Tim Sato at USC's CRCC. And whereas we have been privileged to have interested scholars from other disciplines join us in engaging theologians, we are grateful to Ed Blum and Lynne Gerber for inviting the theologians from the TECC Project onto their disciplinary turf to co-sponsor the 2014 meeting of the California American Studies Association on religion in California. And of course, Sarah Lloyd showed remarkable support for the project early on. We're grateful for her support of theology and its abilities to engage culture, even one as far out as California's.

Fred Sanders and Jason S. Sexton
Advent 2013
La Mirada, California

Introduction

Jason S. Sexton

While recently walking together with one of our state's leading historians on a sunny December afternoon down the University of Southern California's Trousdale Parkway, we both acknowledged that California is not difficult to problematize. Everyone knows this. It is the state consistently *on the edge*. And big problems are right at California's door. The best voices available, then, both new and old, should be active in addressing its major problems. And yet the place is not all problematic. It has held out unusual promises to ordinary people such that many people around the world continue to think on this place with an unusual wonder. North American universities are picking up on this by studying California literature as a theme, recognizing it as a place of hope, surprise, and cultural innovation. And people wonder why.

For quite some time theology has not been part of the broader discourse in the state, neither in the wider academy nor in the public square. And where theology has been present, in confessional institutions and in church communities, and often in less careful ways, it has not consciously been brought into conversation with California. In the present moment of its history, however, a door may be opening for theology to contribute to the good of California's citizens in ways it has not in a long time. California is, of course, the kind of place that is not far from requiring major help in interpreting the various shapes and lines that denote its vast and remarkable culture.

Each of the contributors of this volume has either lived and worked in this place, or else has participated in meaningful community efforts to serve ordinary Californian citizens. Yet each has also lived elsewhere, providing the right kind of critical distance and familiarity, enough detachment and interest, to offer insightful engagement in light of theological considerations offered from various theological perspectives.

This is the first book from our early efforts at exploring California as an explicitly *theological* place, rendering critical and constructive engagement not only with religious and theological phenomena within the state's life, but also with the theological impulses inherent within California cultural icons. Throughout, these essays provide varying degrees of empirical analysis along with critical theological reflection and assessment.

It represents the first installment of the Theological Engagement with California's Culture (TECC) Project's research, flowing from its inaugural session held in San Francisco at the annual meeting of the Evangelical Theological Society, November 16, 2011, and from a workshop held at the Berkeley City Club, March 10–12, 2013. It includes agenda setting essays exploring rationale behind the emphasis on theological engagement with California and methodological possibilities (Part I), as well as expert reflections on some of the state's most noteworthy ecclesial developments (Part II), and also the some of the most exciting and equally challenging cultural phenomena in California's recent history and present situation (Part III). And it aims to contribute new and interdisciplinary ways of thinking about California not reflected in earlier research (Part IV).

All contributors have been deeply shaped by and have reflected on California's various topographies and theologies, although not all are academic theologians. Along with systematic theologians present in this volume (Sanders, Sexton, Farlow, Covolo, Metzger) the book brings together interdisciplinary theological reflection from a philosopher (Mouw), a missiologist (Yeh), a communications theorist and former Hollywood actor (Ganas), a theological ethicist and former entrepreneur (Baker), along with the exchange in the book's final two chapters between a theologian (Sanders), a sociologist (Flory) and an historian (Pointer).

While the various contributors all agree that it is important for theology to exercise itself towards interpreting California, especially in interdisciplinary conversation and reflection (which is at the heart of the TECC Project), the authors here do not all agree on exactly how to do this, neither do they all utilize the exact same conceptual tools at every point. The essays in this volume also employ various quantitative and especially qualitative methodologies. But we're all convinced that robust theological reflection on place—this incredibly diverse and dynamic place of global representation[1]—matters a great deal and has been neglected far too long.

It should go without saying that every view taken in this book is not equally shared by the other contributors or the editors. There is a variety of ways that

---

[1]   See the recent argument made for California's position as a world civilization in Josef Chytry, *Mountain of Paradise: Reflections on the Emergence of Greater California as a World Civilization* (New York: Peter Lang, 2013).

theology (even if exclusively Christian theology) is represented in this book. Additional weaknesses in our approach might be that the theology represented here is not yet reflective of the variegated theologies throughout the state, even Christian ones—a point helpfully highlighted various places throughout the book and also in our earlier collaborative meetings and conversations. Nor can this volume (nor any subsequent volume) be comprehensive of the breadth and depth of the ecclesial or cultural realities identifiable in California's past, present, or future. We accept this, of course, acknowledging that our work has only just begun. And yet in spite of its shortcomings, we are pleased that it has come together at this juncture, seeking to bring theology into the conversations about California and its remarkable culture, attempting to make explicit what is implicit in this incredible place.

Part I: Approaching California's Culture Theologically

This first section offers a series of three methodological sketches for the future work of the TECC Project, beginning with Richard Mouw's chapter. This chapter begins by considering the special enigmatic nature of the state's dynamic and what it all might mean, negatively and positively from a senior statesman of Evangelicalism. Dispelling myths about theology's possibilities, it offers seasoned reflections on the providential care for this extraordinary and yet still quite ordinary place, and creatively engages those who would take to identifying California as a largely sinful place. It addresses matters that have often been on the mind of Mouw, recently retired President of one of the world's largest evangelical seminaries with a home campus in Pasadena. And here California becomes singled out as being not just a matter for theological investigation, but itself a deep theological subject, or a significant theological question.

Fred Sanders then gives a chapter that continues some of the earlier work that was initially generative of this entire project, which began with repeated courses offered each summer at the former Westminster House in Berkeley, where he and colleagues would take students to Berkeley in order to read through California's great texts. This essay then offers a theological investigation of California authors through their own attempts at locating a literary regionalism. After considering a selection of possibilities for developing a regional or localized theology, and possibilities of what even might be genuinely Californian, attention is turned to the Polish poet Czeslaw Milosz for possibilities of borrowing language from California authors to speak in theological language today.

The chapter by Jason Sexton seeks to address key questions about the nature of theology itself, both as an academic enterprise and as the dynamic explication of the church's confession in particular contexts. It highlights the role of theology in California's life, followed by considerations of the nature of what culture and even California culture might mean if framed in some possibly unified manner, and how it shapes things that theology can describe in better ways than have been done here at the end of the continent where things had better work, in Joan Didion's words. The delineation of various promises and possibilities that theology can offer to complement and supplement the traditional disciplines and wider culture are also set forth while showing the fittingness for theology's role in engaging California today.

Part II: California's Culture in Ecclesial Perspective

The second section of this book traverses into the life of the church, agreed upon by all disciplines represented at the TECC Project table to be one of, if not *the*, most significant actor in California's public square. It has uniquely shaped the state and its culture and has also enjoyed various expressions and innovations that could have hardly happened in any other place and yet has been shaped by global bodies and has profoundly influenced the present state of global Christianity and the global church.

Allen Yeh's chapter provides missiological reflections on various features of the Franciscan missions that are set up as somewhat exemplary for Christian missionary engagement today. This remarkably detailed study of the Alta California missions was spurred in part by various commemorations during the 300th anniversary of Father Junípero Serra's birth. And it flows from research conducted during visits to each of the 21 California missions, highlighting the considerable contribution the Franciscans and the missions they left behind made to California's life and culture.

Monica Ganas then considers the California church's struggle to follow Christ today amidst the ubiquitous temptation to mimic the world as expressed in the Hollywood celebrity culture. This epistemology or belief system uniquely developed and strongly promoted in California which she calls *California-ism* brings with it the dubious imperial notion that Evangelicalism has ridden on the back of, following in the wake of Sister Aimee Semple McPherson who gave a marketable shape to the celebrity model of church which many have co-opted and the church today has bought into.

Offering additional critical engagement, this time with a model of a California megachurch that received prominence in the late twentieth century, Matthew Farlow gives an account of Saddleback Community Church in light of the theodramatic model of divine action advocated by the Swiss Roman Catholic theologian Hans Urs von Balthasar. Dependent heavily on empirical research conducted by social scientists who have produced insightful material on Saddleback, this chapter brings these various conclusions under the scrutiny of a theological account of what church actually *is* when understood from a biblical-theological perspective.

Part III: California's Culture in Theological Perspective

On the heels of the section of the book that engaged California's ecclesial situation, attention in this part of the book is turned to a number of significant features present in the state's life. Part of the TECC Project's aim has been to seek to show how theology's ultimate presupposition and claim that Jesus Christ is "Lord" of all contingent realities provides the methodological groundwork for engaging not just ecclesial or religious matters, but enables the church (which does theology by its very nature) and theologians to explore the dynamic intersections between theology and cultural realities of any and every kind.

The first cultural phenomenon taken up is California's surfing culture, explored by Robert Covolo. After charting the Hawaiian origins of surfing and the shape that it took in California, especially in popular culture, this chapter mines the various theological impulses and themes running through surf culture, which are often described in religious language but which are here reinterpreted for theological ends. The chapter places these descriptions into conversation with biblical and theological materials in the attempt to develop a deeper meaning of what is happening in the act of surfing as developed and portrayed in California.

Bruce Baker, a former participant in the ethos of Silicon Valley, explores the culture and key players that made the Valley what it has become, in all of its innovative luster. This chapter frames the anthropology of Silicon Valley in theological-anthropological light, seeking to correlate and distinguish between human creativity and divine creativity according to Christian theology, finding the general spirit of Silicon Valley, while often described in religious terminology, to point toward the reality of being created in the image of God.

Next, Paul Louis Metzger recounts some of his work with African American pastors in the San Francisco Bay Area. He boldly identifies the systemic (even if passive) racism often present in the lives of white evangelicals and their drive-by evangelism strategies of care for those in urban centers like San Francisco, Oakland, and elsewhere. The consideration moves on from here, however, to the deep problem of fatherlessness and gang violence, and how the churches can stand in to embody and nurture family structures in the shape of the church as family, and on the way to making a contribution in community development.

Part IV: Is There a Theology of California?

By way of conclusion, this final section of the book offers a fitting ending, or rather a beginning of the conversations that the editors and contributors to this volume hope to conduct during the course of the ongoing, interdisciplinary, interinstitutional, and interdenominational TECC Project. It commences the conversation with Fred Sanders asking the question of whether there is a theology of California. The question is considered largely in conversation with Josiah Royce's notion of higher provincialism and how that relates to what California is. Continuing with this question, a theology of California is woven through the traditional systematic theological categories with a view towards developing them in ad hoc conversation with a range of significant California cultural phenomena, ultimately concluding that, with the tools of localism and the strategies of regionalism, a theology of California is almost certain to give way to the irreducible diversity of the place, yielding theologies of Californias.

The question Sanders raises and addresses is responded to by two interlocutors working from outside the realm of academic theology. Richard Flory, a sociologist of religion, affirms many of the questions that are beginning to be asked by theologians, but continues to highlight the diversity of matters in the state's life, and additionally the need for an effort like the TECC Project to allow other diverse perspectives a place at the table, even recovering a prophetic voice for others, and perhaps in these ways lead the US on these matters lest the work of theologians be lost in irrelevance and forsake the aim of service for which they hope to offer theology. And finally, historian Richard Pointer continues by also addressing the theologians' need for conducting sound historical work, as well as the ability to offer useful resource material for historians. As Flory did, this last chapter also notes the need for theologians to speak of California theologies, while also acknowledging the additional role of theological engagement with California's culture working to develop a theology *for* California, to bring about more robust Christian living in our broken world in need of redemption.

PART I
Approaching California's Culture
Theologically

Chapter 1

The Enigma of California: Reflections on a Theological Subject

Richard J. Mouw

Joan Didion was born in Sacramento and has spent most of her life in California. In her memoir, *Where I Was From*, published in 2003, she tells us much about her many years of reflecting on what it means to be a Californian. The experience, she tells us, has not been a very pleasant one. "California," she confesses, "has remained in some ways impenetrable to me, a wearying enigma."[1]

Didion finds a kindred spirit in Josiah Royce, who left California in 1885 at age 30 to teach for the next three decades in Harvard's Philosophy Department. Like Didion, Royce also thought much about California. He wrote a book about California history, and he also reflected on his own California origins in a speech that he gave in Philadelphia a few years before he died. Like Didion, he found the effort to understand his native state to be a difficult task. He testified that it had been a significant part of his "life's business" to try to understand the "wonder" of a California that encompasses both the "new" and the "crude."[2]

In thinking about California's "meaning," Didion and Royce are not only exploring their own connections to the state, but they are also trying to see beyond those personal ties to something bigger. What is that bigger something that they are looking for?

As a native of New Jersey I must confess that I have never given much thought to the subject of what the northern New Jersey of my youth "means." I suppose if I were forced to take up the project I could write 10 pages or so about what it meant to grow up not far from the setting for Tony Soprano's escapades. I could say something, I think, about accents and modes of expression, about

---

[1]   Joan Didion, *Where I Was From* (New York: Vintage Books, 2003), 38.
[2]   Didion, *Where I Was From*, 28–9. Didion's citation of Royce is from "Words of Professor Royce at the Walton Hotel at Philadelphia, December 29, 1915," in *The Philosophy of Josiah Royce*, John K. Roth (ed.), (New York: Crowell, 1971), 403.

neighborhoods and their restaurants, and about having one's general outlook on life shaped by a daily exposure to diverse European immigrant communities.

For me, though, none of that would amount to much more than an exercise in nostalgia. I seriously doubt that I would have anything to offer that would interest readers eager to learn something about the "meaning" of New Jersey as such. Nor is New Jersey alone in its failure to evoke this kind of interest.

There are regions other than California, of course, that do seem to elicit more reflective explorations. The American South is an obvious case in point. Some of our best literature has explored the "meaning" of Southern roots—notable examples being *Uncle Tom's Cabin* and *The Adventures of Huckleberry Finn* on the fiction side, and the autobiographies of Frederick Douglass and Willie Morris in the non-fiction category.

What makes California and the South especially interesting is that each of those regions tells us something about the larger "meaning" of America, albeit in different ways. The respective food cultures illustrate at least one key difference. To describe Southern cooking is necessarily to look at history. It is to think about the different food sources of slaves and slave owners, about regional variations on the notion of what it means to be "barbeque," about the nuances of "Southern fried." California cuisine, on the other hand, is an ever-changing phenomenon—its enduring qualities are eclecticism and innovation.[3]

To understand the South is to explore roots; it is to grasp traditions. To understand California is to monitor trends; the task requires a general surveying rather than a serious digging. And it is precisely because of this "surface" quality of what California stands for in many minds that it does not nurture the depth of belonging found among Southerners. Exiled Southerners, even when troubled by their native soil, often still feel an underlying affection, a sense of rootedness.[4] Californians who set out to understand their regional culture's "meaning," on the other hand, often do so with a sense that there is much about that culture that they wish they could shake off. Thus Joan Didion's complaint that her California continues to be "impenetrable to me, a wearying enigma."

---

[3]   Editor's note: Among California cuisine innovators is chef Alice Waters whose globally-acclaimed Berkeley restaurant Chez Panisse was the chosen location for an evening meal during the TECC Project's Spring 2013 workshop. Unfortunately, the meal never happened due to a major fire in the restaurant on March 8, 2013.

[4]   This is evident, for example, in the life of the erstwhile California-based civil rights activist John M. Perkins who, after encountering the black youths in the San Bernardino Mountain prison camps, knew that he needed to go back to the deep South to address the problems there which affected black men who went West to California. At the point of this revelation, Perkins "was never again satisfied in California" (*Let Justice Roll Down* [Ventura: Gospel Light, 2006], p. 78).

Hellish, Heavenly, and Created

While Josiah Royce did not specifically address theological matters in focusing on California and its history, he did employ some biblical metaphors.[5] The folks who ventured to the West Coast around the time of the Gold Rush, he observes, were "going on a pilgrimage whose every suggestion was of the familiar sacred stories."[6] And for Royce, the pilgrims were for the most part on a *sinful* journey. They were, he says, "Jonahs" who "fled from before the word of the Lord" in order to seek "safety from their old vexatious duties in a golden paradise." And, arriving in California, they formed a "community of irresponsible strangers," an aggregate of "homeless" people, who "sought wealth, and not a social order."[7]

Not that Royce was consistently negative in his assessment of the Gold Rush generation. For all of the bad things that we might say about life in California's nineteenth-century mining towns, Royce observes, we can also discern on occasion a healthy desire for a shared sense of community. "Mutual strangers" banded together, he says, with an observable "willingness to compromise on matters in dispute," accompanied by "the desire to be in public on pleasant terms with everybody."[8]

Royce's insistence on seeing some good things at work in the early shaping of California's culture gets at something that is theologically important. He has exercised a kind of cultural discernment, identifying some positive forces at work in the early shaping of the culture of California.

David Tiede, the former president of Luther Seminary, once made a memorable observation in a devotional he gave to a group of academic administrators. The crude and even blasphemous language of the streets, he said, often contains theological meanings that the speakers are oblivious to. His two examples were: "What *in the hell* is going on?!" and "What *in heaven's name* is happening?!" These two expressions, Tiede said, get at important spiritual realities: there is a lot of hellish stuff going on in the world; but we can also on occasion discern things that draw, even if unwittingly, upon heavenly resources.

---

5   Biblical images have often been employed in attempts to describe California, for example, in the poetry of Robinson Jeffers and more recently in the work of Kevin Starr: for example see his *California: A History* (New York: Random House, 2005), 169–70, 282.

6   Josiah Royce, *California: A Study of American Character: From the Conquest in 1846 to the Second Vigilance Committee in San Francisco* (Boston: Houghton, Mifflin and Company, 1886), 246.

7   Royce, *California*, 274–5.

8   Royce, *California*, 280.

Josiah Royce was allowing for a bit of the heavenly amidst much of the hellishness of nineteenth-century mining camp life in California. And it is good for us, as we think in a more sustained theological manner about California's "meaning," to follow his lead. To be sure, I am suggesting that in doing so we honor what for me is an explicitly Calvinist impulse—at least in the "Kuyperian" version of Calvinism. The late Mennonite theologian John Howard Yoder once captured the nature of this impulse quite nicely when, in the course of one of our public Anabaptist-Calvinist debates in the 1970s, he responded to a question from the audience with this comment: on questions of culture, he observed, "Mouw wants to say, 'Fallen, but *created*,' and I want to say, 'Created, but *fallen*.'"

My approach to California's "meaning," then, views the fallenness of the Golden State as a perversion of an original createdness. The general point was put nicely by H. Richard Niebuhr when, in his endorsement of the "Christ transforming culture" approach, Niebuhr argued that human culture as we presently experience it is "corrupted order rather than order for corruption…. It is perverted good, not evil; or it is evil as perversion, and not as badness of being."[9]

This applies nicely, I think, to California. It is always relevant and important to ask these two questions about things that we observe in the Californian experience: What hellishness is at work here? And what might we be seeing that honors the heavenly?

Surface Roots

A Southern California couple were talking recently about a two-week visit, from Oklahoma, of their 20-something granddaughter. "She would love to move here," the grandparents reported. "She just feels that so much is *happening* here, and she wants to find it."

Josiah Royce used the quest motif in explaining the motives of the Gold Rush generation, and it applies equally to the young woman from Oklahoma. Nor is her quest necessarily a bad thing. We are driven by quests as human beings. In the words of Augustine's oft quoted prayer at the beginning of the *Confessions*: "Thou hast made us for thyself and restless is our heart until it comes to rest in thee."[10]

California is an arena for human restlessness—and very often that restlessness is misdirected. And while the restlessness associated with California is a manifestation of a more general human restlessness, we can safely say that

---

9   H. Richard Niebuhr, *Christ and Culture* (New York: Harper and Row, 1951), 194.
10   Saint Augustine, *Confessions* (Peabody: Hendrickson, 2004), 5.

the way in which California manages both to attract and to encourage human restlessness stands out in the broader American culture.[11]

A young Silicon Valley venture capitalist put it well to me not long ago. One of his leisure time activities, following through on a history course he had taken as an undergraduate, is studying twelfth- and thirteenth-century medieval thought, with a focus on the uses made of Aristotle's metaphysics. When I asked him why this interest, he said: "I guess it has to do with the speed of life when you are constantly involved with start-ups. You lose a sense of being a self that has a history. I have to keep working at being connected to something in the past!"

This person is taking definite steps to protect himself from a threat to selfhood that he sees as somehow intrinsic to the preoccupations and pace of his life. He is describing the way in which life in Silicon Valley can be its own version of a surfing culture: a skimming across surfaces without a proper connection to anything stable beneath those surfaces. Albert Borgmann, a Roman Catholic who teaches philosophy at the University of Montana, wrote an excellent book a few years ago in which he discusses the ways in which the postmodern consciousness often limits its attention to the *surfaces* of reality. He addresses this malady with a call to rediscover "the eloquence of things" in their particularity, to recognize "the things that command our respect and grace our life," thus finding "the depth of the world."[12]

We can generalize here on the images we applied to California cuisine: innovation and eclecticism. California means innovative drawing together from diverse sources, perhaps even suggesting some sort of stable locatedness from which to draw. This produces much that is good—there is much to thank God for in what we have received from Silicon Valley and various other things the California imagination and industry has given to the world. But the resulting way of life can sometimes become a surface thing, lacking depth, an absence of rootedness.

HOTEL CALIF.?

Empire Effects or Gracious Promise?

Much of this territory is covered with considerable insight by Monica Ganas in her important book, *Under the Influence: California's Intoxicating Spiritual and Cultural Impact on America*. She approaches her topic with a trained cultural

---

[11] This is not to minimize that California has also attracted the weary and desperate, offering unique forms of hope; yet when this hope is not found, those who were restless elsewhere often become restless once again.

[12] Albert Borgmann, *Crossing the Postmodern Divide* (Chicago: University of Chicago Press, 1992), 51, 82.

eye: she worked for several decades in the entertainment industry before taking up her teaching role in theater, film and communication studies at Azusa Pacific University. Drawing on all of this, she provides a wealth of illuminating cultural information and perspective, both historical and contemporary, including some wonderful personal anecdotes. And best of all, she deals with the complexity of California life out of strongly stated Christian convictions, with many theological and missiological insights.

Ganas sets the stage for her discussion with a clear distinction between the hellish and the heavenly. On the one hand, she says, there is "the delusional and damaging effects of *California-as-a-contrived-religion*"; but there is also, beneath all of the damage, "the promise of *California-the-created-region*." At work in all of the sordid patterns of California life, she says, there are "eternal instincts and longings" that point to "redemptive possibilities." These created yearnings can, if properly redirected, help us to "turn our attention to our real environment, real community, real relationships, and real policies." Without that redirecting, though, we will find ourselves in a trance-like state that "anesthetizes us to actual human experience, relationship, environment, and, I fear, the true God."[13]

Ganas's book contributes much to the project of thinking theologically about California. But she sometimes—and I stress *sometimes*—seems to push things in a direction that makes me nervous, and I think the nervousness is worthy of some theological explication.

I began to experience a little discomfort early on in Ganas's book, when she employed the "empire" image, as set forth in Walter Brueggemann's stark contrast between Christ's Kingdom and our human-created empires. Here is her summary of the contrast:

> The kingdom is based on grace, the empire on earnings. The kingdom is freeing, the empire binding. The kingdom is peaceful, the empire brutal. The kingdom is authentic, the empire deceitful. The kingdom is forgiving, the empire judgmental. The kingdom is renewing, the empire debilitating. The kingdom is imaginative, the empire predictable. The kingdom is filled with second chances and good news to the poor. The empire is filled with power, greed, and injustice.[14]

I have no difficulty with this kind of contrast as such. We do, of course, wrestle, not so much against flesh and blood in California, but against principalities and

---

13   Monica Ganas, *Under the Influence: California's Intoxicating Spiritual and Cultural Impact on America* (Grand Rapids: Brazos Press, 2010), 4, 5.

14   Ganas, *Under the Influence*, 13–14.

powers. We run into problems, however, when we simply identify the actual realities of California culture—its very real "flesh and blood"—with these "empire" characteristics. Indeed, I see the danger here as closely associated with the "empire" talk as such. Empires range over territories and take much of their shape in institutional realities. I think it is misleading to think of California's cultural "territory" as a part of "empire" in that sense.[15]

Back in the 1970s, some of my friends in the evangelical activist movement were taken—particularly in our opposition to the Vietnam War—with the kind of rhetoric set forth by William Stringfellow, who depicted the United States as Revelation's sinful Babylon, embodying and promoting a global "way of death."[16] As a parent in those days of a young child just starting school, I found this depiction difficult to reconcile with my son's daily walking route to and from his inner-city school. Along the way there were stop signs and traffic signals, and at one key point a uniformed crossing guard. His school was regularly visited by fire and safety inspectors. All of these things were life-promoting gifts. There was much that I wanted to criticize in those days about "the American way"—and there still is today. But to characterize it as a "way of death," or as in the more recent rhetoric, an "empire" that is devoted to what is "brutal" and "deceitful" and "debilitating," is to fail to recognize the life-affirming gifts that it makes available to us.

And this shows up in other areas of contemporary life. For example, when I have stayed in European hotels I have often missed the "customer service" orientation that strikes me as typical in California hotels. It's nice to be welcomed by a desk clerk, and to receive a call from her a few minutes later, in the assigned room, asking whether the room is satisfactory. I have no doubt that the display of California friendliness is mandated by a corporate culture that has made decisions about the profitability of "customer satisfaction." But, then, I am not asking to be loved—only to have a fairly comfortable stay for a night or two away from home.

That there is more at stake here than our terminological preferences can be seen in Ganas's account of the continuing legacy of California's Gold Rush. "True

---

[15]   Although with institutional realities shaping the state such as the 1960 "Master Plan" of education, or with various California industries finding institutions competing with one another for survival and often thriving, including the military defense industry and other state-embedded institutions like the California Department of Corrections (and Rehabilitation), the Los Angeles Department of Water and Power, and other institutionalized powers within California with their complex relationship to politics and government (at both state and federal levels) are worth further theological exploration.

[16]   William Stringfellow, *An Ethics for Christians and Other Aliens in a Strange Land* (Waco: Word, 1973).

to gold rush form," she writes, the contemporary person who is intoxicated by California "is still looking out for number one, still staking claims, corporately and individually, whether in traffic jams or grocery lines or crowded gyms or sales bins or church pews. We're still eyeing our neighbor suspiciously, still on guard against the foreign element, which can be anyone who threatens our space."[17] What is missing here is the kind of concession that we saw Royce making about the Gold Rush. He gave us some reason to think of at least some of what went on in nineteenth century mining towns as more like Brueggemann's depiction of Christ's Kingdom than of the rebellious patterns of "empire" sinfulness.

This applies to busy streets in school districts and hotel lobbies as well. And, I must add in this context, it applies to movie theaters. Monica Ganas knows much about the film industry, and her book offers many insights on that important area of California culture. But there are times when I fear that she is too captivated by the notion that somehow the film industry simply is "in" the "empire." Here, for example, is Ganas describing the way we can be tempted to see ourselves as "omniscient and omnipresent" while watching a film:

> Sitting in the hushed darkness of the film cathedral, enjoying our sacramental popcorn for which we've paid too high a price, congregants gaze at the altar of the screen and are given plot information that many characters in the movie do not know and cannot control. We piece together the story we are told, traveling from location to location with or without all the characters, filling in the narrative gaps, and thus it begins to feel as though we ourselves are telling the story. It seems to be our own idea, and thus difficult to refute for the time being, whether or not it aligns with our general beliefs.

All of this is enhanced, she says, by the use of "powerful enough technologies to insure the success of this mystical enterprise." Special effects and the like can invite us into an intimacy with characters who become, Ganas observes, "larger than life," thereby "lend[ing] a supernatural component to the action and serv[ing] to make the narrative at least as vital as the one we're hearing at church."[18]

I have at least two concerns about this kind of depiction. One is that while making a film—and watching one—can indeed be a kind of manner of grasping at omniscience and omnipotence, and thus yet one more way of taking up the

---

[17]   Ganas, *Under the Influence*, 62.

[18]   Ganas, *Under the Influence*, 77–8. See also a similar critique of the kind of liturgical worship taking place at the shopping mall in James K.A. Smith, *Desiring the Kingdom: Worship, Worldview, and Cultural Formation* (Grand Rapids: Baker Academic, 2009), 93–101.

Tempter's challenge that we "can be like God"—while I do think it *can* be that, I do not think it *must* be. The very things Ganas points to as potential instruments of rebellion against God can also serve the cause of righteousness, functioning, for example, as effective tools of moral—and even spiritual—pedagogy. Allowing us to see plot patterns and connections that the characters in the film themselves cannot see—and seeing them "larger than life"—can be a way of alerting us to a narrative unity that provides an alternative, by filling in temporal and spatial gaps, to what would otherwise be a fragmented plot-line.

More importantly for me, though, is my uneasiness with Ganas's use of church-going imagery: the picture of the theater as a "film cathedral" that dispenses "sacramental popcorn," with "congregants gaz[ing] at the altar of the screen," and all of this in the service of a "mystical enterprise."

My worry about this kind of thing was captured nicely by Mark Galli in a *Books & Culture* review essay dealing with writers who are fond of depicting football games and other major sports events in religious categories, as when the Super Bowl becomes a ritualized event that produces ecstasy, creating bonding experiences, fostering communal celebrations, calling for "physical sacrifice," and so forth. Galli rightly rejects such portrayals of a football game as such. Certainly there are many people, he writes, for whom "football has become an idol. Such is the nature of the human heart, that desperately wicked thing (Jer. 17:9)." But it is precisely because many of us experience true religion that we can relax and see a football game for what it is: one of the places where we can often see God's "handiwork and love" being manifested.[19] When that happens, we can be grateful for amazing 80-yard runs, spectacular pass receptions, and a coach's wise use of time-outs in the final minutes of the game. The old anti-Freudian remark that sometimes a cigar is just a cigar has its parallel here. Sometimes a football game is just a football game. And sometimes eating popcorn at a good movie is just eating popcorn at a good movie.

This is not to deny, of course, that there can very well be—and often is—bad football games and bad popcorn and bad movies. And there are indeed cases where football and popcorn and movies can function in obvious ways as "empire"—because they have become instruments of deceit and destruction. But sometimes the badness is of a less cosmic sort: the game is poorly played by both teams. Or the popcorn is stale or much too salty. Or the film's special effects render certain key scenes ineffective.

---

19   Mark Galli, "And God Created Football," *Books & Culture*, Jan.–Feb. 2010, http://www.booksandculture.com/articles/2010/janfeb/godcreatedfootball.html (accessed June 12, 2013).

Much the same holds for the state of California. In many aspects of its life, California is simply a region[20] where many very ordinary things happen on a daily basis: people search for parking spaces, couples get married, writers struggle with finding just the right opening paragraph, and parents are pleased that their teenage daughter got a summer job selling popcorn in the local movie complex.

Sometimes too—often, in fact, in our sinful world—much of this goes bad, as when people fight in parking lots, or when the caterer messes up the food for the wedding reception, or the writer decides to get the readers' attention with a lurid description, or the teenager falls in with the wrong crowd at her summer job selling popcorn.

And sometimes California as a general reality also goes horribly bad, as when it presents itself as a "Golden State" that lures us into false hopes of an earthly paradise of freewheeling self-actualizers who are liberated from the inhibitions that characterize life in other regions. Of course, there is no time in living memory when this kind of boosterism has not been present and fueled by politicians and media moguls. But when that happens, at least some of the language associated with an "empire" ideology may shed light on California's wicked ways.

Yet in all of that it is important to remind ourselves that the Creator—to use a wonderful hymn line that I chose as a title for one of my books—"shines in all that's fair." This is where I find Abraham Kuyper's theology so helpful. Common grace, for Kuyper, is a non-salvific manifestation of divine favor toward the fallen creation. In good part it is a restraining grace, a "leash" on sinfulness that keeps human beings from being as bad as they could be. But it also works positively in unredeemed life. Kuyper sees common grace at work in a positive manner "wherever civic virtue, a sense of domesticity, natural love, the practice of human virtue, the improvement of the public conscience, integrity, mutual loyalty among people, and a feeling for piety leaven life."[21]

The danger of an "empire" approach to the study of California as a complex cultural phenomenon is that it might keep us from noticing those very signs of common grace. Ganas is right to sensitize us both to "the delusional and damaging effects of *California-as-a-contrived-religion*" and to "the promise of *California-the-created-region*." To look for the damage is important. But so is the effort to discern the signs of promise. To miss them is to be left with nothing more than a California that is Joan Didion's "wearying enigma."

---

[20]   For more on reckoning with literary regionalism in California, see Chapter 2 of this volume, pp. 19–33.

[21]   Abraham Kuyper, "Common Grace," in *Abraham Kuyper: A Centennial Reader*, James D. Bratt (ed.), (Grand Rapids: Eerdmans, 1998), 181.

Chapter 2

California, Localized Theology, and Theological Localism

Fred Sanders

Wallace Stegner once said, "Like the rest of America, California is unformed, innovative, ahistorical, hedonistic, acquisitive, and energetic—only more so."[1] As California becomes increasingly self-conscious as a social and political entity, an academic conversation is beginning to take place among historians, political scientists, literary scholars, and others interested in describing this vast place. "California Studies" is now, as they say, a thing. It has classes, courses of study, academic conferences, a journal,[2] and in the inevitable logic of academia, it will no doubt have majors and graduate degrees before long. In this interdisciplinary conversation, theologians have not been prominent so far. As a result, the conversation has lacked a depth and seriousness which theological categories could provide. If theology is a real intellectual discipline, in touch with reality, it ought (at the very least) to be able to find true, interesting, and enlightening things to say in this public dialogue.

But before theologians can contribute to the dialogue, they need to: first, know the Californian dialect: second, clarify their own properly theological reasons for involvement: and third, consider helpful methods from more established disciplines. This chapter will attempt to enact the first (showing mastery of the Californian dialect by working with recognizably Californian sources), pursue

---

[1] Quoted from the editorial of a special California issue from Wallace Stegner, "California: The Experimental Society," *Saturday Review* (September 23, 1967) in Philip L. Fradkin, *Wallace Stegner and the American West*, (Berkeley: University of California Press, 2008), 154.

[2] See the acclaimed, *BOOM: A Journal of California*, published by University of California Press and edited by veteran journalist Jon Christensen; and note the significance of California literature recently highlighted in Larry Gordon, "Students sample the large shelf of California literature," *Los Angeles Times,* January 1, 2012, http://articles.latimes.com/2012/jan/01/local/la-me-california-literature-20120102 (accessed June 13, 2013), and Marisa Silver, "Oh, California," *New York Times*, March 18, 2013, http://opinionator.blogs.nytimes.com/2013/03/18/oh-california/ (accessed June 13, 2013).

the second (explaining theological reasons for theological engagement in the first main section of the paper), and give one extended example of the third, scouting the accomplishments of the critical quest to define California's literary regionalism.

Theological Localism

In the first main section of the chapter, I distinguish between the theological method of correlation on the one hand, which would take culture as either a norm or source for theology, and programmatic apologetics on the other hand, which investigates the culture in order to communicate its message most effectively. The present movement toward developing theological localism is a third thing, an attempt to be aware and self-critical about place, location, and situation. While rejecting correlationism, theological localism attempts to take into account the fact that theological thinking is embedded in the very cultural forms it addresses. It also recognizes that, within the bounds of orthodoxy, a laudable diversity of equally legitimate local theologies have developed elsewhere throughout Christian history, and envisions such possibilities for California.

Correlationism is an approach to theology that gives equal weight to human, cultural questions and to biblical, theological answers. One of its great practitioners was Paul Tillich, who developed it as a method of explaining the contents of the Christian faith through aligning existential questions and theological answers in mutual correspondence.[3] "Philosophy," said Tillich, "formulates the questions implied in human existence, and theology formulates the answers implied in human existence." Tillich was not the first practitioner of correlationism; it is at least as old as classical liberalism, and if Tillich is to be believed, "it is as old as theology. We have not invented a new method, but have rather tried to make explicit the implications of old ones, namely, that of apologetic theology."[4] Tillich said of his own work, "since the split between a faith unacceptable to culture and a culture unacceptable to faith was not possible for me, the only alternative was to attempt to interpret the symbols of faith through expressions of our own culture. The result of this attempt is the three volumes of Systematic Theology."[5]

---

[3]   Paul Tillich, *Systematic Theology*, vol. 1 (Chicago: University of Chicago Press, 1951), 60.

[4]   Paul Tillich, *Systematic Theology*, vol. 2 (Chicago: University of Chicago Press, 1957), 16.

[5]   Paul Tillich, *Systematic Theology*, vol. 3 (Chicago: University of Chicago Press, 1963), 5.

The method of correlation is perennially attractive for theologians of culture because it marks out a clear arena in which culture can make itself heard in theology. It raised theological reflection on culture to a higher level by making it an explicit topic of discussion and by sanctioning it. But already in Tillich's own work, the method showed itself to be unstable. Tillich claimed that culture was neither a source nor a norm for theology, but it proved difficult for him to keep it out of that space. When Tillich was writing, the word "experience" had more cache, and Tillich drew a line there, arguing that experience cannot be a source or a norm for theology. But those who learned the most from Tillich, and carried out his task of reading their cultures theologically and learning their theology culturally, usually drew the opposite conclusion. In the next generation after Tillich, it became standard for theologians of culture to admit categories like experience and culture into their canons of doctrine, both as norms and as sources.

Two other weaknesses of correlationist theology are that, first, only with great difficulty can a correlationist break through the grid of presuppositions built into the questions raised by a culture. And unless they do so, they are stuck with questions no better than that grid permits. But often theology's task is to announce that a culture is not just missing the answers, but asking the wrong questions. Framing a question is often more important than answering it, or at least more determinative of the bounds of discourse. Second, correlationists tend to hurry past the task of describing and elaborating Christian truth, assuming that the proper business of theology is cultural theology. Their sense of excitement and project tend to come from combining theology with the next thing, as if the descriptive and elaborative task of Christian doctrine could be presupposed as already accomplished.[6] The result is that correlationists generally approach their task with an unnecessarily minimized, or thin, theology.

Tillich contrasted correlationism with the "theology of proclamation," especially the approach to theology advocated by Karl Barth. According to Tillich, the theology of proclamation wants to hurl the Christian message like a brick at the head of its audience. This was not, of course, really fair to the theology of proclamation. Even if proclaimers were interested in doing so, they might after all want to know more about the brick they are throwing, and the head at which they are throwing it. One could imagine a theology of California

---

[6] For a critique of this mindset and an alternative to it, see John Webster, "Theology After Liberalism," in, *Theology After Liberalism: A Reader*, John Webster and George P. Schner (eds), (Blackwell, 2000), 52–61. And note also the recently established (regional) enterprise designed to focus on systematic theology itself and its own internal questions in the annual Los Angeles Theology conference, co-sponsored by Biola University, Fuller Theological Seminary, and Zondervan Academic (www.latheology.com).

culture that sought better and better information about that Californian head at which it is hurling its gospel brick.

Which brings us to programmatic apologetics. Tillich called his own method not only correlationism, but also "apologetic theology," by which he meant a theology that helped modern people to answer questions (from the Greek *apo* + *logia*, a word in response, an answer). But in our time, apologetics also names a discipline of recommending and defending the truth claims of Christianity in a public forum. In its advocacy for Christian truth claims, programmatic apologetics is highly interested in the plausibility structures of the target culture. "What will today's culture find believable?" is the operative question. Apologists want to know what presuppositions are held by modern people. Those engaged in apologetics investigate culture in order to communicate their own message to it with maximal effectiveness. Programmatic apologetics has some of the same weaknesses as correlationism—a tendency to let the world set the terms of the debate. But programmatic apologetics is also threatened by the opposite danger, that of failing to notice that the apologist is part of the world they are attempting to persuade; that they can never simply speak to the culture, but always already speak from it, or as one formed by it, as well.

Theological localism is something different from either correlationism or systematic apologetics. Here is a short statement of it by art historian Matthew Milliner, presented in the form of "theses on theolocalism:"

1. When Biblical and Nicene theological norms have been sufficiently internalized, theology can encourage unique regional developments.
2. Localist efforts to combat modern transience should therefore infect theological method.
3. If a given place hasn't yet made a distinct theological contribution, it should consider doing so.
4. Theological localism means thinking with those closest to you—a sort of 100 mile intellectual diet.
5. What theologians thought matters, of course, but so does where they are buried.
6. This is not to be nativist, but to exploit native resources for the sake of the universal church.[7]

---

[7]   http://www.millinerd.com/2011/03/thirteen-theses-on-theological-locality.html (accessed June 13, 2013).

Theological localism is a commitment to regional intellectual resources, both in terms of drawing on them and contributing to them.

Applied to California, the overall intellectual task is somewhere between "A Theology of California" and "Theology from California." Those would be the two bumper stickers. The former, Theology of California, indicates bringing theological reflection to bear on this entity which is California, to offer a theological account of its existence and character. The latter, Theology from California, indicates that we're doing theological reflection about the usual subjects (revelation, God, creation, providence, humanity, sin, redemption, eschatology) in this particular location, intentionally cultivating resources that are Californian.

Theology is going to have to run to catch up here, because several other disciplines are well established in California studies. Or to say it collaboratively instead of competitively, theology has a lot of partner disciplines that it can call on as it begins the investigation. The best case study is literature, which is significant on two levels: first, that distinctively Californian literary art has been produced; and second, that a body of criticism and commentary has been devoted to that art. There are important spiritual elements embedded in the literature (first level) which need to be explored by critics (second level) using doctrinal categories and paradigms which theologians can help provide. A parallel situation exists in the visual arts, where there are important schools and movements of, for instance, California painting. I don't know the field of musicology well enough to comment on the resources there, unless you look at pop and hip hop music where of course a characteristic Californianism is easily discerned. Another discipline that has a lot of synergy with theology is history: there was once a dominant narrative of American history that said we started on the East Coast (pilgrims!) and spread westward (pioneers!). But California-centered historians have long since demonstrated how much that narrative needs to be juxtaposed with our Mexican past, our Russian connections, our Pacific Rim realities: factors which understandably have played a lesser role in an East Coast version of American self-understanding. Theology, partly through church history, has much to learn and much to teach here. Not to leave any disciplines out, sociology is also a field that is doing a good job staying alert to surprising realities that are available for study here in California.

Even philosophy has promise here. There is value in attending to the social-cultural environment in which Christian philosophers work. Localized philosophy pushes against the notion that philosophers are portable brains-in-vats, creatures of pure comprehension who generate concepts that show no traces of local origin. But that's a flawed public image of philosophers, not the way most philosophers actually view themselves. Without taking a hard historicist turn, intellectuals all tend to admit that we're located in multiple ways that influence our intellectual work. My favorite example of a thinker who has reflected well on that is Charles Taylor, and one can easily imagine a really enlightening Californian gloss on *Sources of the Self*: Sources of the Californian Self. To my knowledge, only Josiah Royce has attempted anything self-consciously Californian in the field of metaphysics and epistemology, and few philosophers have followed his lead.[8] But Royce's call for a non-parochial regionalism or a "higher regionalism," visionary though it might have been, seems more like a road not taken in American intellectual history.

Literary Regionalism

The most helpful cognate discipline for initial forays into this project is the field of literature, and this chapter concludes with a few lessons learned in the ongoing quest to identify a California literary regionalism. What counts as California literature?

There is a classic discussion on the subject that is not exactly up to date, but it's a 1955 article full of wise counsel. The article, "California's Literary Regionalism" by Frederick Bracher of Pomona College says "regionalism" is more of a "hypothesis to be tested" than an "unquestionable fact." So it's best to approach California literature by asking of each book or author, "does this represent the authentic voice of California?"[9]

"Voice," of course, is a metaphor, and Bracher laments the "morass of metaphor" that awaits anybody looking into literary regionalism: there are "roots that go down deep into, layers of cultural humus and substrata which lie below, mirrors that catch at a slightly different angle the sunlight of, long immersions in, natural blossoms as opposed to hot-house growths," and so on. That kind of metaphorical description is serviceable when you're talking about the kind of pronounced regionalism that is widely agreed on, like a certain kind of literature from the American South. But when you're trying to name something as ambiguous as "California literature," the morass of metaphor obscures more than it illumines.

---

[8]   See Chapter 10 of this volume for further discussion of Royce.

[9]   Frederick Bracher, "California's Literary Regionalism," *American Quarterly* 7/3 (Autumn 1955), 275–84.

Never mind the question of what geographic region should count as "California" for literary purposes—the spirit of a place doesn't stop at a state line, or even necessarily extend that far, especially if you're sampling literature from before the clear definition of states. Just consider the even thornier question of who counts as Californian. Bracher points out that native birth is not a good criterion, since that would make Robert Frost a Californian (born in San Francisco) and Robinson Jeffers not one (born in Pittsburgh). Living and writing in California doesn't suffice either, since that would transform Thomas Mann, Aldous Huxley, and Henry Miller into California authors (maybe they are). Even writing about California isn't sufficient, since it lets in Evelyn Waugh and John Dos Passos. "Nearly everyone comes to California sooner or later, and many of these temporary settlers dislike the area enough to write about it. But this does not make them regional writers."[10]

What it takes to be a California author, according to Bracher, is a view of the area from the inside "not curiously and from a safe distance, as one might look at animals in a zoo, but with some sense of concern for, or identification with, the region."[11] In other words, California literature is not so much *about* the region as it is *of* the region. And Bracher adds one more requirement: California literature shouldn't be too aware of its regional character. Bracher summarizes Thomas Hardy's rule of thumb for how to know when you're observing a real folk tradition: "the test of an authentic folk custom is the grumpy unawareness of the participants that they are doing anything out of the ordinary."[12]

The sense of identification with the region is hardly demonstrable or analyzable: it must be felt, he says, and goes on to name eight authors in whose work this identification can be felt: John Steinbeck, Robinson Jeffers, William Saroyan, Walter Van Tilburg Clark, George R. Stewart, Hans Otto Storm, Nathanael West, and Budd Schulberg. From among this list, he singles out Steinbeck, Clark, and Saroyan as "the most important of the regional writers."[13]

Even making allowances for the half-century that has elapsed since the publication of Bracher's article, there is a palpable sense of deflation once he has offered this list. Only the most dedicated readers of California literature would have read widely from these eight authors, and some are now minor names indeed.

---

[10]   Bracher, "California's Literary Regionalism," 277.
[11]   Bracher, "California's Literary Regionalism," 277.
[12]   Bracher, "California's Literary Regionalism," 277.
[13]   Bracher, "California's Literary Regionalism," 278.

But Bracher has the wisdom not to be dogmatic about his admittedly somewhat arbitrary choices, and spends the rest of the essay illustrating a few characteristics that he thinks mark California literature at its most regionally distinctive.

First, California authors are not urban; they do not write city novels. "There are no important novels about San Francisco or Los Angeles."[14] California authors have a feeling for the larger landscapes outside the cities, whether it is the long valley of the Salinas River or the whole coastline surrounding Point Sur. No cityscapes or cozy townships for these West Coast authors. Consequently, the characters are people who fit these settings: "The virtues implicit in California heroes are essentially frontier virtues: independence, adaptability, humor, an engaging naivete, and confidence in one's ability to take care of himself."[15] All good novelists make use of local climate, and California authors make the most of California's distinctive weather: the dryness above all, but also the "seasonal alternation of short, cool winters and long dry summers which sets up the rhythm of life in the area."[16]

Second, California literature is non-political. "Despite a distinguished tradition of radical political literature, from Henry George through Frank Norris and Jack London to Upton Sinclair, the best of the present writers seem to be more interested in moral problems than in political problems; in the large general questions of human life rather than in the immediate problems of society, in Evil rather than in particular evils."[17] Here, perhaps, the circular nature of Bracher's procedure is most evident. He picks the least political writers and then declares California authors non-political. But even at that, he has to squint at a great deal of rabble-rousing and social analysis in Steinbeck and Clark to decide that the spirit of California is non-political. For my part, I am struck by the exact opposite trait: California literature is inveterately political, too much so for my taste. Many of the best books have been too invested in too-current events, rendering them period pieces after a couple of decades.

Third, California literature is broadly allegorical rather than tensely aesthetic. The preoccupation with large moral problems brings forth "a kind of naive symbolism—naive in the sense that the authors tend to give their characters symbolic meaning, instead of finding significance in particular characters and

---

14   Bracher, "California's Literary Regionalism," 279. With efforts from writers such as Mike Davis, and Edan Lepucki's *California* (Little, Brown and Company, 2014), this is no longer the case, of course.

15   Bracher, "California's Literary Regionalism," 279.

16   Bracher, "California's Literary Regionalism," 280.

17   Bracher, "California's Literary Regionalism," 280.

events."[18] Bracher cites Saroyan's claim that "everything I write, everything I have written, is allegorical,"[19] and notes Steinbeck's "arbitrary assignment of symbolic meaning to characters" in *East of Eden*.[20] Here I think Bracher has put his finger on something very interesting and surprisingly widespread in California literature: lack of subtlety. I am less sure that it has been a happy trait of the region.

Finally, California literature has "a good-natured ignorance of critical disciplines." The state's best authors "appear to be genially oblivious to the rules of criticism and to critical censure for violations of taste and propriety."[21] Bracher has in mind Saroyan's declared intention to found "a tradition of carelessness" to ensure a plentiful supply of irreverence and creativity.[22] But he also has in mind the besetting bathos that makes itself felt in otherwise fine works: "What other novelist of comparable stature [to Steinbeck] could stomach the over-poetic, pseudo-Irish speech of Samuel Hamilton in *East of Eden*? And what Eastern writer would have been so regardless of possible ridicule as to conclude *The Grapes of Wrath* with its final melodramatic scene?"[23] California writers are naked and apparently unashamed. Bracher warms to his subject:

> The Californians' willingness to let themselves go, their cheerful ignoring of the restraints a writer is expected to impose upon himself, comes fairly close to the traditional stereotype of the Westerner as the child of nature, free from the trammels of tradition and the paralyzing self-consciousness of the hypercritical. There may be a germ of truth in the myth.[24]

Whatever the merits of Bracher's 1955 account of California literary regionalism, he concludes with an interesting note. Many East Coast critics have complained about the "unbuttoned romanticism" of California literature. Edmund Wilson said that the state has a "golden air of death" for the literary mind, owing to "the boundless sunlight which never becomes charged with

---

18   Bracher, "California's Literary Regionalism," 282.
19   Bracher, "California's Literary Regionalism," 282, citing William Saroyan, Preface to "Sam Ego's House," *Don't Go Away Mad and Two Other Plays* (New York: Harcourt, Brace, 1949), 101.
20   Bracher, "California's Literary Regionalism," 282.
21   Bracher, "California's Literary Regionalism," 282.
22   Bracher, "California's Literary Regionalism," 283.
23   Bracher, "California's Literary Regionalism," 283.
24   Bracher, "California's Literary Regionalism," 283.

human energies."[25] Eastern critics from traditioned schools of commentary just can't imagine painting anything human on a canvas as vast as the big Western sky. But perhaps that is because East Coast critics have made the error of thinking that all serious literature has to be urban, political, tensely aesthetic, and critically self-conscious. California literature may just have a chance to be true to itself in a way that could expand the horizons of New York critics.

> The California writers are not hampered by rules or schools; illustrious examples do not intimidate and engross them. They are willing to tackle large and old-fashioned subjects, and they do not worry unduly about partial or occasional failure. At their best, they achieve an easy and unaffected lyricism of style.[26]

Bracher is certainly not the latest word on California literary regionalism. The critical conversation has gone on since 1955, especially with the explosion of diversity in California writing since 1955. It won't do to call California literature non-urban anymore, and it probably never was right to call it non-political. It's also necessary to include assessments of California from outsiders: shrewd observers like Scotsman Robert Louis Stevenson and Polish-Lithuanian Czeslaw Milosz. And I would certainly include some notes about California from the rest of America, because there's no disentangling the state of California from what it has meant to the entire nation. California literary regionalism is certainly, in Bracher's terms, more of a "hypothesis to be tested" than an "unquestionable fact."

Territorial Spirits

To zoom in one level further, I would like to explore at greater length the musings of one writer about California: Czeslaw Milosz. Polish writer Milosz lived in Berkeley from about 1958 until his death in 2004. He looks at California from a long way off, from the Old World, and it is helpful to read him to learn to see the state from that angle. Milosz wants to name the territorial spirits of California, and suspects many of them are demons. Much of his poetry is about things that can't be spoken, or at least things that can't be said quite right, because his view

---

[25]   Bracher, "California's Literary Regionalism," 284, citing Edmund Wilson, *The Boys in the Back Room* (San Francisco: The Colt Press, 1941), 58.
[26]   Bracher, "California's Literary Regionalism," 284.

of the poetic vocation ran along the lines described by T.S. Eliot as "raids on the inarticulate."

Milosz wrote a lot of books. *The Captive Mind*[27] made him famous, but the lectures entitled *The Witness of Poetry*[28] are probably the best place to get an idea of what he's up to artistically. I recommend jumping into the large volume of his *Collected Poems*[29] and finding something that grabs you.

Milosz was no one-trick pony, but he did have a handful of themes and approaches that he kept coming back to in all his work. One of those themes is his own artistic quest to testify accurately about himself. He is always holding up his hand and saying "Here I am," in ways that continually astonish the reader. For our purposes the best book is *Visions from San Francisco Bay*,[30] because though it is a fragmented and flawed book, it is a coherent essay on the spiritual significance of California which only Milosz could write. When he holds up his hand and says "Here I am" from Berkeley, California, he tries to speak for his Lithuanian ancestors, for the continent of North America, for the territorial spirits of California, and for himself after midlife.

His elliptical autobiography *Native Realm*[31] is full of good stuff, too, and mixes some light humor with the heavy brooding and bewilderment that are his signature style. He begins the book by pledging allegiance to his Eastern heritage: "No, I will never imitate those who rub out their traces, disown the past and are dead, although they pretend they are alive with the help of mental acrobatics."[32] He goes on to conjure up all that he has seen during a life in which "new images canceled out none of the old"[33] and he had to speak in spite of "the pressure from this reality I have swallowed."[34] Milosz praises a meticulous biographical essay he once read because it gave such attention to small physical details of the subject's surroundings: "one can get at man only obliquely, only through the constant masquerade that is the extension of himself at a given moment, through his historical existence."[35] He calls his autobiographical work

---

[27]   Czeslaw Milosz, *The Captive Mind* (New York: Penguin Popular Classics, 1953).

[28]   Czeslaw Milosz, *The Witness of Poetry: The Charles Eliot Norton Lectures* (Cambridge: Harvard University Press, 1983).

[29]   Czeslaw Miłosz, *New and Collected Poems, 1931–2001* (New York: Ecco, 2003).

[30]   Czeslaw Milosz, *Visions from San Francisco Bay* (New York: Farrar, Straus, Giroux, 1982).

[31]   Czeslaw Milosz, *Native Realm* (Garden City, NY: Doubleday, 1968).

[32]   Milosz, *Native Realm*, 2.

[33]   Milosz, *Native Realm*, 3.

[34]   Milosz, *Native Realm*, 3.

[35]   Milosz, *Native Realm*, 4.

"a token of respect for those undergrounds that exist in all of us and that are better left in peace."[36]

In speaking from California, Milosz was interested in imagining a world history that jumped straight from prehistory to the industrial revolution in a single year: 1849. That is telescoped a bit, but compared to a Europe that ripened through the middle ages, then made the long voyage to New England, California does seem to have happened overnight, with machines.

Milosz often set for himself a task that he knew in advance was impossible. His poetic vocation was to declare something that couldn't be said straightforwardly, and he advanced toward that goal with a panoply of strange techniques. In the California book, Milosz said "I am always aware that what I want is impossible to achieve. I would need the ability to communicate my full amazement at 'being here' in one unattainable sentence which would simultaneously transmit the smell and texture of my skin, everything stored in my memory, and all I now assent to, dissent from." Why bother trying to say the unspeakable? "Each of us is so ashamed of his own helplessness and ignorance that he considers it appropriate to communicate only what he thinks others will understand."[37]

His goal was to speak his own existence fully, without suppressing the incommunicable mystery of being. He was always looking for "that single phrase which, were it truly weighed, would suffice as a life's work."[38] It wasn't because he thought he was so special, but simply because he was himself, and he as a poet was responsible for bearing witness to that bit of reality about which he had inside knowledge. But he wanted to find a voice or a phrase which would articulate even the parts and layers of himself about which he didn't have knowledge.

> There is nothing degrading in our fundamental incapacity to lay bare all the particulars of our fate. If it were any different, if that chaotic richness, in the presence of which our faculties are like a circle of lantern light in the darkness, did not exist, we would not constantly be aspiring to form, achieved by a process of elimination, and probably the art of writing would disappear. It is enough that we realize to what extent thought and word are incommensurable with reality. Then it is possible to set one's limits consciously.[39]

What Milosz excelled at was speaking in such a way that he and his reader could become aware of what was speaking through him. Was it an epoch, a

---

36   Milosz, *Native Realm*, 5–6.
37   Milosz, *Visions from San Francisco Bay*, 3.
38   Milosz, *Visions from San Francisco Bay*, 5.
39   Milosz, *Native Realm*, 5.

century, speaking through him? A culture, or a clash of cultures, using his voice? Was he identical with his family heritage, his religion, the soil and weather? Were Lithuania and California taking turns talking in his voice? Above all, what spiritual forces were having their say when he freely chose the words and lines of a sentence?

Because he relentlessly sought this goal, Milosz can be a hard poet to read. But he is worth grappling with, because everybody should become more aware of what forces are speaking through them. Milosz is a writer whose whole life's work was to identify those forces.

As I've already said, Milosz thought of some of these forces as demonic. He said of America in general: "this continent possesses something like a spirit which malevolently undoes any attempts to subdue it. The enormity of the violated but always victorious expanse, the undulant skin of the earth diminishes our errors and merits."[40] Later in the book he reports what a European friend said to him about America: "Who knows, maybe this continent was not destined for the white man, and it might have been better to leave it alone." Milosz responds:

> I would have agreed with his divining in those mountains and deserts the powerful presence of vengeful demons with whom only the Indians knew how to maintain alliances. But in California those demons seemed to evince no good will even to the Indians, allowing themselves to be placated only because the Indians remained on the lowest level of civilization, without agriculture or the use of metal. I am also always puzzled why the white man steered clear of California for so long, though word of it had reached him through the accounts of sailors. ... In California, prehistory, millennia of generations passing without chronicle, leaving no other traces than the flint arrowheads found in the clay, collided with the nineteenth century—not the nineteenth century of revolutionaries and poets, but that other, rougher nineteenth century, the century where every many had an equal right to lust for gold.[41]

Sounding nearly Pentecostal, Milosz goes on:

> Call it delusion, but a demonic presence can be felt on this continent whose apparent concern is that Christian man see his own nature revealed and that he unleash all his brutality. Something nameless is concerned with destroying

---

[40]   Milosz, *Visions from San Francisco Bay*, 9–10.
[41]   Milosz, *Visions from San Francisco Bay*, 45–6.

ideology in him and, thus far, has rewarded him not for possessing ideology but for not possessing any.[42]

As he develops the Californian portion of his personal mythology, Milosz enters into dialogue with the poems of Robinson Jeffers, themselves haunted by the territorial spirits of the Carmel coast. And before long he has identified the demons of California, with their struggle between primal nature and technological second nature, with the Moloch of Alan Ginsberg's "Howl": "Nightmare of Moloch! Moloch whose mind is pure machinery! Moloch whose blood is running money!"[43] Indeed, the Moloch of Howl (a poem first published by Bay Area poet and San Francisco bookstore owner Lawrence Ferlinghetti) is curiously in line with "this continent's demons," as Milosz describes them. Their greatest trick, "their leisurely vengeance, consists in surrendering nature, recognizing that it could not be defended; but in place of nature there arose that civilization which to its members appears to be Nature itself, endowed with nearly all the features of that other nature. It is just as alien and hostile to me...."[44]

Conclusion: Toward Theological Categories

With the introduction of the category of demonology, we have made a full transition from literary regionalism to theological concerns. In the early stages of a project like TECC, we can conclude by gesturing beyond demonology to the other traditional doctrinal topics of systematic theology. How do each of the doctrines sound when developed with Californian categories, West Coast intellectual tools, and a local accent? We do not need to embrace Milosz's demonology in order to develop a distinctly Californian doctrine of sin. Outsiders viewing California could easily fill in the elements of our hamartiology. Joan Didion, without calling it sin, has explored this territory at some length, and has linked it to an equally anonymous notion of salvation. Taken together, the ideas of sin and salvation presuppose something about theological anthropology, the doctrine of humanity. What is California man, that God is mindful of him?

Founded as it was by the dream of westward expansion and Manifest Destiny, California's self-understanding has always been involved with a secularized doctrine of providence, and the conviction that God or the gods wanted this very

---

42   Milosz, *Visions from San Francisco Bay*, 51.
43   Milosz, *Visions from San Francisco Bay*, 66.
44   Milosz, *Visions from San Francisco Bay*, 68.

development to happen. That secularized providence is indistinguishable from a cultural eschatology, whether developed in terms of "Continent's End" (the title of a Jeffers poem) or an acceleration toward the end of history. Probably every time the word "paradise" is invoked to describe the place, something eschatological is being conjured. California is usually called a paradise because of its great natural beauty, and its literature and culture are marked by an ecological awareness that runs from John Muir's early conservationism (which he developed with constant use of religious metaphor, in gorgeous latter day King James English) to the host of recent Buddhist and New Age spiritualities. A theological account of creation developed in Californian terms is an obvious desideratum.

But it is the doctrine of God that is the true test for any theology, and this is the doctrinal area which will ultimately determine whether a Californian localist theology will be worth pursuing. Liberal theological method is already fully employed in speaking of a God of California culture, or in "naming toward the transcendent mystery" from this particular place. Such theologies will find the god they seek, as they always have. For Christian theologians who affirm that God can only be known where he has revealed himself authoritatively in Christ through the Scriptures, the whole project of theological localism is admittedly less urgent. But as California continues to develop as a self-conscious regional entity, theologians working here will increasingly ask, "what language shall I borrow?" to speak about the Christian God. Shall we borrow Californian language? Perhaps so.

Chapter 3

Can Theology Engage with California's Culture?

Jason S. Sexton

Introduction to California and Theology

In her earlier attempts to capture the euphoric essence of the Golden State, Joan Didion famously described California as "a place in which a boom mentality and a sense of Chekhovian loss meet in uneasy suspension; in which the mind is troubled by some buried but ineradicable suspicion that things had better work here, because here, beneath that immense bleached sky, is where we run out of continent."[1] Displayed repeatedly in the Sacramento-born Didion's writings, this endeavor to describe a mood, a dream, or perhaps a desperate cry, poured forth from her pen as the theme not only of hope but especially of tragedy recurrently marked her work.

Already pointed out in this volume, California's very existence is paradoxical and enigmatic,[2] as ingenious as disastrous, and as heartbreaking as hopeful. It is the dream turned nightmare for some, still giving enough reason to keep dreaming while uncertain about an exact state of consciousness; hoping that things may soon turn. It is simultaneously imaginative and blinding, as intoxicating as sobering, and often the latter only when options are all but exhausted. California is a puzzle that academics, politicians, writers, poets and paupers, sinners, saints, and even theologians have sought to make sense of and will continue to do so for a while yet.

One recent study exploring California's current civic situation, marking crises facing all Californians, suggested that at the heart of these concerns is "the fear that California lacks even a language, and an understanding, equal to

---

[1]   Joan Didion, *Slouching Towards Bethlehem* (reprint, New York: Penguin, 1974), 144.

[2]   See Chapter 1 of the present volume.

its calamity."[3] Facing scarcity of resources for addressing California's problems, ready and willing to enter the fray to address matters of responsibility and democracy by virtue of sharing a common humanity, perhaps theologians can offer some hope. Fred Sanders has suggested that theologians might even borrow language from the lines of Californian literature for their reflections on matters most critical to theology's remit—even for their ongoing God-talk.[4] Perhaps this is most appropriate because California itself is as much as anything a theological reality—itself an object of deep faith. This suggests in some sense that the question of theology's ability to engage with California is already settled, or may be assumed. Yet the question remains because theology itself is not confined to California and would exist whether or not California ever did (though the modern world as known and experienced would hardly be the same without California). In a sense, theology has already engaged the Golden State in profound ways through the work of countless groups seeking to test their claims of ultimate reality on Californian soil.

At one level, the very question of theology's ability to engage California has been sweepingly dismissed by unbelievers, by which I do not mean naturalists, secular theorists, or atheists. But perhaps because it resists his own version of "Christian America," leading theologian Stanley Hauerwas testifies, "I do not believe in California."[5] Yet whether one chooses to believe or not, the problem is that such a place as California does exist, and people of all kinds don't stop believing.[6] This poses problems of immense significance for its citizens, for others around the world who believe in it, and for the church. The present chapter asks, then, whether theology can begin to helpfully and properly reinterpret and re-engage California's culture in ways that bring the immense resources of the gospel's promises to bear on its reality, thereby laboring for the good of its citizens.

Methods that direct attention to questions of cultural engagement with theology as part of the discourse usually develop what might be called either a top-down or a bottom-up approach, with often very little methodological

---

3   Joe Matthews and Mark Paul, *California Crackup: How Reform Broke the Golden State and How We Can Fix It* (Berkeley: University of California Press, 2010), 2.

4   See Chapter 2 of the present volume, p. 33.

5   Stanley Hauerwas, *Hannah's Child: A Theologian's Memoir* (Grand Rapids: Eerdmans, 2010), 248. What precisely he meant by this is not developed.

6   Interestingly the popular song "Don't Stop Believin'," written by Bay Area band Journey and sung by Hanford-born Steve Perry, has been referred to as "a cultural touchstone" having an "eternal quality" ("Journey song cements status as cultural touchstone," *CBC News*, July 20, 2009, http://www.cbc.ca/news/arts/music/story/2009/07/20/steve-perry.html [accessed June 16, 2013]) and has been sung the world around.

consensus between either proponents, largely conditioned by pre-commitments to particular disciplinary perspectives (consensus even among theologians of the TECC Project will likely be strained). This strain has been a challenge for theology itself, one example of which might be illustrated by the approaches of twentieth-century theologians Karl Barth and Dietrich Bonhoeffer as commonly understood.

It is acknowledged that Barth viewed theology as having no direct responsibility for changing society in any ordinary sense, while Bonhoeffer saw it having robust ethical and social dimensions. The latter's perspective was one that Barth saw as not transcendent enough, and thus he found Bonhoeffer "turning grace into a principle" and "thereby beating everything else to death."[7] During a press conference in May 1962, after lecturing at the San Francisco Theological Seminary, Barth unequivocally displayed his opposition to natural theology. Highlighting society's inability to receive divine revelation, he stressed, "Disaster doesn't bring mankind closer to truth. It has never made any one listen to God's word." With a smile he is said to have then asked reporters, "Do you think the [1906] earthquake here changed the behavior of the residents?"[8] Now, the earthquake was not what brought the greatest destruction of San Francisco, caused more so by negligent political impasse and the inept dynamiting of the city's buildings, as humanly engendered as naturally,[9] which one might suppose Barth was aware of. But his locating of revelation as utterly distinct from these worldly matters is a principle that Barth insisted provides a theology capable of

---

[7]   See the discussion about the disagreement between Bonhoeffer and Barth in Charles Marsh, "Dietrich Bonhoeffer: Under the Constraint of Grace," in *Bonhoeffer, Christ and Culture*, Keith L. Johnson and Timothy Larsen (eds), (Downers Grove: InterVarsity Press, 2013), 133–5. Marsh recounts that Barth viewed theology as bearing no responsibility for changing society, making nothing happen in any "ordinary sense." Responding to post WWI Germany with how theology might be co-opted for certain political propaganda, the early Barth believed that theology ought to be practiced "now as before and as if nothing had happened." Bonhoeffer, on the other hand, especially from his time in America with social-gospel reformers and what he saw from the African-American church leaders, affirmed that "theologians must be willing to speak clearly and pay up personally," and therein he was aggravated by Barth's reluctance to make necessary ethical and social connections for doctrine (see the last quotes in Bonhoeffer, as cited in Ilse Todt et al., "Editors' Afterword to the German Edition," in *Ethics*, Dietrich Bonhoeffer Works, Vol. 6 [Minneapolis: Fortress Press, 2005], 411).

[8]   "*Pressekonferenz in San Francisco [Englisch]*," in *Karl Barth Gesamtausgabe, Gespräche 1959–1962 (GA IV.25)*, Eberhard Busch (trans.) (Zürich: Theologischer Verlag Zürich, 1995), 525–7, from *The San Francisco Examiner*, May 1962.

[9]   See some of the confusion surrounding this event and its immediate aftermath in Kevin Starr, *California: A History* (New York: Random House, 2005), 162–3.

yielding "an anthropology that is ontologically determined by the fellow-human and is ontologically oriented to their well-being." This ontologically-determined anthropology is said to then have decisive political, economic, and social consequences that, rather than engendering the prepolitical atomistic approach of the late-modernist project, cares for the weak and lowly.[10]

Additional approaches to the question of theology's relationship to culture may offer deeper integration of the transcendent with the earthly.[11] Some have suggested, however, that theology is able to engage culture only to the degree that theology resists being shaped in any way by culture, which would thus render theology something less than what any part of the great tradition or ancient creeds would render or recognize it to be. And yet any failure to affirm theology's discursive relationship to all things risks a denial of Jesus' lordship over all that Holy Scripture affirms was "in the beginning" divinely created, *ex nihilo* (out of nothing) which insists that everything is care-fully sustained, providentially-ordered and therefore all matter and events are of immense significance.

But this nevertheless leaves the question remaining about how theology does touch the ground, shaping things in any ordinary sense. Tagged to this is also whether or not a bottom-up theology can indeed be done. This problem is highlighted when theological themes are seen to be ubiquitous in California life and existence (as later chapters in this volume attempt to show), or when transcendent ontologies or philosophies are developed here and disseminated in unique ways across the globe. This is not merely because of the presence of religious people in California, although there have been (and are) many. Many of our cities and towns were named after religious figures, and countless experiences of religious phenomena have flourished here. Indeed California's life can be as much identified by various theological movements and moods as it can with economic, social, and moral booms and crises. Theological impulses and signals have been long present throughout the state's life, in all the California dream holds forth with its forms of eschatological realism, or its protological reflections on individual origins amidst the amnesia, marijuana, psychedelia,

---

[10]   See Brian A. Williams, "Karl Barth's Theology and Politics of Christological Co-Humanity," unpublished paper presented February 22, 2013 at the Winter 2013 meeting of The Kirby Laing Institute for Christian Ethics, Cambridge, UK.

[11]   See, for example, the efforts recently set forth in the following projects: Robin Gill's 3 vol. *Sociological Theology* series (Surrey, UK; Burlington, US: Ashgate, 2012–13); the work of "Ordinary Theology" seen in Jeff Astley and Leslie J. Francis (eds), *Exploring Ordinary Theology: Everyday Christian Believing and the Church* (Surrey, UK; Burlington, US: Ashgate, 2013); and the work of The Ecclesiology and Ethnography Network which has produced a number of vols. with Eerdmans and T&T Clark/Bloomsbury and whose new journal *Ecclesial Practices* (Brill) began Autumn 2013.

conflicted laws, consumerism, and other cultural forces.[12] California art and architecture, sports, technology, politics, and its other cultural innovations invoke theological themes in strong ways, as extremely as any other cultural place. Religious movements likewise were given fertility on California soil and perhaps conscious and subconscious cache as being *from* California that they'd have never garnered in most places. In all these ways and more, California has changed the world. But how does this relate to theology?

Before moving to address this essay's main question, and because I have already claimed that theology exists both apart from inasmuch as within California's existence, a preliminary question begs attention.

What is Theology?

At one fundamental level, theology is the expression of consistent belief and living. It implies "revelation," *theologia vera* (true theology) or divine communication; not the mere reflections of the human mind or Bahktinian projections toward that highest ceiling. It asserts that amidst all the challenges of communicant expressions in our world, language about God may be taken to truly make reference to things as they really are. This is because it contends that God has spoken in Holy Scripture, which speaks truth about whatever it speaks of; and it speaks with unique reference to a self-giving God who has graciously disclosed himself there. Accordingly, theology does not merely affirm this notion but labors to make the matter of revelation plain, ensuring that the truth can be heard, striving to develop sound plausibility structures for this hearing while maintaining a moderate foundationalism reinforced by a hearty realism.

It further maintains the archetypal/ectypal distinction of revelation that correlates to the *homoousios* (same substance) humanity and deity found in Jesus Christ, maintaining a posture that beautifully and capably purports to have the ability to give coherent explanations of all realities. But "all realities" means that theology has been both locally and institutionally nurtured in its variegated expressions, where these realities could be meaningfully situated and interpreted.

In describing "theology" one cannot fail to acknowledge various twentieth-century theologies or descriptive theological systems—feminist, black, Latin American, dispensational, covenant, queer, and others. Because theology flows

---

[12]   See the account of one fortune built on selling this "Dream" in Eric John Abrahamson, *Building Home: Howard F. Ahmanson and the Politics of the American Dream* (Berkeley: University of California Press, 2013).

from a living confession, shaped by the inexhaustible riches found in the gospel with its comprehensive truth claims, various heavily schematizing or corrective theologies can be expected. But rather than the way these emphases tended to compartmentalize and totalize, theology is much better conceived as the expansive rendering of theologies of the whole. To be fair, interdisciplinary theological work being attempted by academics and practitioners in California may very well be ultimately rendered by historians as regional theology, or a theology of more meager proportions. But theology itself does not claim to be satisfied by this relegation or ghettoization inasmuch as its range is not limited to either empirical or the temporal.

Theology's claims regard matters temporal and atemporal, "created" and "uncreated," as the Athanasian Creed states. This shows theology as concerned not just with God, but with all created things, both in their particular relations to God and between one another. Theology deals not with the created order in itself, but the created order in its status as *creaturely*, and thus radically contingent.[13] Therefore theology takes as subject matter all things in relation to God, while simultaneously serving as a witness as it "mirrors, or ... partakes of, the character of its divine subject." In some sense, then, theology is very much both a human creation and a divine one.[14] Admittedly some so-called developments on the human side are simply malformed, perhaps owing to being removed from ecclesial and contextual rootedness, or to having been oppressive to certain groups, or to having proceeded in imbalance by failing to speak out against injustice or things that God's word is concerned with. Committing these errors by failing to pay sufficient attention to God's word marks a negative web of inter-relations characteristic of, quite simply, bad theology. This is one reason why the university's significance for theology remains critical.

Theology as an Academic Discipline

We know that the historical development of higher education in the West had a significant place for theology in its faculties, and the integration of faith and learning.[15] This was the case with the medieval Parisian university which saw intellectual practice as reasonable or rational "*because*, and *in so far as*, it is

---

[13]   A.N. Williams, "What is Systematic Theology?" *International Journal of Systematic Theology* 11/1 (Jan 2009), 47.

[14]   Williams, "What is Systematic Theology?", 48–9.

[15]   In one sense, higher education has always been about moral formation. See Stanley Hauerwas, *The State of the University: Academic Knowledges and the Knowledge of God* (Oxford: Blackwell, 2007), 46.

devoutly Christian."[16] The ordering of human life before God and social life were meant to be developed through the deepening of virtues like humility, piety, and peace through learning. Through the halls of Berlin, Oxford, and Dublin with John Henry Newman, theological reflection on the role of the university has come a long way, but has never lost the notion that the content of confessed faith may yield sound learning able to contribute to the common good. California was no different.

Henry Durant, the Congregationalist clergyman and Yale philosophy professor, moved to San Francisco "with college on the brain," and founded Contra Costa Academy the very same year of his arrival in 1853, which in 1855 became the College of California. Following the 1852-chartered University of the Pacific by Wesleyans in San Jose (formerly known as California Wesleyan College) and the Jesuit Catholic College of Santa Clara established in 1853, Durant's vision, though nondenominational, was to "furnish the means of a thorough and comprehensive education under the pervading spirit and influence of the Christian religion," which was meant to serve the "common interest in the promotion of the highest welfare of the State, as fostered and secured by the diffusion of sound and liberal learning."[17] See also the other academic institutions of great academic significance in California and the nation, including University of Southern California (founded in 1880) and Whittier College (founded in 1887), both private institutions today which began as schools with deep ecclesial sponsorship and support.

Not long after this, however, in the middle of the second half of the nineteenth century, American universities sought reform and ultimately discontinued natural theology courses (University of California's last was in 1871), with moral philosophy being retired shortly thereafter (University of California's last was in 1879), largely because, it was argued, ethical reflection derived reasoning from theological considerations. This reconstitution of departments was meant to give way to the academic study of the science of religion, but nevertheless had a profound influence on the separation between faith and reason.[18] In

---

[16] Mike Higton, *A Theology of Higher Education* (Oxford: Oxford University Press, 2012), 4.

[17] William Warren Ferrier, *Origin and Development of the University of California, Ninety Years of Education in California, 1846–1936: A Presentation of Educational Movements and Their Outcome in Education Today* (Berkeley: Sather Gate Book Shop, 1937), 181, cited in John Aubrey Douglass, *The California Idea and American Higher Education: 1850 to the 1960 Master Plan* (Palo Alto: Stanford University Press, 2000), 38–9 nn. 60–1.

[18] Julie A. Reuben, *The Making of the Modern University: Intellectual Transformation and the Marginalization of Morality* (Chicago: University of Chicago Press, 1996), 88–90.

California, theology went out a long time ago, its departure cemented with the emergence of Edmund G. "Pat" Brown and the promises held out in "The Master Plan" for Higher Education of 1960, which even into the present day has marked theology's ongoing exile from the state's major universities.[19] In one sense, however, this is consistent with the nature of theology, which is no mere compartment of any university faculty.

Theology as the Dynamic Expression of Faith

Theology is something far more audacious than what can be contained in the university, and something much more than merely academic. By "theology" we are referring to the dynamic expression of the body of material and content of Christian faith. Well aware that religious studies and even the social-scientific study of religion have dominated the academic scene, these disciplines do not fully comprehend this dynamic expression. On the other hand, theology is the discipline that holds promise of the integrative work. Pulitzer Prize winning novelist and Fellow of the American Academy of Arts and Sciences, Marilynne Robinson states that, "Theology, of all modes of thought, integrates all the elements of human experience more exhaustively than any of them. Its purpose is to integrate at every level. That in itself means that meaning becomes pervasive rather than being isolated in narrow interests and purposes."[20] In various ways faith matters have continued to play a role in California's public square. But thick theological description has often not been part of the discourse either.

Compare also Higton's critique of John Henry Newman and Hauerwas in *A Theology of Higher Education*, 79–106, 123–8.

[19]   See some of the consequences of secularized knowledge and its relationship to theology and the university in Brad Gregory, *The Unintended Reformation: How a Religious Revolution Secularized Society* (Cambridge: Harvard University Press, 2012), 355–9. And while there are some major universities in the US which still have theology courses in their curriculum (for example, University of Virginia), it seems that California's institutions of higher learning have completely done away with theology as a source of knowledge. And while some like John Aubrey Douglass ("Can We Save the College Dream?" *Boom: A Journal of California* 1/2 [Summer 2011], 41) are calling for a "rebirth" in California higher education, this is largely driven by conversations over economic costs and contain no proposal for a future role of theology. In the opening remarks of his address at the Spring 2013 TECC Project workshop at the Berkeley City Club, March 11, 2013, the eminent California historian Kevin Starr commented that the TECC Project is "doing a favor for the university by trying to reconnect theology back to it."

[20]   See William Storrar's interview with Marilynne Robinson, Center for Theological Inquiry, Princeton, July 10, 2010, http://www.youtube.com/watch?v=wWkOkfN3VAg (accessed November 13, 2013).

It does, however, seem that even some of California's leading sociologists are acknowledging that the more responsible presence of reinvigorated theological reflection is needed in public life, as well as the sound and explicit structural bases for religious expression.[21]

If we can then talk about what this expression might be with the language of a center, it is going to be from this center that the dynamic exposition begins centrifugally moving out and thus regarding both the particular and the expansive. For Christian theology, this center seems to be echoed in the amazingly simple yet profound statement made by the Apostle Paul who wrote, "For I decided to know nothing among you except Jesus Christ, and him crucified" (1 Cor. 2:1 NRSV; see also Phil. 3:8–12). This message of "Christ crucified" is said to contain both God's wisdom and power in its very fabric (1 Cor. 1:22), yet by some is deemed a stumbling block and foolishness for various reasons. If there is something of a recovery of theology to happen—in California or anywhere—complete with its central and wider messages and implications, it is going to need to play a much more relevant role in society and the academy. And if theology indeed is the queen of the sciences, as some today may still want to argue, she must be a queen who, above all, labors to serve the inhabitants of the land, and who deploys her abilities, whatever they may be, in service of others. Theology must be a queen who serves.

Theology is still, however, often perceived to be empirically unsatisfying to the scientific disciplines, unless any particular investigation is genuinely ongoing.[22] In the latter case, investigations follow the world *as it really is* and not as rendered in exclusion by science or any other academic field in isolation, governed inflexibly by certain fashionable rules of any present moment and shut off to new possibilities and the pursuit of deeper questions. But this seems to be exactly the way the universe works, with various longings and impulses met by surprises and wondrously unbeknown satisfactions and discoveries which remain increasingly forthcoming. This is the message and disposition theologians bring to the table as the sobering, hopeful balm that confronts the world with

---

[21] Sociologists of religion seem increasingly aware that theological reflection is a significantly absent part of their work which some are beginning to address. See Wade Clark Roof, "Engaged Faith: My Own and That of Others," in *Studying Religion and Society: Sociological Self-Portraits*, Titus Hjelm and Phil Zuckerman (eds), (New York: Routledge, 2013), 173–4.

[22] See Wolfhart Pannenberg, *Systematic Theology*, vols. 1–3 (trans. Geoffrey W. Bromiley) (Grand Rapids: Eerdmans, 1991–98) as one who in the postwar German universities labored to set forth theology as a hard science and thus challenging the other disciplines to meet with theology on the common ground of historical reality.

a savior who carries a promise of one day healing all that is broken, renewing all that is decayed, and satisfying all longing hearts. In this manner theology is no isolatable academic category or remote body of knowledge easily cordoned off as it has been in some faculties that have viewed "theology" as theoretical and abstract whilst "practical theology" deals with practice and real world affairs. If theology is an exposition of the gospel, it addresses the real broken world we live in with a healing hope that God has chosen to reconcile an alienated world, promising healing of all that is torn in the present.

Theology as Contextual

Theology is shaped by everything else insofar as it—as a confession or internal description of matters of faith—exists as an expression of the Creed which denotes the triune God in action and in relation to all things. To varying degrees and from time to time this comes about as benevolent ectypal expression of the archetypal reality in the life of God, which then leads to the imperfect ongoing construction of models after the reality.[23]

In this way it is right to speak of the medieval distinction made between *theologia viatorum* (theology on the way, or pilgrim theology) and *theologia beatorum* (theology as it really exists, or will be understood eschatologically).[24] In Californian terms, the desire for and attempt to find ultimate fulfillment that has marked so many Californian events and endeavors, and which is true to theology, finds the true paradise remaining ultimately elusive and beyond us.

Of course, theology has had two thousand years of refinement, careful nuance, internal self-critical engagement, and limitless manners of contextual flourishing, aside from its own moral merits and robust claims about the universe. Beyond this it manifests the ability to meaningfully interpret the world, developing wisdom and careful approaches with reference to all matters in every sphere of life. This asserts a distinctly "Christian" theology, which itself displays capable theological descriptions of religions which, in California especially, display unique forms of reality which are subversively fulfilled in the

---

[23]   See John Webster, "Principles of Systematic Theology," *International Journal of Systematic Theology* 11/1 (Jan 2009), 58–64; and John Webster, "Introduction: Systematic Theology," in *The Oxford Handbook of Systematic Theology*, John Webster, Kathryn Tanner, and Iain Torrance (eds), (Oxford: Oxford University Press, 2007), 12–14.

[24]   For a treatment of these categories see the excellent discussion in Richard A. Muller, *Post-Reformation Reformed Dogmatics: The Rise and Development of Reformed Orthodoxy, ca. 1520 to ca. 1725; Vol. 1: Prolegomena to Theology* (2d ed., Grand Rapids: Baker, 2003), 255–69.

gospel of Jesus Christ. And theology implies, again, divine revelation, and the astonishment and wonder that comes with faith in a message as radical as good news from heaven can be, with the full force of its message to wayward children of a father who still loves them and the implications of this message for life now and in the world to come.

No theology is uncontextual, then. It is all shaped by particular cultural needs, conditions, and language. Any pure kind of theology only exists in the being and action of God, and therefore whatever theology is done by any living theologian is entirely second-order, part of a fallen enterprise, and subject to err. Yet it nevertheless participates in the reality of God's saving action in Christ to reconcile the world to himself (2 Cor. 5:19). It aims to shake off various trappings that under scrutiny may be expressions of earlier forms of Christianity which are not essential to the gospel and may indeed prove as unnecessary hindrances to ongoing expressions of Jesus' lordship over all realities. And it remains committed to particular localized expressions of faith in Christ, forged in the reality of the Spirit's constitution of church *qua* church with its intrinsic love for Jesus Christ daily lived out in various community situations and while remaining captive to the word of God. As such, California will have particular expressions of Christianity in its particular contexts. Whether these are in any meaningful sense *unique* in the world remains an area of ongoing exploration.[25]

Theology as Confessional

Theology is dynamic and ecclesial, at home in the church and aiming for the flourishing of all human beings while treating all knowledge as relational, contextual, communal, eschatological,[26] and transformational (understood via soteriology and sanctification). And thus it sees everything as fundamentally theological—containing authoritative sources, traditions, and contexts for furtherance and development—aiming to be explicit and self-conscious about this, deploying rich millennia-tested resources from theology and theological

---

[25] See chapters 10–12 in this volume for a brief conversation on whether there is a "theology of California."

[26] For examples of employing eschatology and anthropology to interpret cultural phenomena, see Luke Bretherton, "Consuming the Body: Contemporary Patterns of Drug Use and Theological Anthropology," in *Public Theology in Cultural Engagement*, Stephen R. Holmes (ed.), (Milton Keynes, UK: Paternoster, 2008), 94–130; and Luke Bretherton, "The Real Battle of St Paul Cathedral: The Occupy Movement and Millennial Politics," *Huff Post*, October 19, 2011, http://www.huffingtonpost.co.uk/luke-bretherton/the-real-battle-of-st-pau_b_1065214.html (accessed November 14, 2013).

discourse (most of which have shaped the world in the twentieth century for good or ill, but rarely acknowledged to have done so) in order to come into closer contact with various topographies.[27]

Because "California," identifiable as such and as a socio-political entity of the United States, is a relatively recent human invention, seeming to endlessly reinvent itself,[28] generated from the most imaginative resources of the human situation, theology offers a unique grasp of these various phenomenological features and innovations with protological, purposive and ultimately eschatological meanings involved.

In these ways, theology as a *confession* affirms all humans as equally significant public actors, with the church as a primary actor in the public square,[29] indicating theology as something uniquely done by the church *qua* church, or as the body of Christ—the concrete substance of what God has spoken to the world. Of course, we are now no longer referring to the academic discipline of theology (although this confession will inform the academy and vice versa), but to the faithful confession of the promise found in the gospel. It expresses amazement at being a direct recipient of the work of divine economic action in salvation history, and having experienced personal ontological change, or a paradigm shift that has awakened this confession. It is not neutral. By the truths inherent in this confession we admit to now seeing things completely different, exclaiming not just "Jesus as Lord" (1 Cor. 12:3; and 2 Cor. 4:5) but also doxologically that "with you is the fountain of life; in your light we see light" (Ps. 36:9, NIV). Setting forth the integrity of the church's faithful confession indicates its exclusive and capable manner of reckoning with all things. It includes responsible stewardship of this confession that has been explicated/enacted for the past 2,000 years and throughout the entirety of redemptive history. The gospel properly confessed,

---

[27]   See the observation of Stanley Grenz's theological work seeking to correlate with sensibilities from an assumed turn to a large-scale postmodern epistemology in Kevin J. Vanhoozer, "Evangelicalism and the Church: The Company of the Gospel," in *The Futures of Evangelicalism: Issues and Prospects*, Craig Bartholomew, Robin Parry, and Andrew West (eds), (Leicester, UK: Inter-Varsity Press, 2003), 67–8. See also a form of correlationism in Tillich that Sanders responds to in Chapter 2 of this volume (see pp. 20–22) which is quite different from what Vanhoozer observes in Grenz.

[28]   See some of this historically chronicled in Starr, *California: A History* and also in the remarkable work, Josef Chytry, *Mountain of Paradise: Reflections on the Emergence of Greater California as a World Civilization* (New York: Peter Lang, 2013).

[29]   For a discussion of various actors in the public square and ways of doing public theology in light of other approaches, see Sebastian C.H. Kim, *Theology in the Public Sphere: Public Theology as a Catalyst for Open Debate* (London: SCM, 2011), 3–26.

then, truthfully addresses the major social, political, and ethical questions of the day.

Because California sits at a crossroads of contradictions[30]—political, moral, ethical, economic, religious, ethnographic, social, and historical—there is nothing better to make sense of its features when the other disciplines exhaust the widest range and farthest reach of their best conceptual tools. Revelation, protological as much as present-apocalyptic and eschatological, is what theology presupposes, labors along with, and lives in light of.[31]

It takes cues often and repeatedly from a transcendent base, affirming things as spiritual and Spirit-wrought, and therefore good; or otherwise some things as displeasing to God from what may be known of this God's character in Holy Scripture (for example, the golden calf of Ex. 32). So theology as a confessional reality may struggle at times to reckon with tools of anthropologists, ethnographers, historians and sociologists. Theology can and will always say more than what these fields can unfold; but must say nothing less than what these say, and will sometime contradict and even confront them, facing whatever consequences may come.[32] Sometimes the conclusions of other disciplines need to be reassessed, or reinterpreted, or reframed in light of a bigger picture— theology most often comes with a different starting point and carries different aims. This ought to settle the question about whether theologians are more akin to academic social-scientists or historians; or else whether they are more like pastors or activists, or something else entirely. In describing claims that "concern the extraordinary in the ordinary," the eternal quickening of human history, Kevin Vanhoozer offers this:

---

[30] See the brief reflections in Richard Flory, "Making Sense of Religion in Southern California," Center for Religion and Civic Culture Blog, December 21 2012, http://crcc. usc.edu/blog/news/making-sense-of-religion-in-southern-california/ (accessed November 14, 2013); Edward J. Blum, "Gods of the Golden Coast," *Boom: A Journal of California* 2/2 (Summer 2012), 82–5; Dowell Myers, "California Futures," *Boom: A Journal of California* 2/2 (Summer 2012), 37–54; with the moral contradictions highlighted in Starr "Intro" to *California: A History*, ix–xiv.

[31] Apocalyptic, however, may be too ambitious [although may be redeemed with realist eschatology] since it displaces church and the very possibility of regional theology, evaporating ecclesial confessional echoes along with various redemptive legacies and good cultural plausibility structures that cohere with the missional shape of this divinely-made and ordered universe.

[32] See, for example, the Barmen Declaration (1934) of the German Confession Church which opposed the practices of the Nazi-regime, an obvious case where the church's action led them to face exile, persecution, and martyrdom. And it is here that theology especially shows its strength, as the voice that remains—speaking for the poor and societally marginalized— when all other discourse is sequestered and stymied.

The vocation of the Christian theologian is to be an interpreter-martyr: a truth-teller, a truth-doer, a truth-sufferer. Truth requires evangelical passion, not postmodern passivity; personal appropriation, not calculation. The theologian is to embody in his or her own person the core of Christian culture, in order to provide a focus for Christian wisdom. Making Christian truth claims ultimately is not a crusade, nor a pilgrimage, nor even a missionary journey, but rather a *martyrological* act. Genuine theology is not only about the art of reasoning well (rationality), but about living well (wisdom) and dying well (martyrdom).[33]

While perhaps being slightly more hesitant than previous eras to speak of theology as queen of the sciences, its apologetic task finds it happily employed as *servant* to the sciences and humanities, although transcending and running through each in complementing and subversively fulfilling ways. While morality remains a significant feature and aim for all disciplines, it is best and most comprehensively built on the basis of theological structures and considerations, which further stress the importance of biblical-theological engagement as high on the priority list (see Gen. 3:4–5), yielding epistemologies of theology which are self-aware and themselves witness to the gospel insofar as they are expositions reflective of the archetypal love of God.

What *in the World* is Theology?

The question must be asked about what theology is for, or what does it aims to do within a culture. It advances the question of particularity, of theology in and for (and from) a particular culture. It picks up the matter of a theology even of California culture. To investigate these matters requires a preliminary consideration of the nature of culture itself.

Defining Culture

Culture often eludes definition, and is notoriously difficult to describe. Cultural critic Raymond Williams noted that the term is "one of the two or three most complicated words in the English language."[34] T.S. Eliot observed that when

---

[33]   Kevin J. Vanhoozer, "The Trials of Truth: Mission, Martyrdom, and the Epistemology of the Cross," in *To Stake a Claim: Mission and the Western Crisis of Knowledge*, J. Andrew Kirk and Kevin J. Vanhoozer (eds), (Maryknoll: Orbis, 1999), 156.

[34]   Raymond Williams, *Keywords: A Vocabulary of Culture and Society* (rev. and exp., New York: Oxford University Press, 1983), 87; emphasis in original.

contemplating remains of a distinct civilization and its influence, culture is what was *"worth while"* for that civilization to have existed; thus he opined that culture is simply "that which makes life worth living."[35] Offering his propositions on culture and how it changes against prevailing views, James Davison Hunter recently suggested that culture is "a normative order by which we comprehend others, the larger world, and ourselves and through which we individually and collectively order our experience."[36]

Emphasizing attentiveness to both inherent systems and practices, Kevin Vanhoozer defines culture as being *"made up of 'works' and 'worlds' of meaning."*[37] Each of these descriptions highlights that culture is a very particular matter wherein humans exist and cultivate life together. Beyond just the nature of humanity is something that signifies and denotes the significance of various beliefs, values and traditions. Once again, much more than the items or things that are created and consumed in a particular context, culture denotes the impulses and rhythms of making and enjoying meaningful life.

Californian Culture and the Theological Place of "California"

If culture is about making and enjoying meaningful life, few places can claim to have held out as robust a promise for a better life in the last 200 years than California. The end of the "out West" phenomena for Europeans and Americans, and "the beginning of the new world" for those in the Far East,[38] California has been perhaps more dreamed about, imagined, and longed for than any other place in recent history, both from a socio-political and economic standpoint as well as from within popular culture. It has also been a place prone to the begetting of dreams and innovation, and the strengthening of the imagination. There is something about this particular region of North America on the Pacific Rim, situated on the San Andreas Fault, that academics have sought to make sense of.[39]

---

[35]   T.S. Eliot, *Notes Towards the Definition of Culture* (2d ed., London: Faber and Faber 1961), 27.

[36]   James Davison Hunter, *To Change the World: The Irony, Tragedy, and Possibility of Christianity in the Late Modern World* (New York: Oxford University Press, 2010), 32.

[37]   Kevin J. Vanhoozer, "What is Everyday Theology? How and Why Christians Should Read Culture," in *Everyday Theology: How to Read and Interpret Cultural Trends*, Kevin J. Vanhoozer, Charles A. Anderson, and Michael J. Sleasman (eds), (Grand Rapids: Baker, 2007), 26.

[38]   This insight is owed to Russell Jeung.

[39]   For example, see the Los Angeles School of geographers which has sought to capture the significance of Los Angeles, chief among them is Mike Davis, *City of Quartz: Excavating the Future in Los Angeles* (New York: Verso, 1990).

It is not as though California's soil has not provided contested religious space for the pluralist and special equity promised to all religious groups under the First Amendment,[40] but a regional "theology of place" is something that theology especially can begin to locate, even while seeking to address questions about why some things happen here in remarkable ways that do not—could not—happen elsewhere. In considering such a question theology begins with the first question God asks of humans: "where are you?"[41]

Any kind of deeper engagement with cultural "place" naturally tempts one toward boosterism or an amalgamated tribalism. It does not have to be this way, especially as there have been copious studies of California from the traditional disciplines that have resisted this. Many of these have sought to understand the inner logic of California. While others have decried, largely due to the intense dynamic of the place, "Anyone who knows enough to define California through culture knows better than to try."[42] But theology offers more, not just in making sense of contingent realities in ways that theology uniquely can, but also offering its language, resources, and conceptual tools to other disciplines for the sake of further insight that true interdisciplinary work may yield.

Any theological investigation into cultural place will affirm *creatio ex nihilo*, and that all other worlds that may be created are contingent upon the omnipotent and *a se* (self-sufficient) reality of the divine being who sustains everything that exists. Every world created by humans carries a *ratio* or logic divinely gifted to the world in such a way that every other world created is derivative of God's ultimate world.[43] In this way, creation is meant to reflect the glories of its Creator—to image God—while humans themselves are meant *to be* that very *imago Dei*. Stephen Holmes says that Christian theology, by its very nature, is both capable of providing and indeed *is* "a coherent account of all created realities in relation

---

[40] See Bret E. Carroll, "Worlds in Space: American Religious Pluralism in Geographic Perspective," *Journal of the American Academy of Religion* 80/2 (June 2012), 304–64.

[41] For an excellent study that theologically examines matters of social and geographical location and matters of natural and built environments, see Eric O. Jacobsen, *The Space Between: A Christian Engagement with the Built Environment* (Grand Rapids: Baker, 2012).

[42] James Quay, "Beyond Dreams and Disappointments: Defining California Through Culture," in *A Companion to California History*, William Deverell and David Igler (eds), (Malden: Blackwell, 2008), 3.

[43] This idea is etched in stone atop the main entrance to the Fisher Museum of Art, University of Southern California: "The True Work of Art is but a Shadow of the Divine Perfection."

to God through Jesus Christ and the Holy Spirit, and of the God to whom we are thus related."[44]

A significant problem, though, is that theology has not been part of the conversations about the particular features of California life. This state's cultural significance reaches the far corners of the earth, in both high and low forms of culture. If various other disciplines can engage California—history, sociology, geography, nuclear astro-physics, aviation, botany, ethnography, environmental science, seismology, law, economics, urban planning, public policy, engineering, public health, conservation biology, transportation and communication studies, and the rest—in order to address the fringes of California's extreme situations, allowances and provisions, then why not theology, which can integrate all these and aims to complement, engage, and enhance them? And all this, especially when religious experience has flourished here and the church as a public actor has been enduringly present and active on the scene at the local congregational level, not merely in the form of institutionally-based organizations enabling religious experiences or religious sentiments tantamount to euphoric or identity-shaping nostalgia, but as a theologically life-giving organism.

Theology is not only the ever-present (tacit) feature in California's culture that should be recognized for its conspicuous nature, as well as for being the discipline that gives the closest categorical language to "make sense of" things (which other disciplines struggle to do), but theology makes claims about things and has potential to change games if its claims are true. And it carries the promise of not only striking chords by rendering what is true, but also what is beautiful and good. Jane Williams has reasoned, "As Christians who believe in God the Creator, anything 'true' is nothing for us to worry about. God is the source of all. So the discovery of anything that is true is simply the revelation of the character of God."[45] Theology further has the capacity to suggest that something may not *really* be what it has been thought to be, possessing potential paradigm-shifting power similar to what was yielded in the Copernican or scientific revolutions. Theology may shed light on things, considering insights from other disciplines that allow theology's categories to further illumine the subject matter under investigation, profoundly shaping the understanding of things. In this, while maintaining confidence in its ability to describe objects, action, and meaning, theology is not dependent on other disciplines for its ability to move forward in its cultural appraisals, but must be tempered in humility when approaching

---

[44]   Stephen R. Holmes, "Introduction," in *Public Theology in Cultural Engagement*, Stephen R. Holmes (ed.), (Milton Keynes, UK: Paternoster, 2008), xi.

[45]   Jane Williams, "Creation, Christology and the Human Vocation," college lecture, March 7, 2013, Ridley Hall, Cambridge, UK.

subjects that theologians have neither been known for engaging nor have engaged in meaningful ways (this does not suggest that the church has not been engaging California but only that academic theology has not been!).

Back to Joan Didion. If things, as she sees it, *had better work here*, and they fall apart, then what? It seems the only answer is to keep searching for a higher order. The truth is, however, that things do *work* here. But the looming question is this: At what (or whose) expense? From technology to church to industry to innovation to sports to entertainment—things certainly do work here. But things also fail here. As much is seen with the world's leading prison state, largely and conveniently relegating these facilities to far out of the way locations. While critics have often suggested California may be a "failed state" with its massive financial problems, Governor Jerry Brown has incessantly looked to creative funding strategies for the state's woes. This materialized in the Spring 2013 trip to China in search of "plenty of billions" of foreign investment dollars whilst local unions also seemed willing to help—for an additional price, of course.[46] Religious groups, especially those with aberrant theologies, have also experienced scandals and bankruptcy, most notably the recent demise of Robert Schuler's Crystal Cathedral in Garden Grove. Hopes of grandeur meet true defeat. Parasitic groups also surface. On the religious level these include advocates of the so-called "prosperity gospel," an especially hubristic form seen on the television series "Preachers of L.A."; and atheist mega-churches like LA's Sunday Assembly have also emerged. But amidst the tragedy and artificiality present on multiple levels, personal and corporate—these religious examples being just one category that has co-opted theology and which a coherent theology might critically and constructively engage—Joan Didion still remained hopeful for a society of a "higher order."

True theology is meant to guide human flourishing. It accounts for the big questions that scientists and leading politicians work to address, which affect ordinary people in profound ways. The John Templeton Foundation has proceeded with the desire to see science and faith work together in fruitful ways, where modern scientific research (especially neuroscience) is meant to yield incredible discoveries for religion and theology.[47] One might suppose,

---

[46]   See Juliet Williams, "Jerry Brown in China: California Governor Heads to Asia Seeking Investments," *Huff Post*, April 6, 2013, http://www.huffingtonpost.com/2013/04/07/jerry-brown-in-china_n_3033523.html; and Saki Knafo, "California Prison Guards Union Pushes for Prison Expansion," *Huff Post*, September 9, 2013, http://www.huffingtonpost.com/2013/09/09/california-prison-guards_n_3894490.html (accessed November 15, 2013).

[47]   For example, see Justin L. Barrett, *Born Believers: The Science of Children's Religious Belief* (New York: Free Press, 2012).

additionally, that this street runs both ways, especially as divinely revealed theology, accommodated to the human capacity and contained in the body of Scripture, comprehends many holy sciences, according to William Perkins. Perkins understood the principal science as theology itself, which yields "a doctrine sufficient to live well."[48] But this, of course poses a challenge for those who would seek to engage theologically with California, or any society. What are the nature and consequences of this higher order of society that Didion was referring to? Californians display a kind of determination boasting the extraordinary capacity for ingenious forms of creativity yet with often less attention to social and moral flourishing.[49] But when can we adequately determine that we have gone too far?

Theology can help with this. It is needed for a coherent grasp of what makes California what it is—diverse and uniform, plural and singular, defined locally in fluid interchange of many realities, and theoretically through media, representative legislation (as anonymous as this can be after Progressive reforms), and the academy. Theology is needed because it stands present on the scene declaring that things are not now the way they're supposed to be. And an essential component of the mission of the church is to reckon with this reality in light of the healing that God will effect for the world through Christ. Theology aims to make all these matters plain, acknowledging that mission doesn't take place apart from the unlimited ranging exposition of the inexhaustible core of our confession and those matters that the core of this message is related to.

While boasting these capabilities, however, it is worth considering how theology resists dominating other disciplines when its claims are so sweeping and its reach so vast, spanning from the transcendent unto the transcendent with audacious promises for this in-between state. It can do so, however, because its discourse is not limited there inasmuch as the transcendent intersects with the contingent, even to the point of becoming one with it, and thereby offering hope amidst the realities of human existence often beset with tragedy.

Theology refers to the relationship of things to one another, which necessarily means prioritizing and regulating things in relation to others that may be more or less significant. For example, a homeless person on Skid Row or in the Tenderloin

---

[48]   William Perkins, *A Golden Chaine: or, The Description of Theologie*, in The Workes of That Famovs and Worthy Minister of Christ in the Uniuersitie of Cambridge, Mr. William Perkins, Vol. 1 (London: John Legatt, 1623–26), 11.

[49]   Kevin Starr observes Josiah Royce as among the first to evaluate the Gold Rush as a social and moral event (*California*, 89). See the additional pressing environment and societal issues (immigration, energy, economics, to name a few) that have plagued Californians in Starr, *California*, 333ff.

District is more important than a famous Hollywood record store. This is not to suggest that music is unimportant, nor the vinyl on which music has been placed, and certainly not those individuals who wrote, performed, recorded, mixed, produced, packaged, marketed and aimed to sell it. Music is an essential part of being human insofar as its production is a *human* action relating material reconfiguration into mathematical sequences that are rendered both fitting and, in some instances, exquisite, for whoever might be the listener or judge.[50]

What theology does is frame things in light of the divine economic action. It shows that the worth of any particular human being, however perceived by society, is given significance as part of the material universe endowed with order and wonderful beauty from the Creator's handiwork, as theologians claim. But further, the significance of such a designation comes not from an investigation into the nature of the subject, as if in isolation. It derives from the truthfulness of the Creator becoming one with creation: *as a human.* A very particular human. A poor one, societally marginalized, treated as a criminal and despised. It is in light of these considerations that the gospel proclamation endemic to the church's mission takes shape, in the language and thought forms that a culture inhabits. But as it does so, it too has something to say about particular cultures.

Theology of California Culture

Before any attempt can be made at drawing theological features from California's culture in a larger effort at rendering a theology of California culture, it must be noted that there seems to be something about California that elucidates theological themes and plays with them in dynamic ways, perhaps even more intensely than any other place. In vibrant ways California's culture co-opts these themes, using them for incredible and often for less than noble aims. In this way there seems to be something quite unique about California's creative culture. But what might a Christian reading of this culture look like?

California's Effects on its Occupants (and Visitors)

From all over the world people have some idea about California, even if they've never been here. If they have been here, the ideas often become more concrete and

---

    50   For a recent theological accounting of music and temporality, see Jeremy S. Begbie, *Theology, Music and Time* (Cambridge: Cambridge University Press, 2000); and also Jeremy Begbie, *Music, Modernity, and God: Essays in Listening* (New York: Oxford University Press, 2014).

even more imaginative, especially since it is near impossible to take in California's vast geographic terrain and kaleidoscopic culture even in one lifetime. But what then does this do to people, both the modern inhabitants of the land as well as its visitors? While we could consider this question by reflecting on the character of its residents, which would be a fascinating study in theological anthropology (especially since hardly anyone has been here more than five or six generations; most are second or third generation), to explore this question momentarily I will briefly consider a few high profile visitors to the state.

T.S. Eliot's visit to Southern California makes something of an interesting picture into the hope and tragedy of a love that never happened. He visited Claremont on one occasion, arriving December 27, 1932 and leaving January 6, 1933 after one lecture at Scripps's Balch Hall on January 5 and a talk at UCLA. But the main reason for the visit was Emily Hale, to spend time together with her, and alone. Hale and Eliot met in Boston in 1913 and some biographers have suggested a romantic relationship that ended when Eliot departed for Oxford in 1915 and married Vivienne Haigh-Wood the same year—a difficult marriage from early on. Hale and Eliot began corresponding in 1927. Hale joined the Scripps faulty in 1932 and invited Eliot out whilst he was lecturing in Harvard. Summer 1933 Eliot legally separated from his wife (who later died in a mental institution in 1947) and was later visited by Hale in England that summer. The relationship altogether is mysterious and will only be elucidated in 2020 when Eliot's staggering 1,000 letters to Hale (written between 1927 and 1957) become available. (Eliot burned all letters from Hale upon marrying his secretary Valerie Fletcher in 1957.) Whatever the relationship, whether platonic or romantic, Judy Harvey Sahak from Denison Library at Scripps College said she was Eliot's "muse" whom he placed on a pedestal as a feminine ideal. In a *New York Times* book review of Lyndall Gordon's 1988 biography of the poet, *Eliot's New Life*, Denis Donoghue wrote this:

> If Eliot was ever in love with Emily Hale, it was in some ethereal and spectral sense, a love beyond desire. It is hard to resist the suspicion that he was morally obtuse: he kept Emily Hale hanging about, full of expectation, as if she had nothing better to do than to maintain his symbolism; he certainly went far toward destroying her life.[51]

---

[51] Much of the material above draws from David Allen's interesting essay, "DAVID ALLEN: T.S. Eliot may have found Claremont the chaste land," *Inland Valley Daily Bulletin*, December 24, 2012, http://www.dailybulletin.com/general-news/20121225/david-allen-ts-eliot-may-have-found-claremont-the-chaste-land (accessed November 15, 2013).

What seems curious about this all was the pivotal moment in California, perhaps where Eliot felt free—free to separate from his wife, free and inspired to imaginatively cultivate the muse—and yet he could never again be as free as he was with Hale for that week and a half in California.[52]

It seems that a similar form of free expression was also experienced when the French philosopher Michel Foucault was invited in 1975 by Leo Bersani to become visiting professor in French at UC Berkeley, marking his first visit to California. According to David Macey, Foucault had taken "a great liking to the West Coast, which was always to have an almost utopian appeal for him." This was the year he took acid for the first time in Death Valley, "an unforgettable evening on LSD" which some have said proffered a paradigm shifting experience. Macey described this occasion as "almost ceremonial, and had as its setting the desert, and as its background accompaniment a tape of Stockhausen." The "pleasures of California," however, would move beyond this. Foucault became involved with the gay community to a degree that "was unimaginable in France" and exhibited "a sexual openness which enchanted and enthralled him," and into which he immersed himself deeply on subsequent trips to the Bay Area. Macey noted that here seems to be where "Foucault began to develop his flirtation with the world of leather and sado-masochism, which were only some of the pleasures available."[53] The other pleasures were also those of the academic freedom he experienced here, and at the time of his death he planned to spend multiple months of the year at UC Berkeley.[54]

Another significant figure who found a temporary home in California was the poststructuralist philosopher, Jacques Derrida. Derrida followed J. Hillis Miller in 1986 from Yale to Irvine to become tenured part-time distinguished professor in Murray Kreiger's Institute of Critical Theory each Spring, a move which he thought would "recharge [his] batteries" and fit with his desire to "win the West," however sub/consciously.[55] Out here people think differently, are perceived differently, and structures work differently. This move that brought him to the West Coast continued to see moods ease away from the earlier hostility toward his deconstructionism, marked especially with a formal lecture

---

[52]   For an account of the relationship, save what may be known from January 1, 2020 when Eliot's letters to Hale become available from Princeton University, see Lyndall Gordon, *T.S. Eliot: An Imperfect Life* (London: Vintage, 1998).

[53]   David Macey, *The Lives of Michel Foucault* (London: Vintage, 1995), 338–40.

[54]   James Miller, *The Passion of Michel Foucault* (Cambridge: Harvard University Press, 1993), 327.

[55]   See these details from an interview with J. Hillis Miller in *Derrida: A Biography*, Benoît Peeters, Andrew Brown (trans.) (Malden: Polity, 2013), 371.

at Stanford in April 1999 where he was warmly introduced by Richard Rorty.[56] In 1990 Derrida agreed to entrust his personal archives to Langston Library at UC Irvine, a matter that became deeply complicated when the University fired Derrida's friend and colleague Dragan Kujundzic for having an intimate relationship with a graduate student. Derrida thought Kujundzic was both a victim of injustice and a mistreated employee. Feeling a betrayal of the trust he had given the University, especially with his archives, he issued an ultimatum in a long letter to the UCI Chancellor, July 25, 2004, that included the cessation of any further materials being gifted. The matter was complicated and Derrida died less than three months later, but it shows at least some evidence of his expectation of a way of doing things differently in California, which in the end simply could not be.[57]

Earlier on, of course, San Francisco had the Bohemian Club which existed as a rendezvous spot for creative personalities from the late nineteenth century, including journalists and artists as well as businessmen, military officers, and others. At its best it celebrated the city as a place where lightheartedness was possible and where, like the later-formed Sierra Club, "the ideality of relationship" was upheld. Oscar Wilde paid a visit to the Club during his journey to "the Occidental uttermost of American civilization." In March 1882 he stepped off the train in Oakland wearing a Spanish sombrero, velvet suit, puce cravat, yellow gloves and buckled shoes. From here he is said to have wend his way to the Bohemian Club where he ably drank his hosts under the table, which was surprising in light of his dramatic self-portrayal as an "enervated aesthetic."[58]

It is often thought that people feel as if they can really be themselves here. People tend to dream differently here, of new possibilities;[59] and here they find new problems, and new ways to discuss the problems, which has led to innovations previously unimagined in leisure, recreation, entertainment, the arts, education, punishment, religion, and countless other categories of culture,

---

[56]   Peeters, *Derrida*, 459 n., which notes Stanford University Press as one US publisher that has published most works by Derrida.

[57]   Peeters, *Derrida*, 534–6.

[58]   Kevin Starr, *Americans and the California Dream, 1850–1915* (New York: Oxford University Press, 1973), 246–8.

[59]   California was where racially-integrated couples would often end up in the postwar era, and was also the place of the first racially-integrated, intercultural church in the United States: the Fellowship of All Peoples in San Francisco, co-pastored by Howard Thurman and Alfred Fisk.

including the ecclesial. The church seems to have also experienced a unique freedom here, as chapters 4–6 of the present volume attempt to highlight.[60]

Affected by Sin/Visitors

By its nature being a discipline that refers to things, and if the Bible has anything to do with informing its content, theology is going to effectively identify some things as sinful. For Augustine, culture is said to be "an end in itself for the earthly city, but merely an aid for the heavenly." It is in this sense "a temporary, this-worldy remedy to cope with the effects of sin until Christ shall come, and sin and death and human culture shall be no more."[61] Yet, in the meantime, rampant forms of sin will exist, about which the Old Testament provides examples of radical eradication, leaving not even a trace of these idolatrous cultures if Israel was to dwell in security.[62] In this way, we might say that there are some forms of culture which are irredeemably and irreducibly sinful.

The pornography industry which has thrived in the San Fernando Valley may be one of these forms. Various cultural pressures weigh in on it that shape it (diseases and health or medical advances, artistic and recreational developments, physiological innovations and abnormalities, music and filming technology, legislative and economic factors, among other things), and other amoral factors may be contained in it such as sound business ethics, health concerns, mutual regard for the "other" when present, athletic fitness and an otherwise healthy view of the human body, and so on. Yet nevertheless, at the root-level is the sexual exploitation of human beings, leaving the pornographic actors and the consumers of this form of entertainment media as those whose own lives are often both underfulfilled (and thus seeking fulfillment in wrong places) and left destroyed in the process.[63]

---

[60]   On recent treatments of innovations in Protestant Evangelicalism, for the first half of the twentieth century see Matthew Avery Sutton, *Aimee Semple McPherson and the Resurrection of Christian America* (Cambridge: Harvard University Press, 2009), and for the latter half of the twentieth century see Darren Dochuk, *From Bible Belt to Sun Belt: Plain-Folk Religion, Grassroots Politics, and the Rise of Evangelical Conservatism* (New York: W.W. Norton, 2011).

[61]   Stephen R. Holmes, "Can Theology Engage with Culture?" in *Public Theology in Cultural Engagement*, Stephen R. Holmes (ed.), (Milton Keynes: Paternoster, 2008), 9–10.

[62]   Holmes, "Can Theology Engage with Culture?", 6–11.

[63]   Even after passing the 2012 "Measure B" ballot requiring Los Angeles County porn actors to wear condoms on film sets, summer 2013 saw multiple instances of actors testing positive with HIV. See Kathleen Miles, "Porn Moratorium After HIV-Positive Test From Performer, Cameron Bay," *Huff Post*, August 21, 2013,

Another irreducibly sinful phenomenon, to keep the matter in the sphere of sexuality, would be an adulterous relationship, which is the vacuous exchange and utter misunderstanding of the nature of marriage. At a basic level, the engagement of other-oriented genital sexual intercourse is intended as an exclusive action and expression of mutual covenantal love that is not open to others in the same way that non-exclusive friendships are, which exist in open kinds of bonding that are not sealed by genital sexual union. In this way, to invite other friends from the non-exclusive friendship category to participate in intimate expressions reserved for the exclusive bonded relationship is the essence of adultery, which is condemned by Holy Scripture. Indeed, marriage honors the other as *sexed other* in manifold non-exclusive ways as with any friendship and affirmation of another's equal human dignity. But only in genital expression within the mutual confines of an exclusive, monogamous covenantal marital union is sexual intimacy supported by the context that yields the fullness of meaning for sexual embrace and the consequent and contingent fulfilment that such an exclusive bonded union brings, which ultimately images something far greater.[64]

On the other hand, there are some cultural phenomena that may seem sinful and often are, but are not so necessarily. For example, street or prison gangs have often been established as means by which to secure flourishing and justice for oppressed groups, the avoidance of victimization, and often show forth allegiances of deep, ongoing solidarity. But with this also comes the flip

---

http://www.huffingtonpost.com/2013/08/21/porn-moratorium-hiv_n_3792761.html?utm_hp_ref=mostpopular; and "Porn star's positive HIV test prompts calls for industry shutdown," *The Guardian*, September 7, 2013, http://www.theguardian.com/culture/2013/sep/07/porn-actor-tests-positive-hiv (accessed November 16, 2013). For how pornography rewires the brain and depersonalizes sexually activity, see Nisha Lilia Diu, "Don Jon: how porn is rewiring men's brains," *The Telegraph*, November 15, 2013, http://www.telegraph.co.uk/men/thinking-man/10441027/Don-Jon-how-porn-is-rewiring-mens-brains.html (accessed November 16, 2013); and also Adam Withnall, "Pornography addiction leads to same brain activity as alcoholism or drug abuse, study shows," *The Independent*, September 22, 2013, http://www.independent.co.uk/life-style/health-and-families/health-news/pornography-addiction-leads-to-same-brain-activity-as-alcoholism-or-drug-abuse-study-shows-8832708.html (accessed December 14, 2013).

[64] While a robust biblical-theological account of human sexuality is well beyond the scope of this chapter and the present volume, yet sorely needed (highlighted especially when reaching for source material during the Proposition 8 campaign), such proposals have been few and far between, especially from evangelicals. For one responsible treatment, see Stephen R. Holmes, "Should we 'Welcome' and 'Affirm'? Reflecting on Evangelical Responses to Human Sexuality," in *Revisioning, Renewing, and Rediscovering the Triune Center: Essays in Honor of Stanley J. Grenz*, Derek J. Tidball, Brian S. Harris, and Jason S. Sexton (eds), (Eugene: Cascade, 2014), 121–34.

of a coin that could yield increased victimization from pre-emptive measures, or else the further removal from the protection of formal societal governance structures.[65] The Wild, Wild West remains such, of course. People escape to here, arriving looking for myth and fantasy, feeding into the economy that provides support for myth-making worlds, and the organization and distribution of such production.

This is the context in which Californian gave birth to Disney. As a storytelling world of wish-fulfilling family entertainment fuelled by postwar American affluence, Walt Disney's great project Disneyland would be a place of knowledge and happiness for its "guests." Producing a sense of overall unity with interweaving pathways and America's first monorail in 1959, Disneyland highlighted "the preponderance of human ambulation" so characteristic of the US and Southern California. Technology aided the creation of Fantasyland and Tomorrowland "designed to awaken emotional or archetypal responses common to everyone," inducing an almost religious experience of happiness, or of feeling alive. And yet through the simulated exhilaration laced with frontier thrills, fantasy, and romance, "[t]he 'Present' was either non-existent or manifested as the emotional experiences of the 'guests.'"[66] It is this powerful inducement that prompted the critical reflections of Umberto Eco and Jean Baudrillard in their understanding of "hyperreality," where simulation destroys the real and obliterates the distinction between the real and the representation, with everything coming down to a sales pitch. This product sounds strangely similar to the San Fernando Valley's other leading industry mentioned earlier, with its subtle song: Do not think about the present, nor of any memorable past or concrete future—only fantasize. While the questions of these industries raise important questions about the composition of California's own political economic makeup, ultimate fulfilment is not found here, in any amusement park, film, or any other fading structures.

---

[65]   For how this work with prison gangs, see the work of political economist David Skarbek, *The Social Order of the Underworld: How Prison Gangs Govern the American Penal System* (New York: Oxford University Press, 2014), Chapter 2; for youth gangs, see the "code of the street" explained in Victor M. Rios, *Punished: Policing the Lives of Black and Latino Boys* (New York: New York University Press, 2011), 55–7, 72–3. See also the remarkable story of John M. Perkins, *Let Justice Roll Down* (Ventura: Regal, 1973), which itself is a story of fleeing west to California for hope, then seeing a deeper need with injustice in the South, and never again being satisfied in California.

[66]   See the chapter on Disney's emotional environment to highlight California's political economy in Chytry, *Mountain of Paradise*, Chapter 5, especially 147–9.

Contingent and Eschatological

The reality of this present world is passing away (1 Cor. 7:31; 1 John 2:17); yet the gospel declares the reality of a world that cannot be shaken (Heb. 12:26–8). That world serves as a critique of the present world since it signals the healing this world so desperately needs, as well as the just judgment of all things that would undermine human flourishing. Accordingly, while it seems that nearly every human community on the face of the earth has some expression somewhere in California, there is "one new humanity" (*kainon anthrōpon*, Eph. 2:15, NIV) that God has willed to create which does not fit with the earlier-erected cultural paradigms and in that sense is properly not of this present world. In a sense, of course, the entire history of California over the last 500 years has been increasingly shaped by something of a vision held out in Scripture, where a new community could exist with its unique form of flourishing, righteousness, and peace. This was been sought by Spaniards, English, Russians, Franciscans, Mennonites, Mormons, Pentecostals, hippies, homosexuals, poststructuralists, to name but a few.

The new human community that the Bible describes, however, is profoundly different than the picture of each culture coming to stake its own claim at an appointed place where it might really experience what it had every hope of becoming, in some culturally hegemonic sense. Alternatively, Scripture speaks of the new human community as cutting

> across all cultures and temperaments. Put another way, it doesn't fit any culture but challenges them all at some point. Christians from more individualistic cultures love the Bible's emphasis on affirming one another and sharing hurts and problems—but hate the idea of accountability and discipline. Christians from more traditional communal cultures love the emphasis on accountability for morals and beliefs but often chafe at emphasis on racial reconciliation and being open about one's personal hurts and financial needs.[67]

About this new humanity Thomas Torrance says that its proclamation "is the most explosive force in the world not only because it is proleptic of the final judgment of holy love and proleptic of the new heaven and new earth, but because in it the last things actually confront man creatively here and now in

---

[67]   Timothy Keller, "Serving Each Other Through Forgiveness and Reconciliation," *Redeemer City to City*, http://theresurgence.com/files/2011/04/10/Keller-Forgiveness_and_Reconciliation.pdf (accessed November 18. 2013), 1.

time."[68] In other words there is a power inherent to the gospel of God that in ultimate ways testifies to the bringing about of the things that ordinary Californian's have been searching for. The desire to find fulfillment, to have a new and better life, to have a new start, to experience true freedom and human flourishing—these are all built into a shared humanity. California has uniquely displayed a "search for higher value" in higher education and religion, a hope for happiness in the world, or for a better life, and for finding a meaningful place in the world.[69] California has indeed succeeded in becoming one of the most diverse places in the world,[70] perhaps following Josiah Royce's "higher provincialism" which Sanders refers to as "A Golden State of Mind."[71] And perhaps there is enough Zen laced through the entire setting to secure a way of journeying through the California terrain believing that such a better situation is possible. But with the wisdom of the ages, Christian theology acknowledges that for whatever gains may be found in this world (which are sadly often at the expense of others), the better life ultimately is only found in the all-benevolent hand of the one who created, and will one-day re-create this particular culture with an innovation that will never disappoint, fulfilling every hopeful longing for all who will truly believe.

But such longings are not fulfilled by human ingenuity or by running as far as land extends before the beach hits the ocean and the sun goes down. These ultimate longings are only fulfilled by sheer grace for those who trust in the one who is the fulfilment of true human existence, who became incarnate, was crucified, buried, dead, rose on the third day, and ascended into heaven where he sits at the right hand of God, from where he will come to judge the living and the dead. None of this denies that there is not something innate about being human, and something about the Pacific region, and especially California, that engenders wonder, hope, dreams, imagination, and innovation—something that perhaps California uniquely captures or embodies, or images somehow. But because this vision experienced in the real state of California is a broken one where dreams are repeatedly shattered as much as they are birthed, the gospel in particular is able to show how these human impulses, very real and unable to be suppressed, are subversively fulfilled in the gospel of the Lord Jesus Christ.

---

[68]   Thomas F. Torrance, "The Modern Eschatological Debate, Pt. 3," *Evangelical Quarterly* 25/3 (1953), 175.

[69]   See Kevin Starr's 2012 "Mission Day" address, January 26, 2012, http://www.lmu.edu/Page82604.aspx (accessed November 18, 2013).

[70]   Kevin Starr, *Coast of Dreams: California on the Edge, 1990–2003* (New York: Alfred A. Knopf, 2004), 141–77.

[71]   See Chapter 10 of the present volume.

Without this kind of particular Christocentric theism, meaning, purpose, and end are features of this present life and human existence that will be completely lost and will continue to undo the particular kind of hope-filled restoration found in the gospel.

Theology's Promise for Culture

If theology—as an exposition of the church's confession of divine salvation offered through Christ—doesn't engage California's culture, it will continue in neglect of its neighboring disciplines in the academy in the pursuit of truth, and will have left the state's politicians and society alone to negotiate the ills that our confession capably and comprehensively purports to be able to reckon with. Seen from this perspective, we cannot *not* engage our culture with theology's claims and promises. Further, it must engage because it has tools that have immensely helped ancient and modern civilizations; and California could use some help. Theology aims to cultivate responsible citizens who in turn model responsible citizenship when the entire population is unwont to. It hardly seems the case that Californians have shed the shallow and irresponsible characterization that Josiah Royce attributed to them in 1886 after the Gold Rush, declaring that they displayed "a novel degree of carelessness and overhastiness, an extravagant trust in luck, a previously unknown blindness to our social duties, and an indifference to the rights of foreigners, whereof we cannot be proud."[72]

A theological reckoning with California identifies a culture that uniquely creates "myth" and re-creates this same vision for others. And what kind of theology can engage with this culture? The kind that doesn't let the siren calling myths have the final say, confronting them by the coherence of the indicative nature of Christian witness (Acts 1.8), and expressing good news in various evangelistic ways, especially in meaningful localized forms of service for the common good. The public work of the church, as Luke Bretherton argues, is to be "an agent of healing and repair within the political, economic, and social order, contradicting the prideful, violent, and exclusionary logics at work in the *saeculum* and opening it out to its fulfillment in Christ."[73] By discriminating between right and wrong then, in society, as it proclaims the gospel, the church labors to establish contexts in which moral and just relations are possible in light of the coming of Jesus

---

[72]   Josiah Royce, *California: A Study of American Character* (reprint, Berkeley: Heyday Books, 2002), 3–4.

[73]   Luke Bretherton, *Christianity and Contemporary Politics: The Conditions and Possibilities of Faithful Witness* (Malden: Wiley-Blackwell, 2010), 210.

Christ. And simply because Christianity is exclusive (maintaining that salvation is found in no one other than Jesus Christ) does not mean it is intolerant.[74] It creates space for various traditions, and even for various religious expressions that are at odds with and parasitic to the truth of the gospel of Jesus Christ. And theological description witnesses in its humility. Consider again Henry Durant's vision for education in the founding of the University of California with what that university became with the "Master Plan" of 1960. Theology, quite early on, left when it was asked to, and has still not been formally invited back to the university. Yet it nevertheless flourished on the streets and in the churches, and is ready to come back and serve wherever it may find willing listeners.

Theology, of course, has no grand vision for what might be accomplished in the present situation which, again, is passing away. It aims in the meantime to know nothing but Christ and him crucified, meaning that those who confess the hope of the gospel would abandon all to see one sinner repent. It views the vocation of theologian, or of social-scientist, or of historian as first of all under the rubric of a divine calling to surrender ourselves in the same way the Lord Jesus did, pouring ourselves into culture in its variable shapes for the good of the church, and for the good of our fellow Californians.

We seem to be living in a moment where the secularization thesis is being shown to be quite a misguided proposal. In 1989 Lesslie Newbigin argued that "the belief in a secular society is an unproven belief accepted uncritically to justify a social institution, and also that the belief is mistaken."[75] Added to the growing dis-ease with secularism are ways that theology is being done responsibly and beautifully in many major university divinity departments around the world, and in seminaries, and by faithful clergy who have begun to carefully articulate theological frameworks for their efforts, in conversation with other traditional categories which have served as theology's replacements, including the arts and sciences.

Coming out of the ghettos in revived fashion, theology is again being shown for what it really is, making sense of the deep matters of the human experience,[76] reengaging from the margins, and experiencing something of what has been

---

[74]   Robert Louis Wilken, "In Defense of Constantine," *First Things*, April 2001, http://www.firstthings.com/article/2007/01/in-defense-of-constantine-47 (accessed November 18, 2013).

[75]   Lesslie Newbigin, *The Gospel in a Pluralist Society* (Grand Rapids: Eerdmans, 1989), 211.

[76]   See Peter J. Leithart, "Death to the Copulative and Long Live the Queen!" *First Things: On the Square*, September 28, 2012, http://www.firstthings.com/onthesquare/2012/09/death-to-the-copulative-and-long-live-the-queen (accessed March 8, 2013).

referred to as a "Lazarus-style comeback."[77] In so many ways then theology is experiencing a moment it hasn't had for quite some time, highlighting that "Christianity is a culture-forming religion, and the planting and growth of Christian communities led to the remaking of the cultures of the ancient world along with the creation of a new civilization, or more accurately several new civilizations."[78] With its retrieved resources, however, theology has a lot of catching up to do with the various forms of academic and public discourse, especially in a place as vibrant as California, and especially in the hopes that scholars, politicians, poets, and ordinary Californians would wake up to find what they've been missing.

Conclusion: Theological Engagement with California's Culture

What has theology to do with California? And how does theology make sense of California culture? How does it engage? There's much more to say, and the efforts in this volume are attempts to begin doing this from various theological angles. The interdisciplinary aspect of it is highlighted toward the end of the volume (chapters 10–12), with Sanders doing as good as anything I've seen, trying to generate a theology of California's culture with systematic theology's tools, which proposal is then responded to by a social scientist (Richard Flory) and an historian (Richard Pointer). If I'd change anything it might aim to supplement Sanders's work with how Stanley Grenz tested his own biblical-theological concepts through the traditional theological loci,[79] perhaps drawing a major theme from California (for example: hope) and bringing it into a full conversation with this idea in Scripture and as it relates to systematic theology. While I anticipate that it will take an extensive and ongoing effort to begin to do this adequately and in a thoroughly interdisciplinary manner, I shall attempt one brief concluding reflection that theology might lend for making sense of California's culture, albeit without the robust biblical exegesis and theological reflection that could also ensue.

---

77 John Milbank, "Lazarus-style comeback," *Times Higher Education*, April 16, 2009, http://www.timeshighereducation.co.uk/story.asp?storycode=406157 (accessed November 18, 2013).

78 Robert Louis Wilken, *The First Thousand Years: A Global History of Christianity* (Newhaven: Yale University Press, 2012), 2.

79 For an account of his methodology for this, please see Jason S. Sexton, "The *Imago Dei* Once Again: Stanley Grenz's Journey Toward a Theological Interpretation of Genesis 1:26–27," *Journal of Theological Interpretation* 4/2 (Fall 2010), 187–206.

In doing this, I'd like to suggest that California uniquely generates "myth."[80] Myth about God, humans, sin, church, Holy Spirit, redemption and reconciliation, Jesus, and the eschaton. It forces a change in the way the big questions are asked, and generates myth to compensate these, providing myths that are perhaps more easily transferrable than other cultural myths because of the dominant forms of irresponsibility and anonymity prevalent among Californians.

People come here from elsewhere looking for a better life, having bought into the myth, whether from boosters or someone else. When they arrive, and are asked "where are you from?" they reply, "elsewhere," causing deep forms of loyalty and identity to emerge (however strong they might have otherwise been) giving shape to the myth of the (in some ways *better*) life that they had. These new arrivers remain loyal to their place of origin, and this is reinforced in various ways. They then aim to import and appropriate mythical features of erstwhile identity in California. When this import of the mythical prior place and its cultural features doesn't work, a dissatisfaction with the present place (California) sets in. Delusion transpires and disenchantment with the present place and the dreams attached with it become shattered. The individual is left with a choice: in what world will he or she live? Many Californians choose not to live in the present world, nor in a truthful appropriation of their memorable past, and choose to remain enchanted, or in the magical land, perhaps with season passes or the annual trip planned to Disneyland.

This is where the church has something very important to offer, even as it seeks to resist the at times overwhelmingly compelling pull of Californian idolatrous myths. Perhaps these are all forms of the American myth of individualism, just expressed in higher forms because of California's unique cultural makeup and pressure? Kevin Vanhoozer expressed one challenge for the church, however: "It is a truism in Christian mission that we must go and address people where they *live*. Quite so. My point is that 'they' (and we) frequently live in cleverly devised mythical world created by media and marketing moguls."[81]

Myths continue developing in the course of California's life, old ones evolving and new ones emerging—myths of educational perfection and state-governed forms of egality; myths of sexual freedom or fulfilling partnership; myths of health and liberalism, wealth and prosperity; the myth of a soundly

---

[80] See Dora Beale Polk, *The Island of California: A History of the Myth* (Lincoln: University of Nebraska Press, 1995) and the recent work on what Californians have done with trees, Jared Farmer, *Trees in Paradise: A California History* (New York: W.W. Norton, 2013). "Paradox" would also be a fascinating conceptual tool to use in examining California's culture.

[81] Vanhoozer, "What is Everyday Theology?" 27.

governed state and security, of a better life; the myth of social/economic boom and overwhelming despair; and endless others. This is not "myth" in the sense of something artificial or sub-real. It's something discerned by inferences. It generates translatable impulses and images that somehow point to the reality without ever presenting its real, super-real substance. It even does this in coherent ways although not in ultimate ways as people are in various ways transported *into* California. Joan Didion has stated that it is indeed a "delusion" to think that California is a mere five hours from New York by air. Indeed, "California is somewhere else." And yet it's not the eschaton, nor tantamount to the promise held out in the gospel. California is rather quite normal, arbitrary, and mundane, even if extremely so. And yet wherever and whatever it is, God is not far from it.

PART II
California's Culture
in Ecclesial Perspective

Chapter 4

The Significance of the California Missions in Californian Theology and Culture

Allen Yeh

This essay attempts to build on the methods and strategies of historical Franciscan missions to construct a modern-day missional theology of California. It contains both descriptive and prescriptive components. Missiology is a field which is by nature interdisciplinary, as it involves the interplay of four components: theology, history, social science, and strategy. To come up with a "Theology of California" is to imply that California has a somewhat of a cohesion to its culture; after all, theology is a cultural attempt to convey a universal truth about God. However, it is not inaccurate to liken California to the story of the blind people and the elephant: one touches the trunk, one feels the tail, another holds the leg, a fourth touches the side, and each concludes something different about the elephant—it resembles a snake, or a rope, or a tree trunk, or a wall—because they've only experienced one piece of the whole. Despite this diversity, stereotypes abound about California as a whole: beaches, Hollywood, "surfer dudes" or "valley girls," the great outdoors—represented by Yosemite National Park, Death Valley, or Lake Tahoe—and negative features such as the obsession with image, body, and the celebrity culture. What most people do not think of when it comes to California, however, is history.

The US has such a short history that there is very little that we can claim as our own. As for the things that are authentically American, there is jazz and rodeo; but much else is borrowed from other cultures. Still, I think that's acceptable. The hot dog is, after all, a variation on the German sausage, and American football is some distant cousin of rugby. Yet both are quintessentially American. These things are a testimony to America's ability to adapt the foreign and make it its own. As such, the history of California is the history of the Spanish missions. They are originally Spanish, yes, but they are unmistakably Californian. The influences of their legacy remain, even if not always recognized. And perhaps it is in the missions where this diverse web of cultures, stereotypes, geographies, and politics can find common ground and a shared history. If California had to be reduced to one thing, to one identity, I want to argue that it is in the historical Franciscan missions of Alta California, because that is where California, as an idea, began. The 21 missions are the geographical backbone of the state of California and gave it its shape.

In the California public school system, during the fourth grade, students do a project on the California missions. This is both a blessing and a curse: it has the benefit of bringing to people's attention the importance of the missions which might have otherwise been neglected; but it lodges in people's minds that study of the missions is strictly for children, and unfortunately children cannot do, for example, cultural anthropology or theology on a high level. Of course, there has been research done on the California missions on a scholarly level, so there is literature available for adults. But these approaches tend not to link the past with the future, nor take the missions prescriptively from a faith perspective, which is how this chapter differs from other scholarly treatments of the missions.

History of the Twenty-One Alta California Missions

What we know as the state of California was originally called *Alta California* (Upper California) to distinguish it from *Baja California* (Lower California). This state is only the upper half of historic California. Today we think of "northern California" and "southern California" but actually everything all the way down to San Diego is "northern/upper California" and everything from Tijuana to Cabo San Lucas is "southern/lower California," historically speaking. California's Spanish roots are evident in many street and city names; it was the last Spanish colony in North America. Alta California was indigenous, then Spanish, then Mexican, and only recently, in historical terms, has it been part of the US. For Americans to claim that Mexicans are illegally "invading" the state of California is historically problematic. Mexicans have a popular saying: "We did not cross the border; the border crossed us."

So perhaps the first characteristic to consider in a missional theology of California combines *language and immigration* together for consideration. Who was here first? Who gets to name the land? Just as many Americans wrongly think of Jamestown, Virginia, as the first European settlement in the US (the first was actually St Augustine, Florida, which was a Spanish settlement founded in 1565; Jamestown was the first *British* settlement founded in 1607), the US should not be thought of solely in Anglo terms. John F. Kennedy celebrated

Fr Serra's 250th birthday on November 24, 1963 as a "reminder of our Spanish heritage whose values were exemplified in the piety, courage, and vision of Father Serra."[1] However, not even Mexicans or Spaniards can claim precedence; it was the Native Americans first. This conjures up images of the Jews and Palestinians in Israel jockeying for a historical claim to the land. Truth be told, the land has belonged to many, and it is often difficult to discern who really came "first." Today it must be shared by all who have historical roots there, and it must welcome those who do not yet have historical roots there but will do in several generations, in much the same way that Boston is "Irish" and Miami is "Cuban" and Vancouver is "Hong Kong Chinese" (its nickname is "Hongcouver") but can embrace so many more ethnic groups than those names imply. There is no one ethnicity or nationality that is *the* face of California. Some might say Hispanics, but California also has the largest Asian population in the US, along with significant white and black populations. It is a truly multiethnic state. This is borne out historically by the fact that California has been claimed by at least seven governments: England, Argentina, Spain, Mexico, Russia, the Republic of California,[2] and the US.

The 21 Alta California missions were founded between 1769 and 1823. This covers a period of 67 years during which time the current state's city-structures began to emerge. Here are the missions in the order of their founding:[3]

1. Mission San Diego de Alcalá founded in 1769
2. *Mission San Carlos Borromeo de Carmelo founded in 1770*
3. *Mission San Antonio de Padua founded in 1771*
4. Mission San Gabriel Arcángel founded in 1771
5. Mission San Luis Obispo de Tolosa founded in 1772
6. *Mission San Francisco de Asís (Mission Dolores) founded in 1776*
7. Mission San Juan Capistrano founded in 1776
8. *Mission Santa Clara de Asís founded in 1777*
9. Mission San Buenaventura founded in 1782
10. Mission Santa Barbara founded in 1786
11. Mission La Purísima Concepción founded in 1787

---

[1] *The Fresno Bee* (June 3, 1963), 16

[2] California's independence was launched from the doorstep of the last of the missions, San Francisco Solano. The so-called Bear Flag Revolt declared California an independent republic on June 14, 1846, which eventually led to California's statehood on September 9, 1850, as the 31st state of the Union.

[3] David J. McLaughlin, *The California Missions Source Book* (Scottsdale: Pentacle Press, 2012).

12. *Mission Santa Cruz founded in 1791*
13. *Mission Nuestra Señora de la Soledad founded in 1791*
14. *Mission San José founded in 1797*
15. *Mission San Juan Bautista founded in 1797*
16. *Mission San Miguel Arcángel founded in 1797*
17. Mission San Fernando Rey de España founded in 1797
18. Mission San Luis Rey de Francia founded in 1798
19. Mission Santa Inés founded in 1804
20. *Mission San Rafael Arcángel founded in 1817*
21. *Mission San Francisco Solano (Sonoma) founded in 1823*

Though it is true that the first mission (San Diego) was the southernmost and the last mission (Sonoma) was the northernmost, this gives the impression that all the missions were founded in geographical order. This is actually misleading, as the second mission was the Carmel mission near Monterey Bay, and the missions were founded almost alternating from South to North in equal measure (the list above gives the northern California missions in italics to show how they alternated geographically in their founding). The commonly noted fact that the missions were a one-day walk from each other also seems to suggest that there was a logic, rhyme and reason to their establishment. Yet it was largely coincidental that they were so evenly spaced.

This suggests a second characteristic to a missiology of California: *geographical unity*. The California missions provide an argument for the state's cohesion. If the southern missions were founded first, and the northern missions were founded later, then perhaps a case could be made for the state's segmentation, but historically this cannot be supported. This is further strengthened by the fact that people mistakenly think that Fr Junípero Serra founded all 21 missions. He actually only established the first nine; then his successor Fr Francisco de Lasuén founded the next nine;[4] and the last three were established by others. Thus, Frs Serra and Lasuén did not distinguish between north and south in their minds as they set up the missions—to them, it was all one piece of land. As such, Fr Serra, Fr Lasuén, and the other Franciscans can be viewed as establishing California by uniting the 21 missions in the same way that the Founding Fathers can be viewed as establishing the US by uniting the original 13 colonies. Perhaps this can be a good historical rethink of California and the British colonies framing the founding of our nation—it was not just a one-directional sweep

---

4   McLaughlin, *The California Missions Source Book*, 18.

from East to West, but rather Spain landed on the West, Britain on the East, and they met just over the Sierras.

The last mission was San Francisco Solano, often simply called "Sonoma" because of where it is located to distinguish it from San Francisco de Asís (aka Mission Dolores). The reason for the similarity in name is because it was named after another Francis: St Francis Solano. It is the only mission built not under Spanish rule but under the Mexican government.[5] There is a plaque on the wall of Mission San Francisco Solano which reads:

> The End of the Mission Trail: 1523–1823. The Mission Trail marked three hundred years of Spanish-Mexican settlement. It travelled as far south as Guatemala and traversed Mexico to advance through eleven of our present day United States. In 1823 Mission San Francisco Solano was founded, marking the last and northernmost outpost on the historic mission trail.

California's geographical unity, therefore, extends not just from the top of Alta California to the bottom of Baja California, but really all the way down to Guatemala.[6] Though the missions belong to California, they also belong to the Americas, and to think of them hermetically sealed in isolation is to remove them from historical context.

History of the Thirty Baja California Missions

The 30 missions in Baja California were actually founded prior to the 21 missions in Alta California. The difference is not just geographical, in the fact that Baja is on the peninsula and Alta is on the mainland; there was also a religious difference: the Baja missions were mostly founded by Jesuits, whereas the Alta missions

---

5   McLaughlin, *The California Missions Source Book*, 20.

6   Though Fr Serra did not found any of the Baja California missions, he did found five missions in Mexico, in the Sierra Gorda region of the state of Querétaro (just north of modern-day Mexico City), prior to establishing the ones in Alta California: Santiago de Jalpan; Nuestra Señora de la Luz de Tancoyol; Santa María del Agua de Landa; San Francisco del Valle de Tilaco; and San Miguel Concá. The mission at Jalpan was Serra's home base from 1750–58. This provides a definitive and indisputable genetic relationship between California and Latin America. According to Steven W. Hackel, *Junípero Serra: California's Founding Father* (New York: Hill and Wang, 2013), 84: "He would leave the Sierra Gorda an experienced administrator who knew how to organize missions and win the support of the Spanish political authorities." These missions were crucial and foundational to his later success in California.

were founded by Franciscans.[7] Thus, the third characteristic of a missiology of California is found in *the distinct Franciscan vow of chastity, poverty, and obedience.* When one thinks of the state of California today, often the opposite of chastity and obedience come to mind. Rather, Hollywood and the moral degradation glamorized in films are often thought of, along with the protest mentality that has come from disestablishment movements.

As for poverty, it is ubiquitous. Los Angeles has the largest homeless population in the US, and San Francisco is not far behind. Part of it probably has to do with the warmer weather, where homeless people can survive winters in California better than they can in New York or Chicago, for example. Yet, whenever one is confronted by a homeless person in California, or sexual immorality, or anarchy, perhaps it would be worth thinking about the legacy of the Franciscans.[8] They came with a charge to confront these three social ills.[9]

Among the 30 Baja California missions, half of them are practically nonexistent today because they've fallen into such states of disrepair, in contrast to the 21 Alta California missions which have all been nicely restored by the US government.[10] Three of the Baja missions worth highlighting are: Loreto ("The Mother of the Missions"), San Javier ("The Jewel of the Baja California

---

[7]   After Fr Serra founded the Sierra Gorda missions in Mexico, he arrived at Mission Loreto, the first of the Baja and Alta California missions, on April 1, 1768. He reorganized 15 of the Baja missions then proceeded to found the Alta missions under the same title. The area of Baja California was more than 10 times larger than Mallorca or Sierra Gorda, so this prepared him to later govern a similarly vast tract of land with the Alta missions. Thus, the Sierra Gorda missions, the Baja California missions, and the Alta California missions, all bear the handprint of Fr Junípero Serra, though in different ways. A significant difference between the Sierra Gorda missions and the Alta California missions, however, was that many of the Indians in Sierra Gorda had already encountered Catholicism, so it was not "frontier" missions, whereas Alta California was totally fresh soil as far as the gospel was concerned.

[8]   Mission Santa Clara was named for the woman who was the female counterpart to St Francis. St Clare (1194–1253) was from Assisi as well, and a follower of St Francis. She established her own order of Claretian sisters and they also dedicated themselves to the poor. Mission San Buenaventura is named for the most famous Franciscan other than St Francis of Assisi himself, and he carried on the mission and spirit of his predecessor.

[9]   Unfortunately, discipleship prior to baptism was not a large concern for the Franciscans. They tended to baptize as many as possible (equating baptism as conversion), and harshly disciplined the "converts" for any behavior that did not conform to Christian behavior, viewing that as backsliding. See James A. Sandos, *Converting California: Indians and Franciscans in the Missions* (New Haven: Yale University Press, 2004), 82.

[10]   This effort was led by Abraham Lincoln, who recognized the legacy of the missions to the history of California even though he never personally set foot in the state; we have him to thank for the fact that all the Alta missions are intact today and do not just exist in historical memory like most of the Seven Wonders of the Ancient World.

Missions"),[11] and San Ignacio. Right above the doorway of Mission Loreto is inscribed these words: *"Cabeza y Madre de Las Misiones de Baja y Alta California."*[12] Loreto was the first mission founded in the Californias (1697), which is why it is the Mother of the Baja and Alta California Missions. This further reminds us that the national and linguistic ties between Alta California (now part of the US) and Baja California (now Mexico) are strong, if Loreto is historically the mother of the 51 California missions. To discuss the Alta missions without taking into account the history of the Baja missions is like reading the New Testament without the Old Testament. Seeing the actual "Mother" Mission, where it all started, is thus even more significant than visiting Mission San Diego, the first of the Alta missions, similar to visiting Jerusalem over Rome in the deeper historical roots of the faith. Due to this being the originating point of the 51 missions, it fittingly has an on-site museum dedicated to the history of the Spanish missions in the Californias and containing many artifacts. Mission San Javier was founded as an extension mission to Loreto, and to get there, one has to drive inland for almost two hours for 30 kilometers, of which only two-thirds of the way is paved. The last 10 kilometers is rough dirt road and extremely slow going, but the goal is worth it. The San Javier mission building is one of the two most beautiful and best-preserved of the Baja missions. The other is Mission San Ignacio. Interestingly, these were named for Francis Xavier and Ignatius of Loyola, the co-founders of the Jesuits, just as San Francisco was named for St Francis of Assisi, the founder of the Franciscans. The San Ignacio mission is located in exactly the halfway point of the entire peninsula of Baja California (both widthwise and lengthwise), and is situated in a lush green oasis which is completely surprising given the stark desert surroundings.

The history of California missions bears an interesting connection to recent events in the Roman Catholic Church. Significantly, in March 2013, Cardinal Jorge Mario Bergoglio became the first Catholic Pope from Latin America. He chose the name "Francis," the first time in history that a pontiff has taken such a name. There was much speculation as to whether he was naming himself after Francis of Assisi because of his identification with the poor (which would link him with the Alta California missions) or whether he was naming himself after Francis Xavier, the co-founder of the Jesuits, because Bergoglio is the first Jesuit Pope, thus linking him with the Baja California missions. Pope Francis has since revealed that

---

[11]   Edward W. Vernon, *Las Misiones Antiguas: The Spanish Missions of Baja California, 1683–1855* (Santa Barbara: Viejo Press, 2002), 26.

[12]   "Head and Mother of the Missions of Lower and Upper California."

it is Francis of Assisi that he had in mind,[13] showing that the patron saint of Alta California still has modern relevance because "the poor you will always have with you."[14] In other words, helping the poor will never become irrelevant. While this truth is timeless, the state of California is still embodied temporally in physical space and ever-changing culture, which leads to the next point.

The Makings of the California of Today: Transport, Architecture, and Culture

The Spanish created three types of settlements when they first came to Alta California: missions, presidios, and pueblos.[15] Missions, of course, were religious establishments. Presidios were military forts with probably the most famous in California being the one in San Francisco near where the Golden Gate Bridge now sits.[16] And pueblos were secular towns. These three represented religion, politics, and economics, respectively. As was the case with much of missions during the colonial era, the missionaries were often at odds with the secular colonists because they had differing goals with respect to the indigenous people; the former wanted to convert, the latter wanted to exploit.[17] Unfortunately the indigenous often could not see the difference between the two, as the missionaries arrived on colonial ships. In addition, unlike in the British and French colonies,

---

[13]   Pope Francis, March 16, 2013, http://www.vatican.va/holy_father/francesco/speeches/2013/march/documents/papa-francesco_20130316_rappresentanti-media_en.html (accessed July 15, 2013)

[14]   Matt. 26:11; Mark 14:7; John 12:8.

[15]   McLaughlin, *The California Missions Source Book*, 72. There were only four presidios: San Diego, Monterey (corresponding with the first two California missions, though the mission itself was across the bay from the presidio, in Carmel), San Francisco, and Santa Barbara. There were only three pueblos: San José (in a different location from the mission despite the same name; the mission was in Fremont while the pueblo is the eponymous modern-day city), Los Angeles, and Villa de Branciforte.

[16]   For a discussion of the early history of the area see Kevin Starr, *Golden Gate: The Life and Times of America's Greatest Bridge* (New York: Bloomsbury, 2010), 18–32.

[17]   Part of this came from the different anthropological view each group had of the Indians. According to Sandos, *Converting California*, 64: "Indian violence against missionaries was misguided behavior and not a deliberate rejection of Christ. To Serra Indians were Satan's pawns. That Indians also could be Franciscan pawns was a point Serra could not admit and perhaps not imagine... Secular men saw the Indians as murderers, thieves, cattle killers, and rebels, not misguided followers of Satan. Indians were real or potential insurrectionists...."

the *conquistadores* came bearing both the cross and the sword, so it was not as clear-cut with the Spanish conquest what their ultimate intentions were.[18]

Los Angeles is unusual because it is one of the only major cities in California that was not founded as a mission but rather as a pueblo. There is a plaque at Olvera Street which signifies the founding location of Los Angeles.[19] Yet, LA would not have been founded without the prior influence and establishment of nearby Mission San Gabriel, so a case can be made that San Gabriel is the true birthplace of Los Angeles.

El Camino Real, or The Royal Highway, was the road that connected all 21 Alta missions.[20] Today El Camino Real roughly corresponds to Highway 101.[21] All along El Camino Real were mission bells, and even today the state of California has preserved some of them, which can be seen while driving along Highway 101. The bells further support the claim of Baja and Alta California as a geographical entity (characteristic 2): each one is inscribed with the words "Loreto Oct 25 1697, Sonoma July 4 1823," thereby linking the first mission in Baja California with the last mission in Alta California. The new Catholic cathedral of Los Angeles, built in 2002, was intentionally situated alongside the 101 as a reminder of the mission's legacy and has an El Camino Real mission bell in its courtyard. Also worth noting is that the current archbishop (appointed

---

[18]   However, the intentions were certainly different. Serra and his Franciscans did everything they could to oppose the murder and rape of the Indians that was being carried out by the Spanish troops. The Santa Barbara mission, for example, was often at odds with the Santa Barbara presidio. The soldiers despised Serra so much for this that there were two unsuccessful attempts on his life by his countrymen. See Sandos, *Converting California*, 52. This led Serra to support the very un-Catholic idea of the separation of church and state. According to Hackel, *Junípero Serra: California's Founding Father*, 143: "One thing that clearly differentiated some of the Jesuits in Baja California from Serra was their seeming disregard for the calamities that befell Indians under Spanish rule ... With attitudes like this it is little wonder that the Jesuits' efforts in Baja California bore 'little fruit.' By the 1760s, from the Spanish perspective, the missions of Baja California were failures."

[19]   The city's full name is La Ciudad de Nuestra Señora La Reina de Los Angeles del Río Porciúncula—or, the City of Our Lady, Queen of the Angels, by the River Porciuncula (Porciúncula is the old name for what is now known as the Los Angeles River). Despite the fact that Los Angeles's name is actually a tribute to Mary, it was founded as a secular settlement, and the proximity of the mission helped to determine its location and helped to populate it.

[20]   Hereafter in this chapter referred to as the California missions.

[21]   Ironically in Southern California this is called the "Hollywood Freeway" which, considering characteristic 4, seems to go counter to the intent of the original missions; I wonder what the Franciscan founders would have thought about the fact that their mission's road is now the road through Hollywood.

in March 2011) of The Cathedral of Our Lady of the Angels is José Horacio Gómez, the first Mexican-born archbishop of the city of Los Angeles. This is surprising that it took so long, considering that LA is the second-largest Mexican city in the world by population after Mexico City.

Roads have historically been a major help to missionaries. Many people ask why Jesus Christ came to earth when and where he did. One possible explanation is that the Roman Empire was at its height, and one of its glories was the intricate network of roads that connected the entire Mediterranean region. The gospel message spread all over the Roman Empire utilizing the unprecedented road network, much as the gospel spread via ships during the period of European colonialism. California's version of the Roman roads was El Camino Real, precursor to Interstate 5 and other major arteries that run throughout the state and to the rest of the country. And Los Angeles, for better or for worse, is known as a city of automobile drivers, with the most extensive network of highways of any city in the world. Technology is not just that which is created in Silicon Valley; the original information superhighways were literal paved (and unpaved) roads.

A fourth characteristic of a missiology of California is found in *its architecture*. Physical structures are not often something which comes to mind when thinking about missions in general, but the visual images of the California missions are so integral to their identity that a major part of the California missions projects for fourth-graders is building missions models. The Spanish missions have extended to influence architecture of many universities, including two of the state's most world-renowned, the California Institute of Technology and Stanford University, as well as public buildings like LA's Union Station. Though Los Angeles's City Hall is not built in mission style (it is modeled on one of the Seven Wonders of the Ancient World, the Mausoleum at Halicarnassus), the building was constructed from materials including sand from all of California's 58 counties, and water from all 21 missions. Ironically however, the missions architecture has not greatly affected the architecture of most churches in California, not even the Catholic ones (the current Our Lady of the Angels Cathedral in LA is modern and completely asymmetrical by design). Prominent evangelical Protestant church structures such as Saddleback Church and the Crystal Cathedral[22] do not have Spanish architectural elements in them. And many California megachurches just meet in the equivalent of a warehouse. However, architecture should signify something, and while a church is really the community of gathered believers and not the building, to deny the building completely is to miss out on one

---

[22]   Now owned by the Catholic Diocese of Orange [County] and newly renamed, "Christ Cathedral."

component of a church's embodiment. Perhaps architecture is something that we need to recover in a missional theology of California.

Considered the greatest architect in American history, Frank Lloyd Wright had a massive influence on Californian architecture, and his primary contribution was the California Craftsman style. But Mission Revival Style, the immediate predecessor to Spanish Colonial Revival Style,[23] is just as important to California's image, if not more so. The Mission Inn in Riverside[24] is the most famous example of this style, and it is such a renowned hotel that President Richard Nixon, the only California native son who ever became President of the US,[25] was married there on June 21, 1940. There is an anonymous poem that is relevant when talking about the influence of the missions on California's architecture:

> Give me neither Romanesque nor Gothic;
> much less Italian Renaissance,
> and least of all English Colonial—
> this is California—give me Mission.[26]

Historically, San Juan Capistrano (which bears the moniker "The Jewel of the Missions"), known for its sheer beauty, is also the most significant architecturally. It has the Great Stone Church (nicknamed "America's Acropolis") which was heavily damaged in an earthquake but stands Parthenon-like in its ruined splendor, and Fr Serra's chapel, the oldest building in California still in use and the only one extant in which Serra personally led mass.[27] The images of the missions are so crucial to California that they have been captured in serial detail by artists such as Edward Vischer (in the 1860s he was the first artist to depict all 21 missions through painting) and Edwin Deakin, and photographers such as Carleton Watkins and Adam Clark Vroman (founder of the well-known Pasadena bookstore; in his store, he sold prints of all 21 missions).

Architecture does, however, also have bearing on functionality, and one criticism is that the idea of "mission stations," which the California missions undoubtedly were, was not the most effective or respectful of the indigenous

---

[23]   Kevin Starr, *California: A History* (New York: Random House, 2005), 148.

[24]   The Mission Inn has a collection of over 800 bells but in the lobby of the hotel is displayed the biggest gem of all: "the oldest bell in Christendom" dating from 1274.

[25]   Though California has two Presidential libraries, Ronald Reagan was actually born in Illinois even if he did serve as Governor of California. He also has a marriage link to the Mission Inn: he and his wife Nancy honeymooned there.

[26]   Felix Rey, "A Tribute to Mission Style," in *Architect and Engineer* (October 1924).

[27]   McLaughlin, *The California Missions Source Book*, 17.

culture.[28] Though the missions are impressive to visit because each one was a self-contained community with kitchens, bedrooms, a library, wine cellar, cemetery, courtyard, agricultural fields, among other things,[29] the idea of a cloistered monastic existence seems antiquated and unhelpful in today's societies. One cannot be incarnational or a respecter of cultures behind closed doors.[30] Missions must necessarily be going out to the people and contextualizing to their situations, not forcing the people to come to them and molding them in their image.[31] In Greek, the word "apostle" means someone who is sent out. California is a crossroads of the world and naturally attracts global attention, but it should never rest on its laurels. Myopic Christianity does not serve well in an increasingly globalized, international world. California can continue to be at the vanguard of culture and technology if it innovates by looking outward. Ralph Winter, a leading missiologist of the latter twentieth century, was the founder of the US Center for World Mission in Pasadena. Pasadena is also home to Fuller Seminary, arguably the most well-known evangelical seminary in the world. California has definitely shown that it can lead in mission and theology if it is willing to be adaptable,[32] but this is in spite of the original "mission station" idea of the Franciscans.

---

[28]   One of the main proponents of mission stations in Africa was Robert Moffat. His son-in-law, David Livingstone, was a much more famous and arguably more effective missionary because he was itinerant and went out among the people rather than expecting them to come to him. See Ruth A. Tucker, *From Jerusalem to Irian Jaya: A Biographical History of Christian Missions* (Grand Rapids: Zondervan, 2004).

[29]   McLaughlin, *The California Missions Source Book*, 18–19.

[30]   According to Sandos, "Fraternizing with settlers, Serra believed, would harm new Christians. Franciscans like Serra believed that keeping Indians in the missions protected them from exploitation by colonists; colonial authorities, however, came to see Indian isolation as missionary exploitation that prevented Indian assimilation into the empire. Such conflicting views colored the entire missionary experience in Alta California" (*Converting California*, 54; see also n. 56).

[31]   "Indian love of liberty lay at the core of the missionary problem... Religious instruction and more efficient production of food at the missions through sowing and harvesting of grain and cereals three times annually, however, did not fully satisfy Indians who yearned for their homelands, for visits to relatives and friends, and for access to native foods.... Yet the missionaries feared that visits to the gentiles would prove near occasions of sin for their neophytes... The Indian struggle to endure culturally, despite population decline and externally directed change, would persistently oppose Franciscan evangelization efforts throughout the mission era" (Sandos, *Converting California*, 93–4).

[32]   Editor's note: One stream of research the TECC Project proposes to explore is Californian ecclesial innovation and how the present church can learn from past efforts for knowing how to continue to imagine church in an ever-changing context on the Pacific Rim.

Nevertheless, to be fair, though the strategy of mission stations was perhaps misguided, the motivation of the Franciscan friars was sincere and true. On November 20, 1542, King Charles V of Spain issued a code of "New Laws"[33] which was to dictate the strategy of the California missions:

1. Indians should have their own land;
2. Indians should choose their own leaders;
3. Indians should not be enslaved;
4. Indians should not live outside their own village;
5. Spaniards should not stay in an Indian village beyond three days;
6. Indians should be Catholicized.[34]

Even more progressively, according to Spanish law, the missions' lands and resources belonged to the natives and would be put in their control when they had learned to manage themselves in the Spanish way. So as soon as the Indians had converted to Christianity and were educated and learned to grow crops with more advanced methods, the missionaries turned over the mission property to the Indians. This is seen in the 1986 film about Jesuit missionaries in South America, *The Mission*, as opposed to the secular governments of Europe which continued treating the Indians as incapable of maturity and independence. The intention all along was not for the missionaries to seize the Indians' land but for the missionaries to essentially work themselves out of a job and for the missions to become independent. This is a precursor of what today is known as the Three-Self movement[35] among indigenous churches: self-sustaining, self-governing, and self-propagating. Again, though the missionaries' intentions were good, sometimes the practical outworking of this did not have the intended consequences, as the secularization of the missions by the Mexican government essentially shut down the missions and took away the only lifestyle that the Christianized Indians had ever known, and thus left them bereft.[36] If a Western culture and lifestyle is part of what it means to be Christian, essentially

---

[33] This was an attempt to treat the Indians more humanely, largely as a result of the reform efforts of Bartolome de las Casas. It was a reaction against the cruel encomienda system.

[34] Hubert A. Lowman, *The Old Spanish Missions of California* (Arroyo Grande: John Hinde Curteich, Inc., 1989), 3. NB: as in much of the scholarly literature, the term "Indian" is commonly used in this chapter to refer to Native Californians, also known as Amerindians.

[35] This idea was first developed by Henry Venn, General Secretary of the Church Missionary Society from 1841–73. See Max Warren (ed.), *To Apply the Gospel: Selections from the Writings of Henry Venn* (Grand Rapids: Eerdmans, 1971).

[36] McLaughlin, *The California Missions Source Book*, 67.

missionaries are alienating the indigenous from their own people and the ability to reintegrate into their own society.

In addition, the problem of the "rice Christian"[37] was rampant. Many of the neophytes were converts in name only, receiving material goods and living a syncretistic life with indigenous religions and superstitions. Converts would initially receive baptism, a blanket, and a shirt. There were not only positive reinforcements, there were negative ones: when they did not show up or work, they would receive at least a dozen lashes. And many were frightened by Spanish technology exemplified by gunpowder—guns and cannons.[38] This is why the Three-Self concept is necessary for verification of authentic faith—especially the self-sustaining feature, which means continuing without outside funds and supplies.

The endeavor to accomplish the Three-Self idea included some money set aside for the purpose of sustaining the Jesuit missions in Baja California, called the Pious Fund of the Californias. Later, as the Jesuit missions were transferred from Spain to Mexico, the Pious Fund was diverted to support the Franciscan missions of Alta California instead.[39] Eventually, this fund, which was set up for a good reason—separation of church and state so that the three selves could become a reality among the missions—became a source of bitter controversy as it no longer became about benefitting the California Indians but rather a dispute over the "inheritance" of this fund between Mexico and the US. It became such an international incident that it made history as the first dispute to be settled by the Permanent Court of Arbitration at The Hague.[40] Sadly, well-intentioned Western involvement eventually devolved into Western greed over the proceeds of the Fund. Again, this is a concrete example of the mixed legacy of missionary involvement in the Californias.

A fifth characteristic of a missional theology of California is *culture-making*. Culture studies is integral to missiology, as it is embodied by how people speak,

[37]   This term comes from missionary work done in Asia where rice was offered as an incentive for natives to convert to Christianity. However, this can refer to anywhere the motives of the converts were suspect if one could never be sure if their "faith" was real or done for the sake of material benefits. The only way to ascertain the truth is if the material goods stopped coming in and to see the reaction of the people, if they should fall away or continue as Christians.

[38]   Antonio María Osio, *The History of Alta California: A Memoir of Mexican California*, Rose Marie Beebe and Robert M. Senkewicz (trans.) (Madison: The University of Wisconsin Press, 1996), 66–8.

[39]   Osio, *The History of Alta California*, 17.

[40]   William E. McDonald, "The Pious Fund of the Californias," *The Catholic Historical Review* 19/4 (January 1934), 427–36.

eat, dress, celebrate, and more, which are essentially vehicles of communication. While missionaries usually try to communicate the gospel through the culture of a people, in Californian history it has sometimes gone the other way— the missions have sometimes *dictated* the culture of California rather than *contextualized* to the culture of California. Unfortunately much of the religious significance on the culture has been lost as California grows ever more secular. The San Diego Padres baseball team are named thus because the San Diego mission was the first in California and the baseball team name is an homage to the Franciscan friars who established the missions which became the foundation of the state.[41] Beyond pop culture, however, the missions no longer seem to have much of an influence on contemporary Californian culture. Christians leading the way in creating and cultivating culture is something which needs to be recovered,[42] as Californian culture seems to be dictated more by Disney, Apple, Hollywood, the beach, the Green Movement, and other cultural innovators.

Yet, history offers some hope with regard to the arts. The Franciscans viewed singing as an approach to the sacred. Mission San Jose was especially well-known for its orchestra and choir composed largely of Ohlone Indians, and credit goes to Fr Narciso Duran who formalized the musical education of Indians in the California missions. Another mission famous for its music[43] was San Juan Bautista, though today it is more known for being the filming location

---

[41]   The Minor League (Double-A) affiliate baseball club of the Padres is the San Antonio Missions, named after the Alamo and the other four Spanish missions that were founded in the city of San Antonio, Texas.

[42]   Andy Crouch, *Culture Making: Recovering Our Creative Calling* (Downers Grove: InterVarsity Press, 2008). Crouch argues that creating and cultivating culture, where Christians lead the way, are preferable to the early twentieth century Fundamentalist posture of condemning culture, the mid-twentieth century neo-evangelical posture of critiquing culture, the 1970s Jesus Movement posture of copying culture, or the current evangelical posture of consuming culture, all of which are reactionary.

[43]   Sandos, *Converting California,* 130: "Music played an important, but heretofore largely overlooked, role in converting California Indians to Roman Catholicism. Music's importance lay in its centrality to the Mass, and the Mass, in turn, lay at the religious center of the Franciscan mission.... The Mass performed the ongoing function of integrating, or attempting to integrate, participants of the Mass into the Church and thereby into the Mystical Body of Christ to which all baptized members of the faith automatically belonged. Song involved the congregation and the choir directly in this integrative act." Again, Sandos, *Converting California,* 181: "Music helped to bond those Indians who were not choristers, although to a lesser degree. By bringing diverse Indian groups together to worship and work, the Franciscans taught Indians the rudiments of 'keeping together in time,' of cooperative action by many people."

for Alfred Hitchcock's *Vertigo*.[44] Mission San Gabriel has the Mission Playhouse right next to it which is still currently in use for performances. A plaque on the side of the Mission Playhouse reads:

> The Mission Playhouse, now the San Gabriel Civic Auditorium, was built by John Steven McGroarty to present his epic *Mission Play*. The play told the story of the California Missions and the lives of the people around them. Beginning in 1912, it drew people from all over the world to San Gabriel. The Playhouse was planned and completed for the 1927 season, with stage and dressing rooms large enough to accommodate the cast of 150 for the 4½ hour production. The exterior is patterned after the Mission San Antonio de Padua and the interior décor is a blend of Spanish, Indian and Mexican influences. In the courtyard on the north side are replicas of all 21 Missions. The Playhouse was acquired by the City of San Gabriel in 1945, fulfilling McGroaty's wish that it belong forever to the people. He went on to become a two term Congressman, and was Poet Laureate of California from 1933 until his death in 1944 ... [plaque dedicated] November 4, 2006.

The Mission Playhouse courtyard has miniature replicas of all 21 California missions, but even more impressive are the models at the official California Missions Museum at Cline Cellars in Sonoma, near the last of the missions.[45]

Literature about the missions has also made its mark on California. Called the "Queen of the Missions" because of its unique architectural style (it is pink and resembles a Roman goddess temple), Santa Barbara has the unmarked grave

---

[44]   More Hollywood connections: Mission San Antonio de Padua is located very near to Hearst Castle, the former estate of media mogul William Randolph Hearst (whose life served as the basis for the Orson Welles film *Citizen Kane*, voted the number one movie of the twentieth century by the American Film Institute).

[45]   The plaque at the museum reads: "The museum was built to house permanently the entire collection of the California Mission Models. These 21 intricately detailed models were crafted for the Golden Gate International Exposition of 1939, and were exhibited in the California Pavilion. The models were built by German craftsmen under the direction of the Italian artist, Leon Bayard de Vale. The models were meticulously researched to represent each mission as it was originally built and designed by the missionaries. This museum hopes to impart to all who visit it a sense of awe at the ingenuity, dedication, and tenacity of those who have gone before us. Built and donated by Fred and Nancy Cline, 10 September 2005." Why are the mission models at Cline Cellars? The sign at the entrance to the property explains: "The Last Mission. At this site, on July 4, 1823 Father Altimira set up a camp altar and planted the Holy Cross. The troops fired a volley, and the padre sang in adoration of the cross. A mass was celebrated in gratitude, and the place was named San Francisco Solano. The mission was later built at its present site in Sonoma." St Francis of Solano, "The Apostle of Peru," is to be differentiated from St Francis of Assisi. Both Francises were heroes to Serra.

of the real-life heroine of the book *Island of the Blue Dolphins* by Scott O'Dell. Her name in the book was Karana but she was baptized in real life as Juana Maria. The plaque at the mission reads: "Juana Maria, Indian woman abandoned on San Nicolas Island eighteen years, found and brought to Santa Barbara by Capt. George Nidever in 1853 ... [plaque dedicated] 1928." She is not the only significant person to be buried at the missions. Fr Serra himself is buried at the Carmel mission. Santa Clara, the only mission to reside on the site of a university (Santa Clara University; today the mission is the chapel of the university), has the grave of Peter Burnett, the first American governor of California. Mission Soledad has the grave of José Joaquín de Arrillaga, the first Spanish governor of California.[46] And Mission San Fernando hosts the grave of Bob Hope. Juana Maria, Peter Burnett, José Joaquin de Arrillaga, and Bob Hope are quite an eclectic group, but it just indicates that the missions belong to everyone.

The book *Ramona*, written by Helen Hunt Jackson in 1884, is often regarded as the *Uncle Tom's Cabin* of Native Americans. Jackson defended Indian rights and brought her literary talents to bear in highlighting their plight and victimization. Not only is this a classic piece of California literature, but it surpasses the Mission Playhouse in San Gabriel as another piece of theater associated with the missions. *Ramona* has been turned into an outdoor play, the longest-running outdoor drama in the US, shown continuously since 1923 in the town of Hemet in Riverside County. In fact the play was so influential that the San Bernardino Freeway was called the Ramona Freeway for a while, and the town of Ramona in San Diego County was named for the novel. *Ramona* tells the story of the titular character, a half-Native American woman, her adoption by a Mexican family, and her romance to an Indian man. Though fictional,[47] this story helped Native Americans recover some dignity and seemed to have parallels with the real-life first marriage in California.[48]

As mentioned above, the city of Riverside is the site of the hotel built in faux-mission style, the Mission Inn. Riverside was also home to the Mission Indian Federation, founded in 1919, which was one of the longest-lived grassroots political organizations of California Indians, fighting for civil rights, self-governance,

---

[46] Osio, *The History of Alta California*, 30.

[47] Although some have traced the "real" Ramona to Ramona Lubo of Cahuilla Reservation in Riverside County, and she became a minor celebrity as a result.

[48] On the outer wall of Mission San Antonio are painted these words: "First Marriage in California took place at this Mission between Juan Maria Ruiz of El Juerte, Sonora, Mexico, 25 years of age, and Margarita de Cortona, 22, a Salinan woman of Mission San Antonio, on the sixteenth of May in the year of Our Lord 1773." So the first official marriage in California was cross-cultural, interracial, and international.

and land ownership. The Sherman Institute, a US Indian school, was also built in Riverside in the same architectural style as the Mission Inn, and furthered the work of education among the California Indians.

In the historical missions, not all of the cultural contributions were positive, however. An unintended consequence—done more out of ignorance than malice—was bringing European culture and imperialism along with Christianity. When the Franciscan missionaries came to California, though they brought a great deal of Christianity with them, there was also a corresponding loss of Indian languages and culture. Essentially, Indians went into the mission compounds to become European, not just to become Christian. They learned to play the violin, they learned to speak Spanish, and they changed the way they dressed.

Nonetheless, during the late 1800s and early 1900s, the missions were California's biggest tourist attractions, and their fame was aided by the art, photography, fiction, film, and drama depicting their life and architectural splendor. Unfortunately, much of the picture painted of the missions was inaccurate. When the missions were secularized by the independence of Mexico from Spain in the 1830s, the missions era faded into nostalgia and myth. Much of the history was obscured by romanticization of a bygone era, and a lot of the conflict was sanitized into historical amnesia by the subsequent culture.

Fr Junípero Serra and St Francis of Assisi

If there is one name synonymous with the California missions, it is Fr Junípero Serra[49] (1713–84),[50] the "Apostle of California,"[51] who was beatified by

---

[49]   His birth name was Miquel Joseph but he took the name Junípero Serra in 1731. He was born in the town of Petra on the island of Mallorca, Spain. Much of what we know of Serra today is credited to his good friend and official biographer, Francisco Palóu, who published an account of Serra in 1787. For a recent biography, see Steven W. Hackel, *Junípero Serra: California's Founding Father* (New York: Hill and Wang, 2013).

[50]   2013 marking his 300th birthday. Thanks are due to the Huntington Library in San Marino, California, which had an impressive temporary exhibit dedicated to the tercentenary of Fr Serra's birth entitled "Junípero Serra and the Legacies of the California Missions," August 17, 2013–January 6, 2014. The Huntington also hosted a three-day conference from September 19–21, 2013 on the theme of "Junípero Serra: Context and Representation 1713 to 2013" featuring many leading scholars of the California missions. Both the exhibit and the conference helped me tremendously in preparing this chapter, as did actual in-person visits to all 21 missions.

[51]   Serra was far from being the first missionary in the Americas, however; that honor belongs to Pedro de Gante. And he is not the first Catholic in America to be considered for

Pope John Paul II in 1988.[52] His name is now found in multiple street names throughout California. If one visits the US Capitol building in Washington, DC, there are 100 statues in the National Statuary Hall because every state in the union was allowed to contribute two statues of the most important figures in their history. California contributed, unsurprisingly, Fr Junípero Serra as one of the two statues. The other statue originally was Thomas Starr King, "The Orator Who Saved the Nation," because of his efforts in saving the national parks and keeping California from seceding from the Union. In 2009, California decided to replace King's statue with former President Ronald Reagan.[53] Interestingly, King was a Unitarian Universalist and Reagan dabbled with astrology, strong contrasts with the Christian roots of Fr Serra's missions. There is a statue of Fr Junípero Serra in front of all 21 California missions—the same statue mold as the one in DC. Fr Serra's favorite mission was the second one he founded, Carmel, and it is where he is now buried. A visit to Mission San Carlos Borromeo de Carmelo will include his magnificent tomb. Though, as mentioned above, Fr Fermín Francisco de Lasuén (1736–1803) founded as many missions as Fr Serra did (nine each), there is only one statue of Lasuén on the grounds of any of the 21 missions, and that is at Mission San Fernando Rey where his statue is hidden in the bushes! Fr Serra is depicted widely in sculpture and painting throughout the state, but a popular image is of him holding a rock in one hand and a cross in the other—the former symbolizing his willingness to punish himself for his sins and take on the sins of others,[54] and the latter to show the sacrifice of Christ for the salvation of the world. None of the images depicting him, unfortunately, are accurate. There is not one likeness of him which is historical, and in reality he had a lame leg which he suffered from chronically, making him a frail and sickly individual, not the robust champion that we so

---

canonization; the first saint was actually St Rose of Lima.

[52]   His body was exhumed in 1943 as part of the canonization process in becoming a saint. He was declared "Venerable" by John Paul II in 1985, and "Blessed" three years later, two steps toward sainthood.

[53]   History links these two men. It is not coincidence that Ronald Reagan, when he was sworn into office on January 2, 1967 as governor of California, took his oath of office on Fr Serra's Bible, in the same way that Barack Obama took his Presidential oath of office on Abraham Lincoln's Bible in 2009. In both cases there was a deliberate attempt at making a symbolic statement of successorship to an honored and established historical groundbreaker.

[54]   This self-sacrificial attitude must be considered alongside the immense death toll of the California Indians. The missionaries would never do anything that they didn't require of their converts, so at the very least they were consistent and their integrity was intact. In fact, the Franciscans deeply venerated missionaries killed in Indian rebellions, believing that their deaths, and the miracles that followed, would attract Indian converts.

often see in paint and stone. In this sense, he is more of an Apostle Paul figure, one whose "bodily presence is weak, and his speech of no account" (2 Cor. 10:10–11) even if our historical memory of the man sees him as a towering hero.

Fr Serra's influences must be understood in order to make sense of his mission as well. In addition to Duns Scotus and St Francis of Assisi who are mentioned below, Ramon Llull (1232–1316) was a first-class philosopher and apologist who evangelized Muslims and Jews. Obviously there were no Muslims or Jews in the Americas during Serra's time there, but today that fact has certainly changed, so perhaps Serra's vision can be fulfilled today even if it was not fulfilled during his lifetime. Another profound influence was Sor María de Jesus de Ágreda (1602–1665) whose writings motivated Serra to become a missionary to Mexico and California. The reason is because of her mystical bilocation in which she was reputed to have been instantaneously transported to the American Southwest, even though she never really ever left Spain. While in what is today Texas, according to legend, she evangelized the Indians. Her writings, such as *La Mistica Ciudad de Dios* and her *Vida*, were often to be found in the libraries of the California missions.

However, if there was one person who even more so embodied California and the missions, it would be St Francis of Assisi himself, the founder of the Franciscan order, because it was his ideas that shaped the theology and ministry of the California missions. Serra looked not just toward Llull's conversion of Muslims as an example, but also Francis's attempted conversion of Sultan Melek-el-Kamel. Even more than Fr Serra, St Francis is the historical "soul" of California. Between Fr Serra, Fr de Lasuén, and St Francis of Assisi, it is the last who is the most important to the state of California though he never came to American soil. But really, all of them were important. It was a collaborative effort amongst many which helped the missions (and thus the state) to become what it was. California can trace roots back to Italy, St Francis's home; to Spain, Fr Serra's birthplace; to Mexico, the country which governed California immediately prior to the US and where the predecessor missions were located; and to the US. This seems to go against the individualized celebrity-status or single-culture mentality that dominates much of the California church today. Thus, the sixth characteristic of a missional theology of California is *collaboration*. Collaboration was seen in the ministry of William Carey, the "Father of Modern Missions," who could not have done what he did without the aid of Joshua Marshman and William Ward, the three of them forming the famous Serampore Trio. Even the Apostle Paul needed Barnabas, Timothy, John Mark, and others to aid him in his efforts. Mission is most successful with the contributions of many people and cultures, and California is no exception.

Missiology

St Francis of Assisi lent his name to one of the most important cities in the state, San Francisco. A few blocks away from the SF mission is the so-called Golden Fire Hydrant. During the earthquake of 1906, which resulted in a fire (which actually did more of the damage and largely contributed to the death toll of about 3,000 people), the only fire hydrant in the entire city that still worked was on the corner of 20th and Church Streets. Firemen used that and saved the entire Mission District from burning, which is why Mission Dolores is still intact today, despite much of San Francisco itself not surviving the quake and fire. Today, the city painted the hydrant a golden color in honor of its role in SF history, and there is now a plaque next to the hydrant which reads:

> Though the water mains were broken and dry on April 18, 1906, yet from this Greenberg hydrant on the following night there came a stream of water allowing the firemen to save the Mission District. Dedicated to Chief Dennis Sullivan and the men who fought the Great Fire and to the spirit of the people of San Francisco who regardless of their losses brought our city from its ruins to be host to the world with their 1915 Panama Pacific Exposition and the building of our Civic Center. May their love and devotion for this city be an inspiration for all to follow and their motto "The City That Knows How" a light to lead all future generations... [plaque dedicated] April 18, 1966.

Almost all the buildings in the Mission District today are pre-quake architecture[55] due to the golden fire hydrant saving them. But even more significant than architecture in this example is a seventh characteristic of a missiology of California: *holistic mission.* The juxtaposition of the mission and the fire hydrant suggests a biblical definition of mission, as Jesus' mission in Luke 4 (reading the scroll of Isaiah, the so-called "Nazareth Manifesto") was holistic, to offer both spiritual and physical salvation to people. The apostles likewise in Acts 6 had a division of labor because they realized they needed to offer preaching as well as food to people. Every year on April 18, the anniversary of the quake, the hydrant gets a fresh coat of gold paint by the San Francisco Fire Department by firefighters who commemorate its special place in the city's history. The San Francisco mission and the golden fire hydrant symbolize so well the holistic mission of the Franciscan friars, as they sought to improve the

---

[55]   Especially the mission building itself, which is the oldest intact standing structure in San Francisco.

physical lives of the Indians they encountered, no less an expression of the love of Christ as preaching the gospel to them. Today, Latin American *evangélicos* are known for their contribution of *misión integral* (holistic mission) to worldwide missiological theory and practice.[56]

Holistic mission involved both improving the spiritual lives of the Indians as well as their physical lives. Junípero Serra's Franciscan compassion for the poor extended to the indigenous and women[57] as well. It is no wonder that the image of the Virgin of Guadalupe,[58] "the Patron Saint of the Americas," who is both indigenous and female, is found in abundance in California. And Serra, whose chief theological influence was John Duns Scotus,[59] a Franciscan theologian from Scotland, was a strong advocate of women[60] because of Scotus's view of the Immaculate Conception[61] of the Virgin Mary. Serra's other chief theological influences besides St Francis—Ramon Llull and Sor María de Ágreda—also defended this doctrine.[62] Not only did Duns Scotus advocate a Marian theology, but his other contribution to Franciscan thought was a vivid Johannine apocalyptic vision but in a geocentric universe.[63] Mary in the book of Revelation

---

[56]   C. René Padilla (ed.), *Misión Integral: Ensayos sobre el Reino y la iglesia* (Kairos: Buenos Aires, 2012).

[57]   For an oft-omitted discussion of the indispensable role of women in California during the missions era, see Jack S. Williams, "Vidas Perdidas: The Forgotten Lives of the Women of the San Diego Presidio," in *Archaeological, Cultural and Historical Perspectives on Alta California* (Proceedings of the 20th Annual Conference of the California Mission Studies Association, Santa Cruz, California, February14–16, 2003), 45–89.

[58]   The Basilica of the Virgin of Guadalupe in Mexico City is the second-most visited Catholic pilgrimage site in the world after the Vatican itself.

[59]   Sandos, *Converting California*, 37.

[60]   Sandos, *Converting California*, 99: "Franciscan attitudes toward Indian women reflected the medieval expression that sin entered the world through a woman and the world would find salvation through the Virgin. Franciscans devoted themselves to the perfect woman in the form of Mary Most Holy even as they discounted and sought to control her profane sisters."

[61]   In fact one of the missions is named La Purísima Concepción, and two others are named for the Virgin Mary: Soledad (Our Lady of Solitude) and Dolores (Our Lady of Sorrows—the nickname for Mission San Francisco). Three others are named for women: Santa Clara, Santa Barbara, and Santa Ines.

[62]   On the façade of the Landa mission (one of the five Sierra Gorda missions) shows an image of Duns Scotus and Sor María de Ágreda, who were often paired together.

[63]   Sandos, *Converting California*, 80: "Serra and his students could not accept a challenge to the Scholastic geocentric universe because it would destroy their theological explanation of how the universe behaved. God had Angels motivate the seven spheres described in the Apocalypse of John.... Tampering with Scholastic science meant tampering with Scholastic theology—it meant violating the Apocalyptic message and the need for

was seen as a transcendent cosmic version of the Nativity,[64] and portrayed in California as either the Immaculate Conception or the Guadalupe.[65] Images of the Virgin taught the Indian females the importance of maintaining family unity. For men, instead of a Madonna birth image, they were given cross images which taught them suffering for the sake of the family.[66] Another important contribution of Scotus to Serra's thought was the theology of pilgrimage in order to reach unity with God. Serra interpreted this as leading the Indians from itinerancy to settled conversion, an express goal of the California missions. He did not view conversion as sudden but as gradual.

Holistic missions also did not just imply spiritual and physical aid, but also evangelism and discipleship. Franciscans loved to baptize, and Fr Serra performed over 500 baptisms. The Franciscans were excellent at record-keeping and they recorded over 80,000 baptisms in total. However, other Catholic orders such as Jesuits and Dominicans often felt that Franciscans baptized too quickly, without enough education prior to the sacrament. There was initially no bishop so Serra himself performed confirmations which is akin to discipleship. Fr Serra's brand of mission was keen to stress education. The Franciscans' education, however, sometimes was misguided as their approach was to "civilize" (or, "Europeanize") them. The missionaries viewed the Indians as children and sought to use fear by

---

Indian reparation assisted by the Franciscans, which Serra would not and could not do. Enlightenment thinking, however, advocated the Copernican system that Serra abominated. Copernicus's system and later Newton's law of inertia, if accepted, would wreck [*sic*] havoc upon the Scholastic worldview and the critical role of and need for human reparation for Christ's suffering in preparation for His return."

[64] Sandos, *Converting California*, 44–5. This was the doctrine of reparation, where Indians were taught they must help the cosmic Christ-child atone for the sins of the world in His battle against Satan. Thus the idea of personal responsibility on the part of each individual Christian was a large part of the missionary education of the Franciscans. This reparation idea was not only due to the influence of Duns Scotus, but also St Bonaventure, upon Serra. One of the missions is named San Buenaventura after him.

[65] According to Sandos, *Converting California*, 45: "As La Purísima, Mary stood on a crescent moon, usually without the Christ child, a halo with stars above her head and clothed in finery, usually white. As Guadalupe, the dark Virgin who allegedly appeared to the Indian Juan Diego outside Mexico City in 1531, Mary, a blue cloak embroidered with stars around her shoulders, stood on a crescent moon crushing the serpent beneath her feet. Any image of Mary, however, could be converted into a Purísima by adding a halo with stars, as Serra did when he brought such a device along with two statues of Mary with him to California, only one of which was a Purísima. Mary's flexibility of representation enabled the Franciscans to communicate a variety of her role models to churchgoers."

[66] Sandos, *Converting California*, 45–6. This is why art was so important; it played a huge role in the education of the Indians.

way of punishment (sometimes enforced by the military) to discipline them in work, trade, and morality. On the good side, they did support the vernacular languages,[67] so while Spanish was definitely taught, most of the education of catechisms and prayers was done bilingually.

Sometimes, however, good intentions can lead to bad results, as was the case with many of the Indians' health. As the gospel was brought to this new land, along came with it physical death for most Indians: European diseases such as cholera and smallpox wiped out some 80–90 per cent of the native populations of the Americas. Between "Guns, Germs, and Steel"[68] (borrowing the famous title by author Jared Diamond), germs were by far the deadliest. There were about 310,000 Indians in California when the Europeans arrived.[69] Over the course of the missions era, the native California Indian population declined by a staggering 74 per cent.[70] Thus, some scholars view Serra negatively, in much the same way that many view Columbus Day today, and protest the furtherance of the process leading to his canonization as a saint.[71] Within the realm of things the missionaries could control, though, they would set up hospitals and other healing clinics for the people.[72]

---

[67]   There were nearly 100 native languages in California, including Rumsen, Esselen, and Chumash. These languages helped to preserve their culture, ironically, even though the intention was to Hispanicize them.

[68]   Though European presence as a whole was destructive to the Indians, the missionaries surely were not as fatal as the secular colonists, according to Sandos, *Converting California*, 183:

> Gold seekers waged a war of extermination against Indians, a race war that received the financial backing of the state of California and the US government to pay the expenses of Indian killers. One historian, after careful consideration of the evidence, has concluded that the only word to describe this episode is genocide.... For the long-term history of California, former mission Indians adapted and survived the American onslaught occasioned by the gold discovery in 1848, something that gentiles, innocent of European contact, did not.

[69]   Sandos, *Converting California*, 179.

[70]   Sandos, *Converting California*, 102: "Procreation was critical to mission success. Since deaths routinely exceeded births, Indian women suspected of aborting a fetus, voluntarily or involuntarily, suffered particularly severe punishments." But women were affected the worst: "In California, Indians as girls and women suffered disproportionately more than men from the new diseases. Female Indians bore the brunt of the colonial experience, while children simultaneously suffered the greatest fatality rates in the missions" (127).

[71]   For example, Rupert Costo and Jeannette Henry Costo (eds), *The Missions of California: A Legacy of Genocide* (San Francisco: Indian Historian Press, 1987).

[72]   These opposing views of the Franciscans are known as the "Christophilic Triumphalist" view and the "Christophobic Nihilist" view, where either they are regarded hagiographically as being selfless saints who helped the natives, or destroyers of life and

Missionaries throughout history, especially Protestant, have not only tried to help heal physical woes but also have striven for higher education. After all, literacy was the foundation of the Protestant Reformation, because only when everyone can read the Bible in their own language can there be the priesthood of all believers. Though Mission Santa Clara is the only mission currently on a university campus, it is actually Mission Santa Ines (located in the faux Danish town of Solvang) which has the original claim of being the birthplace of California universities. They have a sign in the garden which reads:

> Did you know that you are standing where the first institution for higher education in California was built? In May 1844, the first seminary of the future state of California was established here. Built within the Mission Santa Ines quadrangle it was named The College of Our Lady of Refuge of Sinners. Here you can see a portion of the original floor of that two-story building which ran north and south. Just like the Church it was made of adobe with a tile roof and was about 120' long and 50' wide. The lower floor was divided into classrooms and rooms for the instructors. The upper floor contained the dormitories with a porch over the ground floor. The exposed floor that you see is asphalt and is typical flooring of the period. The Chumash used asphalt for many purposes prior to the Spanish Colonization period and gathered it from natural petroleum seeps or from the beaches.

Education was as much a part of holistic mission as feeding the poor and healing the sick were. In order for a church to be self-propagating, self-sustaining, and self-governing, it must be educated.

Mission San Juan Capistrano is famous for the Cliff Swallows which historically have migrated here every year from Argentina on St Joseph's Day (March 19). Inspired by this, Leon Rene wrote a hit song called "When the Swallows Come Back to Capistrano." There is a replica of Rene's recording studio on the mission grounds. Unfortunately, due to development and urbanization which has destroyed a lot of the swallows' natural habitat which is the nearby river bed, they no longer migrate to San Juan Capistrano in the manner they used to, and one can no longer view the amazing sight of the swallows descending in a cloud upon the mission. The mission was once not only a refuge for sinners but for the birds of nature. This conjures up the image of St Francis of Assisi, the inspiration and patron saint of the 21 California missions, who famously was

---

culture. See Sandos, *Converting California*, xiii. The truth probably lies not in the in-between but in the both/and.

a lover of nature and preached to the birds. Francis's care for nature is a natural extension of his care for the poor: to reach out to the least of these, the most helpless, the ones who have most been ravaged by power and oppression, and to offer them hope and sanctuary. His love of nature has been immortalized in the fact that St Francis often appears as a garden statue today. This is a parallel with another missionary, William Carey, who was a passionate nature lover. Not only did he preach and translate the Bible into many languages but he was also a botanist and agriculturalist. Another household name who did something similar was William Wilberforce, the MP in the British Parliament who successfully fought for the abolition of the slave trade.[73] What many do not know, however, is that he was also the founder of the Society of the Prevention of Cruelty to Animals.

Historically, the California Indians were mainly hunter-gatherers.[74] The Franciscan friars not only taught the Indians agricultural methods but even developed their own varietals and hybrids, such as the "mission grape" which has contributed to today's burgeoning wine industry in Santa Barbara, Sonoma, and Napa Valley.[75] California is the "bread basket of America." Perhaps not for wheat (which the Midwest produces more of), but certainly for everything else: avocados, tomatoes, oranges, olives, strawberries, almonds, grapes, and other produce. California's San Joaquin Valley is the largest patch of the most fertile soil (Class 1) anywhere on earth[76] and with its Mediterranean climate (hence the similarity to Italy's and Spain's food, which also makes it a suitable progeny of St Francis of Assisi and Fr Junípero Serra) it generates more produce than any

---

[73] On Indian slavery, see Sandos, *Converting California*, 178: "Were the Indians slaves? … the answer is no: there was no sense of ownership of the Indian by the Franciscan. The Indian, once having accepted baptism, however, was not free to come and go as he pleased, was not free to resume or continue his native way of life. The Indian's new spiritual and physical obligations to the mission made him unfree but not a slave; the term 'spiritual debt peon' more accurately describes neophyte status."

[74] McLaughlin, *The California Missions Source Book*, 13.

[75] The film *Bottle Shock* is based on the true story of how California's wine industry took on the French and beat them in an international competition, thus securing its foothold as a world-class wine-producing region. The first recorded California wine was from Mission San Juan Capistrano in 1782. See Michael R. Hardwick, "Changes in Landscape: The Beginnings of Horticulture in the California Missions," in *Archaeological, Cultural and Historical Perspectives on Alta California* (Proceedings of the 20th Annual Conference of the California Mission Studies Association, Santa Cruz, February 14–16, 2003), 109–112.

[76] Mark Bittman, "Everyone Eats There: California's Central Valley is our greatest food resource. So why are we treating it so badly?" *New York Times*, October 10, 2012, http://www.nytimes.com/2012/10/14/magazine/californias-central-valley-land-of-a-billion-vegetables.html?pagewanted=all&_r=3& (accessed December 3, 2013).

single state in America. Much of this is attributable to the aqueducts and farming techniques initially brought over by the Europeans. Today, the missions continue to be identified with Creation Care in the fact that Santa Cruz, La Purísima, and Sonoma are the three California missions which are part of California's State Park system. Leading missiologist Andrew Walls lists Creation Care as one of the five marks of twenty-first century mission,[77] and this is certainly another crucial aspect that rounds out holistic mission. Missions and Creation Care are natural partners.

Toward a Missional Theology of California

These are the beginnings of the making of a missiology of California. The seven characteristics that can begin to define a missiology of California (lessons from history) are:

1. language and immigration issues
2. geographical unity
3. poverty, chastity, and obedience
4. distinct architecture
5. cultural-creation
6. collaboration
7. holistic mission

These seven are certainly not meant to be all positive examples either, as the Franciscan missionaries failed on many of these fronts. But perhaps it is not a story of total success that we are meant to emulate; rather, we can learn from an acknowledgment that these characteristics have been descriptions of Christian missions in the early life of our state.

Regarding Fr Serra's ongoing consideration of canonization as a saint in the Catholic Church, James Sandos has this to say: "Serra had a medieval Franciscan utopian dream that he tried with all his being to institute in Alta California; his dream—along with many other dreams of Indians, Spaniards, Mexicans, and Americans in what became the American West—ended in failure." Yet, "Sainthood means that his is a universal example for all Catholics to follow;

---

[77]   Andrew Walls and Cathy Ross (eds), *Mission in the 21st Century: Exploring the Five Marks of Global Mission* (Maryknoll: Orbis, 2010). The other four marks are evangelism/ proclamation, discipleship, social service, and social transformation.

it means that the eighteenth century expression of Serra's medieval worldview would judge the twenty-first century and whatever centuries are to come."[78] As such, these seven characteristics of a missiology of California are *descriptive*, yes. How *prescriptive* and characteristic they will be for life as the gathered church in the future, however, is up to the church today.

---

[78] Sandos, *Converting California*, 184.

Chapter 5

"I Have Adonis DNA":
Californian Entertainment, Celebrity
Culture, and Evangelicalism

Monica Ganas

In a recent book reflecting on California and its significance for the rest of America's culture,[1] I argued that the unique phantasmagoria of California culture, with its potent distillation in the entertainment industry, can shape our theological assumptions in numerous ways, even though everyday Californians may resist such assumptions. From its love affair with spectacle and broadcasting to its emphasis on eternal youth, celebrity, and most importantly, human perfection, the culture has provided heady material for an ad hoc belief system I have called, for lack of a better word, *California-ism*.

Among other things, this belief system allows for the propagation of man-made forms of transcendence, especially in and around Hollywood, based on *the imperial idea* that people and their manufactured systems can be their own gods.[2] The path to godlikeness lies chiefly in the power of influence and the sacred imprints of cultural technologies. Several seasons ago, as the newest revelations of Apple and Microsoft were being met with a breathless anticipation befitting the tablets of Moses, greater still was the anticipation of Charlie Sheen's recent Caligula-like ranting in various media. In California's version of Rome's imperial cult, Sheen's short-lived tirades (drug induced or not) were in many ways merely the outward sign of inner assumptions in and around Hollywood—that the emergence of demigods is not only possible but also probable. It coincides with the very promise of Scientology and its "Celebrity Centre" located in Hollywood. With his claims

---

[1]   *Under the Influence: California's Intoxicating Spiritual and Cultural Impact on America* (Grand Rapids: Brazos, 2010).
[2]   Brian J. Walsh and Sylvia C. Keesmaat, *Colossians Remixed: Subverting the Empire* (Downers Grove: InterVarsity Press, 2004), 162–4.

to possess "Adonis DNA" and "tiger blood,"[3] Sheen was demanding his place in the imperial cult as, granted, a tiny, temporary Dionysian god of addiction and licentiousness, but a god nonetheless, a "rock star from Mars" whose "perfect and bitchin'" existence towered over that of ordinary mortals.

The man-made transcendence system, the imperial idea, creates gradations of humanity that can be used to determine human worth. In the imperial state of mind described by Walter Brueggemann,[4] such assumptions make no room for (imperfect) humans, but find ever more scathing ways to judge and humiliate them—as evidenced in the gladiatorial arena of Reality Television, for example. The fall out of the "human perfection" model is in fact judgment—an exquisitely crafted evaluation process that has been taught to us in one form after another, from *Toddlers in Tiaras* to *The Biggest Loser*. On the other hand, the *kingdom* idea, as revealed in Holy Scripture, is that there is only one God—with no negotiation, and the path prescribed for life in this kingdom is faith in the redemptive work of Christ. This involves confession, forgiveness, grace, and the freedom (finally) to be merely human; perhaps even fully human.

However, like the early church, we in the Californian church have difficulty living in tension between the two big ideas. Accordingly, certain aspects of Evangelicalism have been prone to negotiation. California-ism provides Christians the hope of proving that we can serve two masters after all. The *negotiated* idea is that people can be like God, or at least stand in for God, while proclaiming there is only one God. The path once again involves influence and technology now placed in service to God, but retaining the essential characteristics of the Hollywood industry since ultimately they share the same goal: to gain an audience. In Evangelicalism the goal is not (usually) financial but spiritual, yet the transaction is much the same. And in this transaction, in the minds of the audience at least, God's spokesperson that we can see often becomes a greater focus than the true God that we cannot see.

Nearby Idols, Far Off God

The replacement of the real God with a preferred god is automatic to humans. Both John Calvin and Martin Luther noted that the human heart is a natural

---

3   See a recounting of the interview on NBC's Today Show, http://www.today.com/ id/41824830/ns/today-today_entertainment/t/sheen-demands-percent-raise-two-half-men/#.UbyEY5z9U6w, February 28, 2011 (accessed June 15, 2013).

4   Walter Brueggemann, *The Prophetic Imagination* (2d ed., Minneapolis: Fortress, 2001).

idol maker.[5] So natural is this behavior that the first two commandments delivered to Moses on Mount Sinai forbid it.[6] Theologian Richard Keyes has observed that the real God is impossible to grasp because by nature God is *both* personal (nearby) *and* all-powerful (far off) and people simply cannot take this in.[7] Thus the preference is to split God in half and create our own nearby, accessible gods to provide us with the hopes offered by our own far-off gods. If we make them up, chances are we can better understand—and control—them. Jesus dealt with this issue while on earth. In a land of false Messiahs, he did not "fit the part" of the Son of God that some wanted him to play. The focus was on his public image and even his passing popularity, rather than on the redeeming, eternal work of Christ.

The creation of nearby gods in the form of celebrity evangelists with winsome personalities is a historical phenomenon in California, with Aimee Semple McPherson having paved the way for future generations. Though herself Pentecostal, "from her location in Hollywood, McPherson's integration of politics with faith set precedents for the religious right, while her celebrity status, use of spectacle, and mass media savvy came to define modern evangelicalism."[8] McPherson built upon a base created by several influences, one of which was the ongoing interplay between Pentecostals and evangelicals. Edith Blumhofer notes:

> Pentecostals drew on themes with deep roots in American evangelicalism, reviving hopes that had surfaced repeatedly in the past. Restoration, health, and empowerment were common concerns in American society and religion. Early

---

5   In Book 1.11.8 of his *Institutes*, John Calvin says that "... man's nature, so to speak, is a perpetual factory of idols" (*Institutes of the Christian Religion*, vol. 1, John T. McNeill [ed.] and Ford Lewis Battles [trans.], [Louisville: Westminster, 1960], 108); Luther's view of humans as "image makers," referring to Ps. 135:15–18, is discussed in Oswald Bayer, *Martin Luther's Theology: A Contemporary Interpretation*, Thomas H. Trapp (trans.), (Grand Rapids: Eerdmans, 2008), 110–11.

6   "You shall have no other gods before me. You shall not make for yourself an image in the form of anything in heaven above or on the earth beneath or in the waters below. You shall not bow down to them or worship them; for I, the LORD your God, am a jealous God, punishing the children for the sin of the parents to the third and fourth generation of those who hate me, but showing love to a thousand generations of those who love me and keep my commandments" (Ex. 20:3–6, NIV).

7   Richard Keyes, "The Idol Factory," in *No God but God: Breaking with the Idols of Our Age* (Chicago: Moody, 1992), 29–48.

8   From the publisher's summary of Matthew Avery Sutton, *Aimee Semple McPherson and the Resurrection of Christian America* (Cambridge: Harvard University Press, 2007).

Pentecostal views on such themes mattered deeply to the constituency and were shaped in part by radical evangelicals in the last quarter of the nineteenth century.[9]

The restoration she mentions is connected to "restorationism," or "the impulse to restore the original order of things revealed in Scripture,"[10] and it lay at the heart of much Pentecostal thinking. One emerging assumption was that "God had long since abandoned organized religion,"[11] an idea that still resonates with many Californians. Restorationists "believed they had discovered the biblical way to transcend the struggles of daily living," offering "not only certainty and divine immediacy but also a new way of perceiving reality." Some groups came to "regard themselves as a spiritual elite by insisting that they had recaptured more fully than others the dynamic, the message, or the form of the early church."[12]

These notions made their way to Los Angeles, home to the Azusa Street Revival of 1906 led by William Seymour. While newspapers complained of noisy, weird and wild fanatic activity at the neighborhood mission, Pentecostal leaders concluded that God had chosen Los Angeles to be the exact location where he would restore the Church to its former place and power. The "fervor, intensity, and a pervasive sense of the divine immediacy"[13] held great appeal for Los Angeles' turbulent, burgeoning population in 1906. Searching for religious connection and community, and frightened by the April 18 San Francisco earthquake as a possible sign of judgment, they sought immediate religious experience and the surety of signs and wonders. Over time, the transience and uncertainty of everyday life in Los Angeles became emblematic of the believer's pilgrimage on earth as *aliens* who belonged, after all, to another world. Interest in the things of this world—society, culture, economics—gave way to imagining the coming days of heaven on earth. "Yet the spirit of the age shaped Pentecostal's understanding of the Holy Spirit's presence among them, and they mirrored their culture in significant ways."[14]

---

[9]   Edith L. Blumhofer, *Restoring the Faith: The Assemblies of God, Pentecostalism, and American Culture* (Champaign: University of Illinois Press, 1993), 12.

[10]   Blumhofer, *Restoring the Faith*, citing Daniel G. Reid, et al. (eds), *Dictionary of Christianity in America*, (Downers Grove: InterVarsity Press, 1990).

[11]   Blumhofer, *Restoring the Faith*, 14.

[12]   Blumhofer, *Restoring the Faith*, 14.

[13]   Blumhofer, *Restoring the Faith*, 59.

[14]   Blumhofer, *Restoring the Faith*, 96.

Toward a Sunbelt Religion

Migration from the Southwest also shaped Evangelicalism in California. The early years of the twentieth century saw a steady exodus from the Old South to states west of the Mississippi including Texas, Arkansas, and Oklahoma, and little by little, a tough-minded, scrappy philosophy emerged among the plain folk populace there based on conflated doctrines of "Jefferson and Jesus."[15] They drew from Thomas Jefferson the "entwined values of localism, individualism, volunteerism, and free enterprise";[16] and from Jesus, moral imperatives and the need for revival. "Plain folk pioneers thus became pilgrims burdened with the responsibility of evangelizing and civilizing ... the dark, secular reaches of Southern California."[17]

For a variety of socio-economic reasons, the ensuing decades would eventually see more Southern-born residents living in California than in any other non-Southern state. And they brought with them a flinty, pragmatic theology with a political edge that left an indelible brand on the Golden State. Moreover, California's "Hollywood culture and competitive marketplace of ideas, resources, and influence drew out this faith's innate inventiveness and combativeness" and "Texas theology's encounter with a Southern California style forged a vigorous cultural force, one that melded traditionalism into an uncentered, unbounded religious culture of entrepreneurialism, experimentation, and engagement—in short, into a Sunbelt creed."[18]

Strains of both restoration theology and the Sunbelt creed are found in the work of Aimee Semple McPherson and other celebrity evangelists. McPherson's Angeles Temple, dedicated New Year's Day, 1923, was a massive undertaking, designed to hold 5,300 seats. At one point, the mega-church was filled three times a day, seven days a week, its popularity stemming not only from McPherson's imaginative, elaborate, sometimes militant theatrics during church services, but as a result of her broadcasts on the newly minted radio. "The evangelist even talked about building a hotel for church visitors,"[19] many of whom were tourists encouraged by the Los Angeles Chamber of Commerce and other city boosters to make Angeles Temple a "must see." She in turn promoted California

---

[15]   Darren Dochuk, *From Bible Belt to Sunbelt: Plain-folk Religion, Grassroots Politics, and the Rise of Evangelical Conservatism* (New York: W. W. Norton, 2011), 13.

[16]   Grant Wacker, "California Dreams—A Review Essay," Christian Scholar's Review 40/3 (Spring 2011), 311.

[17]   Dochuk, *From Bible Belt to Sunbelt*, 13.

[18]   Dochuk, *From Bible Belt to Sunbelt*, xvi–xviii.

[19]   Sutton, Aimee Semple McPherson, 88.

onstage and on the air. McPherson was the second woman in America granted a broadcast license.

In 1932 journalist Morrow Mayo wrote that Los Angeles was "not a mere city [but] a commodity; something to be advertised and sold to the people of the United States."[20] Even though some writers warned that LA had become a place of "decadent religions and cults ... apt to get the better of one, both materially and spiritually,"[21] city boosters worked hard at creating quite a different image.[22] McPherson joined the effort, penning a song titled "I Love You California" that included the lyrics:

> Garden spot of God and Man,
> Favorite Child of Uncle Sam,
> That's my sunny, that's my honey,
> That's my sunny California.[23]

Often compared to movie starlets, McPherson screen-tested well and negotiated a film project with Universal Studios; the newsreels loved her. She was larger than life. Biographer Matthew Sutton writes: "She was ... a living, moving image that embodied the blend of conservative faith and modern technology, made possible in the land of Hollywood. In effect, McPherson was redefining the relationship between conservative Protestantism and American culture by working to harness the religious potential of the new mass media."[24]

Word and Image

One contemporary of McPherson, California-born Charles Fuller, also made use of the media, but, importantly, his media was more reliant upon word than image. The would-be citrus farmer and lover of California's natural landscapes and wildernesses, having played an important part in Sothern California's citrus industry and having served a variety of tasks in his local Presbyterian church, was ultimately called to one of California's first Bible colleges, B.I.O.L.A. (Bible

---

20   Morrow Mayo, *Los Angeles* (New York: Alfred A. Knopf, 1933), 319.

21   Louis Adamic, *Laughing in the Jungle: The Autobiography of an Immigrant in America* (New York: Harper Brothers, 1932), 219–20.

22   Glen Gendzel, "Not Just a Golden State: Three Anglo 'Rushes' in the Making of Southern California, 1880–1920," *Southern California Quarterly* 90/4 (2008–2009), 366.

23   Sutton, *Aimee Semple McPherson*, 27.

24   Sutton, *Aimee Semple McPherson*, 157.

Institute of Los Angeles) and a life of full-time church ministry. When his travelling and preaching schedule became untenable, Fuller developed "The Old-Fashioned Revival Hour," an hour of teaching focused on Scripture, evangelism and soul winning.

It was first broadcast on B.I.O.L.A.'s radio station, and then moved to a station founded by the Santa Ana local newspaper, the *Register*. The paper ran an editorial stating, "Movies have failed to be educational, and radio so far, but it is hoped that this unique venture will be the reverse of all that."[25] Fuller's Scripture-based, Christ-centered teachings, the kind he hoped to foster with the founding of Fuller Seminary, were geared toward individual listeners rather than large crowds, and while in time his radio program amassed an international audience, he carefully eschewed the expensive airwaves of television, and hence, most of the trappings of celebrity.[26]

Quentin Schultz has observed that, historically, American evangelicals have rarely if ever met a mass medium they didn't like.[27] This makes sense, since a central goal of Evangelicalism is to spread the gospel as widely as possible; and time and again, all mass media have presented tantalizing opportunities for kingdom growth. Just as Christianity can affect media however, media can affect Christianity. Schultz makes a distinction between old-fashioned religious broadcasting such as Charles Fuller's and that to which it has given way: televangelism, or the electronic church. The latter broadcasts are characterized as "audience-supported ... personality-led ... experientially validated ... technologically sophisticated ... entertainment-oriented ... [and] expansionary-minded," adopting a grow-or-die approach during an era in which the television industry realized the financial gains to be made by such programming.[28]

"Not having a theology, however, is key to the success of the electronic church" writes Richard Kyle, adding that "some individuals even contend that theology is an elitist discipline."[29] As in Hollywood, there is a general disdain for higher education that "squares with evangelicalism's populist and pragmatic character"[30] and also squared with Aimee Semple McPherson's philosophy. According to Kyle, theology, which tends toward discussions too complex for

---

25   Daniel P. Fuller, *Give the Winds a Mighty Voice* (Waco: Word, 1972), 77.

26   Fuller, *Give the Winds a Mighty Voice*, 48, 77.

27   Quentin Schultz, *Televangelism and American Culture: The Business of Popular Religion* (Grand Rapids: Baker, 1991), 47.

28   Schultz, *Televangelism and American Culture*, 29–43.

29   Richard G. Kyle, "The Electronic Church: An Echo of American Culture," *Direction* 39/2 (2010), 166–7.

30   Kyle, "The Electronic Church," 170.

the airwaves, is replaced by emotionalism, nationalism, and even sensationalism that include hyperbole, drama, and ongoing descriptions of the cosmic battle raging around us. Importantly, evil is characterized as something outside of us; something to be feared from others, rather than from ourselves.[31]

The need to deny our daily vulnerability and/or inclination to sin seems to me the first step in the creation of American Christianity's own brand of super-humanity and the resulting judgment against those humans we deem the *real* sinners in the world (thus creating our own version of *The Biggest Loser*). Does the world need the gospel or a self-improvement plan, a spiritual makeover, so to speak? Robert Schuller's "theology of self-esteem"[32] presents an interesting case in point. The first two points of Schuller's basic theology, as outlined in a letter to Jesse Jackson, were these:

1. I am a believer in Jesus Christ, and have accepted him as my personal Lord and Savior. In that sense, I am of the evangelical theological tradition.
2. I believe in positive thinking. It is almost as important as the resurrection of Jesus Christ. A negative-thinking Christian isn't much good to God or to his fellowmen.[33]

The pragmatic leap Schuller makes here seems at home with the Sunbelt creed, as does his introduction to *Self-Esteem: The New Reformation*. It invokes a Gallup poll listing all the ways in which self-esteem is tied to higher ethics and morality, stronger family life, success, productivity, volunteerism and generosity.[34] Referring to self-esteem as "the universal hope"[35] seems another leap from the gospel of grace to the gospel of self-improvement. It is uncertain whether this is Schuller's intention, but at the very least it is an example of the ongoing tension between gospel basics and the various applications of the gospel that have (erroneously) sprung from some of California's ministries. Schuller's message was ideally and inevitably suited to television, in both its content and form. "The Hour of Power," became "a driving force in Christian television,"[36] and the program's producer Michael Nason stated:

---

[31] Kyle, "The Electronic Church," 168–9.
[32] Michael Nason and Donna Nason, *Robert Schuller: The Inside Story* (Waco: Word, 1983), 151.
[33] Nason and Nason, *Robert Schuller*, 152.
[34] Nason and Nason, *Robert Schuller*, 17.
[35] Nason and Nason, *Robert Schuller*, 145.
[36] Nason and Nason, *Robert Schuller*, 128.

If you go to television, you had better be television, you had better give the viewer what he has come to expect from television. Television is not the route to go if you want to project the poor, humble Christian image. You may have a wonderful message to communicate, but no one will listen to you long enough to find out what it is .... They expect it to be fast paced, entertaining, and colorful.[37]

Schuller has helped many people, and time will tell what his legacy will be. Yet there seems something oddly fleeting about California's spiritual enterprises. Schuller was the first to establish a drive-in church, the popularity of which set the foundation for what became the Crystal Cathedral in Garden Grove. There, at one time, one could enjoy theatrical spectacles that rivaled Broadway productions, as well as beautifully landscaped grounds with statues of a friendly Jesus happily playing with children. (The statues closely resembled the fare at nearby Disneyland.) One could also visit a gift shop brimming with spiritual self-help slogans, many of which encouraged us to pull ourselves up by our spiritual bootstraps, so to speak. Emblazoned upon a far wall were the words, "If you can dream it, you can do it!" (a phrase later to be co-opted by the Will Ferrell ice skating satire, *Blades of Glory*). Yet this opulent campus just off the Interstate 5 Freeway has since become the stuff of bankruptcy courts and other legal battles, being purchased by the Roman Catholic Diocese of Orange on February 3, 2012.[38] So much seemed to ride on Robert Schuller the person, or the personality, that the ministry began to unravel as he faced retirement.[39]

Stars in Our Eyes

David Shaw of the *Los Angeles Times* once wrote, "Americans have a unique hunger to identify with personalities, larger than life personalities especially. No country in the world is as driven by personality as this one."[40] And Richard Kyle agrees. "Lacking religious traditions, Americans, especially evangelicals," he

---

[37]   Nason and Nason, *Robert Schuller*, 132–3.

[38]   Ronald Campbell, "Crystal Cathedral sold to Catholic church," *Orange County Register*, February 3, 2012, http://www.ocregister.com/news/cathedral-338810-diocese-congregation.html (accessed June 15, 2013).

[39]   It might also be argued that the theological drift from gospel at the core of Schuller's ministry made it vulnerable to collapse without the authority it drew from Schuller's powerful presence.

[40]   David Shaw, "Hunger for Heroes, Villains Routed in American Psyche," *Los Angeles Times*, February 17, 1994, G7.

writes, perhaps unfairly, "have always been obsessed with celebrities. They are not primarily interested in issues and ideas but in people and personalities."[41]

Years ago, Mel Gibson came to my university to promote, discuss and screen his film *The Passion of the Christ*. It was a remarkable moment at school, generating great excitement. The last time I'd seen such a thing was when Kirk Cameron came to campus to speak in chapel. On both occasions, there was giddiness in the crowd that I rarely see, and it obviously threw our guests, who seemed to have expected something else from the believing community. During the interview with Gibson, the event host asked him if making the film had changed him personally. His diffident response, "Well, I quit smoking," pulled such cheers and applause that he widened his eyes and said, "Wow, if you think that's a big deal, maybe I shouldn't tell you the rest." Though this drew laughs, it turned out that Gibson really was in a confessional state of mind. Yet each time he attempted to describe the chinks and stains in his character the host cut him off with a winsome chuckle and a quick quip. At one point Gibson said, "I have a lot of problems, you know?" and was met with "But ... you're Mel Gibson!" In all, I can't remember much conversation about the actual film we were about to see. The focus was not Gibson's work, but his personal character, indeed, his personality.

I believe this desire to keep our Christian celebrities bright and shiny stems from a few understandable impulses, a couple of which might seem obvious. To begin with, Christian celebrities tend to be used to legitimize our faith; that is, it makes us feel less culturally awkward when pop cultural icons believe what we believe. But in order for them to retain this authority, there's often an expectation that they become models of Christian faith and practice, precisely because of their high visibility. This is what creates such disappointment in some evangelicals when, for instance, Christian artists don't "use their gifts to glorify God" by confining their material to Christian themes. Newly converted celebrities (or those, like Gibson, who have expressed a return to faith in a public way) seem especially vulnerable to this treatment, often with damaging effects.

Moreover, if we can compete on a cultural level with other famous opinion makers by offering our own, Christians might become more legitimate and even more influential in society's eye, and hence more effective in various evangelical campaigns. And this may work best when we have folks who are seen to have "made it" in both the kingdom of God and the kingdom of man. A 2010 "Spotlight" in *Christianity Today* titled "American Idols and Saints" featured five Christian *American Idol* contestants that the magazine referred to as "instant celebrities." It quoted a Beliefnet blogger: "There was a time when

---

41 Kyle, "The Electronic Church," 169.

a worship leader performing on a show like *American Idol* would have caused Christians to question his [*sic*] faith. But with the culture of celebrity becoming more common in the Christian community, the idea of a Christian making it big in the mainstream isn't so distasteful anymore." It probably helped that one of the contestants, Jordin Sparks, "made headlines defending promise rings on the MTV Music Awards."[42]

Famous Christian life coaches, financial gurus and motivational speakers show us how we too can make it big here on earth while sports stars, beauty queens and rap artists who thank God for his support provide credence that God is keenly interested in our earthly success. I am fully supportive of thanking God publicly and I have no doubt that God does indeed bless our earthly efforts. The point here is that fame lends authority to evangelical claims regarding both a faithful God and the power, or rightness, of Christian faith and practice. And, according to Ted Smith of the Vanderbilt Divinity School, the authority of celebrity has been an ongoing need since the days of Charles Finney, not a Californian, but a powerful influence.

Finney's preaching reached many because he found ways to express emotions usually limited to private life in respectable public forms and he employed an extemporaneous style that bridged public and private forms of discourse.[43] Yet, during the mid-nineteenth century, in order to display a private persona in public, and thus register as more genuine and trustworthy to everyday folk, a preacher had to set aside the trappings of traditional authority such as high pulpits, distinctive dress, and mannered rhetoric—practices that legitimated a preacher by showing connections to institutions "whose legitimacy could be taken for granted."[44]

In the absence of traditional authority, Finney borrowed authority from "the emerging 'star system' that appeared most clearly on the stage but also arose in religious and political spheres."[45] These stars found ways "to combine the intensity, passion, veracity and heightened reality of a private self with the prestige, reason, power and widespread presence of an alienated public representation. That amalgamation gave stars a distinct kind of authority." While working "miracles of popularity" which also lent Finney authority, he "showed

---

[42]   "Spotlight: American Idols and Saints," *Christianity Today* 54/5 (May 2010), http://www.christianitytoday.com/ct/2010/may/27.11.html (accessed June 16, 2013).

[43]   Ted A. Smith, *The New Measures: A Theological History of Democratic Practice* (New York: Cambridge University Press, 2007), 190–1.

[44]   Smith, *The New Measures*, 194.

[45]   Smith, *The New Measures*, 194.

a celebrity's dependence on routinized mass images and measures."[46] Handbills promoting his appearances hawked the number of conversions he'd made just as similar handbills might promote an actor who'd "played to throngs" elsewhere.

Still, "[Brother] Finney ... took great pains to show his followers that he was just like them." And while they reckoned him to have "extraordinary qualities ... they saw him as one just like them ... only more so. He was an icon of their aspirations." And it was "the interchangeability of the star's persona with that of audience members that helped ground the authority of a star."[47] Then as now, the great appeal of stars is that they are like *us*. They are *People*, as today's gossip magazine titles imply. We can have what they have, be who they are: a kind of super human. It's a tantalizing notion, especially here in California, where brushes with greatness, or at least brushes with fame, seem always within reach. After all, we breathe the same air, pay the same utility companies, drive the same roads, use the same airports, and occasionally shop at the same markets as celebrities. Who knows, we might even stumble onto a TV show one day. In Southern California, at least, the studios are part of the landscape.

Christ and the Celebrity Model

Ultimately, the tie between celebrity and authority makes its way back to the very person of Christ. The University of Southern California historian Richard Fox finds that when "new realities demand a new view of Jesus or a return to an old one that has been forgotten [Americans] reconfigure his identity to renew or restore his authority."[48] And when celebrity became a dominant cultural value, "it was inevitable that Jesus would be pressed into service." Fox cites John Lennon's famous line comparing the popularity of Jesus to that of The Beatles, and notes that while there was a hailstorm of criticism over the remark, the essential reconfiguration of Jesus as celebrity figure was rarely the issue, only that he was called *less* popular.

Similarly, when the rock opera *Jesus Christ Superstar* was released, critics railed more about the obscure ending that did not include a clear resurrection than about the central conceit of the story: again, Jesus as celebrity figure. Fox surmises "articles written about the opera in *Christianity Today* actually disclose

---

[46]   Smith, *The New Measures*, 195–6.
[47]   Smith, *The New Measures*, 195.
[48]   Richard W. Fox, "Jesus as a Celebrity," lecture given at Sophia University, Japan, June 2006, http://ci.nii.ac.jp/lognavi?name=nels&lang=en&type=pdf&id=ART0008406154 (accessed June 16, 2013).

that evangelicals had come a long way toward accepting celebrity as a fact of life in America, and even toward finding spiritual power in it."[49] The focus was not on the work of Christ, most importantly his finished work on the cross, but upon his personal character, his personality. Hollywood has made a significant contribution to the celebrity Jesus, Fox observes, adding that "on film, Jesus as image tended to crowd out Jesus as Word, no matter how much he preached. He became more familiar, predictable, unmysterious."[50] This was Aimee Semple McPherson's goal as well, to humanize Jesus, "making him come to life as a real person,"[51] like us ... only more so. This seems to be the definitive appeal of celebrity, the promise of some sort of human divinity. And while Christ truly was utterly human and utterly divine, this phenomenon has happened only once on earth, no matter how much we would like to duplicate it. That is the kingdom idea, the new idea.

While it can be argued that the Church has always created celebrities, in the form of saints, for example, there is an important distinction. True, statues of saints were crafted from the statues of pagan gods and goddesses and may have functioned similarly as human models of divinity. But their veneration stemmed less from what they were than from what they did. Like the famous saints of the modern world, from, say, Martin Luther King, Jr to Mother Theresa, they sacrificed and suffered. They served. We focus on their work, really, rather than their personalities. Saints inspire us *because* they are human, and not despite the fact. We want their strong spirits, not their super lives; in fact, we rarely wish to share their fates: the costs of their actions.

Here in California, there are thousands of saints from whom to learn. At one time, I was privileged to hear two famous Californians discuss their film *The Way* after its screening in the ordinary auditorium of a Catholic university. They were Martin Sheen, who acted the film's leading role, and his son Emilio Estevez, who directed him. Their film is about a flawed and distant father who comes to France to collect the remains of his adult son, killed in a storm while travelling the 500-mile El Camino de Santiago (The Way of St James). The Internet Movie Database (IMDb) states: "Tom decides to embark on the historical pilgrimage to honor his son's desire to finish the journey. What Tom doesn't plan on is the profound impact the journey will have on him and his 'California Bubble Life.'"[52]

---

49   Fox, "Jesus as a Celebrity," 5.
50   Fox, "Jesus as a Celebrity," 11.
51   Fox, "Jesus as a Celebrity," 20.
52   *The Way* (2010), "The Storyline," http://www.imdb.com/title/tt1441912/ (accessed July 27, 2013).

Unlike Mel Gibson, who was interviewed before the screening of his film, Sheen and Estevez were interviewed afterward. And because we were focused on the profound and moving story, the questions were about their honest work as faithful artists, rather than about their celebrated selves. They fielded them with humility and warmth. "Hollywood thinks no one wants to see this film," Estevez observed, and that is, in part, because the film is about real humans. Characters who walk the way with Tom in the hopes of losing weight or their cigarette habit fail in those goals, but encounter a greater miracle: grace. "We're all beautiful wrecks," Estevez said. "No one in the movie gets cured in the film," only accepted by fellow pilgrims in ways that are denied them amid the constant demands of commoditized culture, one that makes little room for imperfection.

Estevez is a micro farmer who lives down the street from his parents and has been acting and directing for 30 years. When an audience member mentioned the many sacramental moments in the film, he responded, "holy moments happen and you just hope the camera is rolling." He was content to serve the bigger story rather than becoming a bigger star. I thought of Martin Sheen's other son, Charlie, and couldn't get over the fact that this family, at the time, operated as such a compelling metaphor for all that is most inspiring and most challenging in the Golden State. As California's Christians make their uneasy way through the streets of today's Corinth (in terms of lifestyle) *and* Ephesus (in terms of influence), theological engagement with California culture bids the Church to ponder whether we will learn to live contentedly as faithful humans who have come to believe in a gospel of grace and who are called to lives of humble service, or whether we will attempt to trade true godliness for the fleeting lure of god*like*ness.

Chapter 6

In Pursuit of the Consumer Crown or the Crucified Crown?

Matthew S. Farlow

Opening Curtain

The performance of Christ—his incarnation, life, death, and resurrection—is, according to Dorothy Sayers, "the greatest drama ever staged." The biblical script communicates the relational reality of faith that is "the most exciting drama that ever staggered the imagination of man."[1] If this is true, then how should God's drama, as revealed in Christ through the Holy Spirit, influence and guide the way Christians *are* church, especially in one of the leading places of ecclesial imagination and innovation, the Californian church?

The language of the Bible is best understood as interactive, calling for a participation in the Being and act of God. The church is called to *be* the community of faith that not only learns from, but lives out, the biblical script. With this in mind, then, it is important to ask: Is today's church living out Christ's incarnational performance and thereby promoting first our being *in* Christ so as to then establish our own act (purpose)? Or, in its quest for the "unchurched," is church, especially the megachurch, subtly promoting an individualistic and consumeristic lifestyle that seeks to "win at all cost?" This "win at all cost" ideology is a manifestation of California's early culture that was both pioneering as well as entrepreneurial; a mentality that embodies the mantra "There it is. Take it."[2] As John S. Hittell, author and Forty-Niner, writes, "The people who come to

---

[1]   Dorothy L. Sayers, *The Greatest Drama Ever Staged* (London: Hodder and Stoughton, 1938), 1.

[2]   David Ulin, "There It Is. Take It." *Boom: A Journal of California* 3/3 (Fall 2013), 28–37. Ulin highlights the type of entrepreneurial energy and consumeristic mindset that fuels California culture. In 1913 William Mulholland, a major player in the creation of the California Aqueduct, dedicated the aqueduct to the people of Los Angeles. There Mulholland proclaimed, "this is an altar and on it we are here consecrating this water supply and dedicating this aqueduct to you and your children and your children's children—for all

California are bold adventurers naturally. We were dissatisfied with life in Europe and the Eastern states, because it was too slow. We came here to enjoy an exciting life and make money rapidly."[3] In light of the aforementioned, one wonders, how deeply California's pioneer spirit has influenced the vision of the megachurch thereby impacting its pursuit. In other words, is the purpose of the church today the pursuit of the consumer crown or the pursuit of the crucified crown?

The crux of this chapter is to investigate the theological focus of the megachurch, paying special attention to Saddleback Church in Lake Forest, Southern California. The investigation considers two possibilities. Is the model of the megachurch driven towards the empowerment of the individual and their consumeristic mindset? Or does it promote and embody a Christ-centered reality that seeks to participate in Christ so as to elevate the "other" as opposed to commodifying them? This chapter suggests that the theological underpinnings of the church are dramatic in that they require participation as opposed to observation. That is, God's interaction with his creation—his Theo-drama—is the example (model) for the church; it is a relational model that seeks to live in the fullness of community as it lives out service toward the other. From the church, society has a window of seeing who God is and thus who the human is. Created in the image of God, the human is a relational being created for fellowship with others, the created world, and the Creator. The created reality of the human should have as its focus Christ, and thus community, as opposed to self and the consumption of the "other."

The church remains true to its being and act when the church's theologians seek to refer the church back to its source. As Karl Barth states, "I believe the Church as the proclaimer and the hearer of the divine Word ... the Church could not ever be exempt from seeking after the Word and asking for the Holy Spirit which alone leads it to all truth."[4] It is only through careful and constructive

time." Concluding his thoughts, "Mulholland gestured toward the aqueduct, and—to the crowd, to history, to whomever—shouted: 'There it is. Take it.'" The point to consider here is between a life lived by someone whose purpose is derived from oneself—he sees life as a conquest, to see something and seek to take it—contrasted with one who is "more than a conqueror" based solely on being a participant in Christ's own life, death, and resurrection because Christ is our refuge and the one to whom our lives should seek to grab hold of (Ps. 73:25–8).

    3   John S. Hittell, *Resources of California, Comprising Agriculture, Mining, Geography, Climate, Commerce, etc. etc. and the Past and Future Development of the State* (San Francisco: A. Roman and Co., 1863), 333–4, quoted by H.W. Brands, *The Age of Gold: The California Gold Rush and the New American Dream* (New York: Doubleday, 2002), 441.

    4   Karl Barth, *Theology and Church* (trans. Louise P. Smith) (New York: Harper & Row, 1962), 285, 295.

dialogue within the academy and the church that the message of the church will guard against becoming merely the voice of humankind as opposed to the dynamic revelation of God in Christ through the Holy Spirit.

The chapter is broken into five sections. The first section opens the curtain on the current discussion concerning the church by providing background to the make-up of the current script. The second section sets the stage regarding the megachurch by looking at its focus and pursuit, and how this pursuit is beginning to play out in church culture. The third section illumines the movement of the stage in light of the church's "purpose driven" pursuit. The fourth section looks in on the cast of characters that will play a role in this drama and how they work (or stumble) as a collective whole. The fifth section concludes with a look at what can be the church's curtain call if it seeks to participate faithfully in Christ's act of reconciliation. The world is in need of the church to understand its being, so as to apprehend the essence of its ecclesial role in the divine drama.

Preparation of the Stage

Seeing the Focus

No doubt one could claim that the megachurch has thrived in recent culture. Popularity of the megachurch movement and influence is evidenced in the visible "Christian subculture" that has arisen. This culture has established and maintained a "Christian identity, providing an exciting and entertaining experience, and not really requiring much in the way of commitment beyond showing up and enjoying the experience."[5] Polls continue to show that while we have entered a post-Christian era "churches like Saddleback are growing in size and influence while older, mainline churches and denominations continue a decades-long decline in membership."[6] Looking into the success keys into a major component or focus of the megachurch—marketing.

---

[5]   Richard Flory and Donald E. Miller, *Finding Faith: The Spiritual Quest of the Post-Boomer Generation* (New Brunswick: Rutgers University Press, 2008), 78–9.

[6]   Justin G. Wilford, *Sacred Subdivisions: The Postsuburban Transformation of American Evangelicalism* (New York: New York University Press, 2012), 3. Editor's note: according to recent reports from Saddleback staff members, one way that Saddleback is apparently not growing at present is with 20- and 30-somethings who simply do not live in Lake Forest and cannot afford to, posing a future problem for this church, although perhaps displaying foresight in its commitment to tent-ministry instead of large buildings throughout the campus.

Marketing the church is popular in the evangelical world as attenders are often referred to as consumers or customers and an ethic of consumption—of products and experiences—has often been encouraged. Foundational in the megachurch model is the emphasis on "individual choice and consumer culture as an organizing ideal."[7] Driving the marketing mentality is the seeker movement, which has institutionalized its approach through market research that helps to "make church and the Christian message 'relevant.'"[8] Furthering the need to be relevant, many churches today have intentionally sought to capitalize on the consumerist culture prevalent in society as well as the church today. Concerning a "consumer Christianity," Richard Flory and Donald E. Miller note that "one can wear their identity through a T-shirt, bumper sticker, or tattoo, have coffee at their church café, and have what amounts to Christian vacations, all without really giving up any part of an American middle-class consumer lifestyle."[9] Churches purposely have their own slogans printed abundantly over their material. They brand their logos, symbols, and creative marketing captions on t-shirts, bumper stickers, license plate holders, window decals, Facebook, and more. Fading fast and near gone are the days of the community church, house visits, church directories, humble presences, and denominations.

What does this movement in the Christian church indicate for religion and faith today? Interestingly we have indeed entered into a time of "posts": postmodern, postreligious, postchristian, postsuburban, and postdenominational. For the church, the focus has seemingly shifted from being a "regular" sized church to becoming a "supersized" or "mega" church. While bigger does not always mean better (nor worse, necessarily), what all of this talk about church numbers, marketing schemes, and campus square footage seems to insinuate is that in the church today, bigger does mean better.

When looking into the megachurch model, influence and size are key factors in deciding who and where to go to investigate this phenomenon. There are roughly 1,600 megachurches, and the largest portion of them is found in California and the South (Texas and Georgia).[10] With this in mind, it is being argued that a look at Saddleback will not only shed light on the church culture and theology of California, but will also illuminate much of the current trend of

---

[7]   Flory and Miller, *Finding Faith*, 74.

[8]   Flory and Miller, *Finding Faith*, 65.

[9]   Flory and Miller, *Finding Faith*, 82.

[10]   Nearly 15 percent of all megachurches are located in California. These statistics are in accordance with the Hartford Institute for Religion Research, 2011. Records of research can be found at: http://www.hartfordinstitute.org/megachurch/megachurch-2011-summary-report.htm (accessed December 1, 2013).

thinking within the church walls. It is no stretch for one to make the following two claims: first, California is one of the most diverse states in the US; and second, it is one of the richest.[11] The combination of these two factors makes what happens in California exceptionally influential across the greater US (and even the world). Situated in the third most populous county in California, Saddleback Church is arguably one of the most notable churches in the US, and its senior pastor one of the most recognizable and influential pastors in the US and around the world. According to Justin Wilford:

> Saddleback Church is one of the largest and most influential evangelical megachurches in America. Its pastor, Rick Warren, is the author of *The Purpose Driven Life*, a book that has sold more than 40 million copies, as well as *The Purpose Driven Church*, the best-selling church-growth manual in the history of the genre. In fact, "purpose driven" has become a popular brand of its own in American evangelicalism.[12]

What is the lure, the appeal, the popularity of the megachurch? Being "purpose driven" continues to be fashionable. Much research has been done on this phenomenon because, like in high school, people want to be like the big kid on the block (or at least somewhat like the big kid). Behind the megachurch model rests the idea of meeting the needs of culture. As evidenced by Saddleback's growth, one could readily argue that the megachurch model works. This is in large part due to the fact that the leadership of the megachurch are "savvy cultural observers who are able to see what is appealing to current and potential Christian believers in both the larger culture and within the church."[13] While it is agreed that the church should be aware of the culture that surrounds it, this should not come at the expense of the gospel. Leaders should continue to question their focus and methods of equipping lay leaders and evangelism while always assessing if it is the church leading culture or culture leading the church. Flory and Miller observe:

> In one sense, these churches are truly postmodern organizations. Their identity is based on appropriating the experiences, consumption patterns, and the need for

---

[11] According to the current Census Bureau, California ranks in the top five most diverse states demographically, as nine out of the top 20 most diverse cities in the US are in California. Ranked the ninth wealthiest state, California's Gross Domestic Product (GDP) is the richest of the top ten richest states at almost 2 trillion. The next closest state's GDP is 430 billion. These current stats are in accordance with the latest data released by US Census Bureau's American Community Survey for 2011, which is valid for 2012 and 2013.

[12] Wilford, *Sacred Subdivisions*, 2.

[13] Flory and Miller, *Finding Faith*, 163.

belonging, as found in both the larger culture and in the Christian culture, and then marketing these back to their members, with the intent to provide a place for them to find individual fulfillment and shelter from life's difficulties.[14]

A look into Saddleback Church, which again is one of the largest churches in the US, illumines that the church "has most of the characteristics we associate with such a large enterprise, such as a large suburban physical plant complete with a large multipurpose worship center, several semi-permanent 'pop-out' tents that house different styles of worship, a children's center, an educational wing, an administrative building, and of course acres of parking."[15] Many megachurches today respond to culture like Saddleback does, seeking to meet needs expressed within the wider culture, thereby promoting a church model known as the "religious market model."

The Saddleback model functions as both an ecclesial and a business model. Primary to this model is the focus of being seen as both compelling and relevant. Saddleback, like other churches following its lead, seeks to "create these experiences (compelling and relevant) through imitating, or appropriating, trends found in larger culture and ultimately popularizing these through their networks into a particular form of pop-Christianity that is primarily oriented toward an individual spiritual experience."[16] Saddleback's influence is evident through its conferences, publications and online presence. The model of what "church" is as promoted in and through Saddleback is a "bureaucratized and consumption-oriented, franchised form of Christian expression and belief."[17]

In his book *Sacred Subdivisions*, Wilford critically examines the Saddleback model that deals in "supernatural goods," thriving in "an open religious market so long as they respond effectively to the needs and desires of local communities as potential customers."[18] But what does this do for any understanding of the theological impact of the Saddleback model? A model promoted through international conferences in which "hundreds and sometimes thousands of pastors and staff from around the US and the world would come to learn about the 'purpose driven' methods of church planning and growth." As Wilford highlights, through these conferences, as well as website resources and consulting, Saddleback has led more than "500,000 pastors in 'purpose driven

---

14   Flory and Miller, *Finding Faith*, 163.
15   Flory and Miller, *Finding Faith*, 172.
16   Flory and Miller, *Finding Faith*, 14.
17   Flory and Miller, *Finding Faith*, 14.
18   Wilford, *Sacred Subdivisions*, 5.

training."[19] What is the theological foundation of the church being promoted and marketed by Saddleback that is molding, shaping, and influencing today's postsuburban, postdenominational churches both in and outside of California?

Playing out the Focus

Saddleback, and megachurches like it, strive to bring the "unchurched" into the realm of faith and should be commended for this. It is the way in which the church is seeking to reach out to the "unchurched" and the insinuating results that are being questioned. Reaching out to culture with the hope of finding people who are "lost" so as to help them find purpose is good in and of itself, but what do the "lost" find and how is their purpose defined? "The goal of Saddleback pastors is to draw 'the community' and 'the crowd' to the campus and keep them engaged there long enough to begin the individualized postdenominational evangelical journey back out into the world."[20] Such focus sounds good, but in order to remain true to Barth's notion of "seeking after the Word" the church must ask if this focus is an adequately Christ-centered, trinitarian approach? That is, does the Saddleback model promote an incarnational, self-giving model as represented by the triune God of the Christian Scriptures? As mentioned earlier from Sayers, Jesus' entry into human history—his earthly life, his death, and his resurrection from the dead—marks the climax of the biblical drama. Jesus' life also marks the essence of transformation and mission. Being in Christ is the only way to close any gaps created by our turning away from God, an action that perpetuates the continued division between identity and role. In other words, our purpose (mission) is the recognition of our identity (being) and our role (participation) in Christ. Christ does seek to draw in humanity by inviting us to participate with his ongoing reconciliatory performance. But unlike a major emphasis in today's megachurch, Christ's desire is not based on the people coming to him; quite the opposite, he goes to the people. Jesus makes himself present amongst the people—not requiring them to first find him—and then beckons them to come and lay their *burdens* at his feet (see John 3:16; Matt. 11:28). He is a pursuing God.

Is the Saddleback model presenting to culture its God-given purpose or instead, allowing customers/consumers to determine what they desire to be their purpose? Much of what occurs in a megachurch intentionally creates an experience which can provide purpose, but is this a purpose devoid of an

---

19   Wilford, *Sacred Subdivisions*, 10.
20   Wilford, *Sacred Subdivisions*, 80.

understanding of what it means to be a participant in the kingdom of heaven? Flory and Miller note, within such a megachurch, "there is much more of the spectator approach ... a type of individualistic experience of the divine, however, the community and participatory experience is missing."[21] Instead of participating in an experience that embodies a Christ-centered approach to worship and faith, a megachurch attender is given want they want, like a consumer having their needs met.

Saddleback is not only a pioneer in this new movement of churches that Wilford identifies as postdenominational evangelical (PDE) churches,[22] but is a primary leader. To understand better what is meant by a PDE church, Wilford lists eight characteristics and then informs us that Saddleback Valley Community Church "embodies each of these."[23] What is interesting to note is that none of the eight characteristics listed explicitly identify the church as Christocentric or Spirit-led. Wilford does observe that the PDE churches hold to "a highly conservative and traditionally evangelistic theology" which historically has led to a heavy reliance on Scripture. This might not seem detrimental at first, but over time, a primary and exclusionary focus on Scripture as over and against Christ can tend to overshadow the dramatic action and interaction of Christ with his church. In the worst case, the result is an undramatic Messiah who is a primary character of a story as opposed to the Savior of the world who calls his followers into a participatory role that seeks to embody the biblical script instead of merely observing it.[24]

---

[21]   Flory and Miller, *Finding Faith*, 164.

[22]   PDE is the term devised to "categorize a subset of evangelical churches that share important religious, organizational, and geographic characteristics" whose overarching characteristic is in the "unbending concern with engaging contemporary secular life with the goal of converting the 'unchurched' and retaining the already churched" (Wilford, *Sacred Subdivisions*, 8–9).

[23]   Wilford, *Sacred Subdivisions*, 9. The characteristics are: (1) a loose denominational or nondenominational structure; (2) guiding concern with evangelizing to the unchurched and underchurched (Wilford notes that while it is unintentional growth typically occurs from transfer membership); (3) weekend and weekday services produced in multiple contemporary idioms; (4) services and programs with a markedly therapeutic style and message; (5) internal church structures highly segmented to accommodate smaller demographic niches in church; (6) highly conservative and traditionally evangelistic theology; (7) location on extreme periphery of large cities; (8) reliance on small groups which meet in homes as opposed to church campus.

[24]   Examples of this may be found in the programmatic nature of what the church has become. After school Bible programs, summer Bible camps and the like all promote the Bible. In this promotion these programs often subtly allow the Bible to overshadow the one

PDE churches offer "therapeutic and easily applicable sermons, upbeat, and cutting-edge worship services," and again at first glance this appears to be an acceptable approach to church, but what is being argued is that in time, such a model continues to mold into culture so much so that eventually one cannot tell the difference between church and culture. The theological concern then rests in the influence of PDE churches and specifically Saddleback, who according to Wilford, has "pioneered or perfected over the years many of these postdenominational elements."[25]

It is important to consider the reason for the church's existence in the divine economy, and to remember the mission of the church. Theology is crucial to the whole of the church and those who are "churched" must think theologically with regards to the church's mission. In doing so, the church should seek to keep accountable not to the popular marketing and consumeristic trends of society but to the foundation of the church—Jesus Christ—who is in no way marketable. Saddleback's marketing strategy and purpose driven focus should be looked into and investigated to determine whether what is being promoted is indeed the essence of what the Christian church is called to be and do.

There is no denying that focusing on what gives humanity its purpose or mission is essential. What I am arguing for is that the church's primary focus should be on Christ and not that which makes people comfortable, or that which keeps them entertained. The question is not if Christ is relevant for people today, but are people relevant to him? Saddleback, like much of California, thrives on cultural relevance. San Francisco, San Diego, Los Angeles—these cities are petri dishes of cultural relevance, and Orange County (where Saddleback is located) is no exception. It is no surprise that a model of church that would be massively concerned with Christ's relevancy to the world would flourish in California.

When thinking of or speaking about Saddleback, their pastors "consciously create and structure the church so it mirrors its environment." While acknowledging that Saddleback pastors would reject this characterization since they surely don't want to mimic "the world," their pastors rather speak in terms of "relevance." One former Saddleback pastor noted, "Our job is not to be like the world, but to be relevant to the world. We need to show the world that what we are doing here directly relates to their lives."[26] It is true that the world needs to know that God loves them and cares about them. The problem comes, though, when speaking of Jesus, the apostles, prophets, and the whole

---

to whom the Bible primarily points. Memorization of Scripture rather than participation in Scripture's drama can be a tendency of such programs.

25 Wilford, *Sacred Subdivisions*, 10
26 Wilford, *Sacred Subdivisions*, 97.

biblical cast—we should not try to relate simply their actions to ours but more importantly the hearts behind the actions (see 1 Sam. 16:7). How does a life of intentional, emotional torture, physical suffering, personal sacrifice, and selfless living relate to the consumer driven, self-made individual who has been brought up in an affluent Orange County context that proclaims personal independence and the right to life, liberty and the pursuit of happiness? Relevance is a cultural concern; reconciliation, a divine one—can the two exist in a happy union inside the church of Christ?

Center Stage

Misdirection of the Stage

What is the result of promoting a "purpose driven life"? It is true that in finding purpose the church will be active. That is, in order for the church to find it purpose it must act and will also act as a result of finding purpose. However, the root of such action is the key. The action of the church *qua* church insists on a theo-praxis that stems directly from the performance of Christ through the Spirit. The action of the Christian finds its criterion of quality in "both the *action* itself and the character of the agent."[27] Such character can only be rooted in the action of the Godhead—action that often defies the logics or relevance of society, finding its clarity, strength, and character in the dramatic event and in-breaking of the Son of God through the Holy Spirit. Humanity is invited to participate in God's theater of glory, not because of any merit of its own, but because of the Being and act of the Godhead.

Rather than being Christocentric in its perspective, purpose driven living tends towards an anthropocentric perspective. The focus becomes the self in a somewhat unhealthy way as attenders are encouraged to find and fulfill their own "spiritual niche" which occurs through a "customizable Christian experience that is in many ways consumer/choice driven. In fact, the church website, a key entry point and resource for Saddleback attendees, encourages this sort of customizability in which the member/attendee can set up a 'my Saddleback' account containing certain 'personalized Saddleback features,' such as worship preferences, which campus of the church they call home, and

---

[27]   Reinhard Hütter, *Suffering Divine Things: Theology as Church Practice*, Doug Stott (trans.), (Grand Rapids: Eerdmans, 2000), 32 (italics added).

on and on."[28] Focus on self is important, of course, if it stems from the proper foundation—believers are told they must love self somewhat if they are to love their neighbor. However, what must not be absent from this reality of loving neighbor and loving self is the foundational component of loving God. The love of God exposes the reality of who people are. In this way, purpose should stem from being. Church is not meant to be a "customizable Christian experience" but an entrance into the Being and act of God here and now.

The implications of the church illuminating who God is directly relates to who we are. That is, the church, in its revelation of who God is, is not so much about purpose as it is about *being*. Humanity comes to understand itself when it first realizes that freedom and truth of humanity comes only from being *in* Christ. The church's perspective should be oriented from top down and then flow outward rather than bottom up. Even Warren admits that life is not about "you." The opening sentence in his best seller *Purpose Driven life* says as much: "It's not about you." But is this the case with PDE churches? Wilford writes, "The design of the PDE megachurch is carefully crafted to meet the highly differentiated, individualized needs of the postsuburban self .... For these PDE megachurches it is unswervingly and painstakingly *about you*. More precisely it is about a set of performances that center on *you*."[29] The megachurch is set up with the intention of focusing on the individual. And while this seems perfectly "Christian" at first, because in truth God does care about each person as an individual, this is never at the exclusion of his communal care. The problem comes with the result of such an individualistic mentality:

> The postsuburban dreamscape has nostalgically held fast to the older suburban version themes (escape, social advancement, and self-fulfillment), except in the new version the negative sides of suburban cultural binaries—poverty, ethnic minorities, crime, heterogeneity—have lost their geographical bearing in the city center. The "other" does not map onto an urban center-periphery as easily ... PDE megachurches have built their institutions on concerns for the individuated self and its (real or ideal) nuclear family.[30]

Focus on the individual leads the church to be more concerned about its marketing schemes and consumer mentality than its Lord or the active transformation of culture. It seems that in the repeated attempts to remain

---

28   Flory and Miller, *Finding Faith*, 173.
29   Wilford, *Sacred Subdivisions*, 71.
30   Wilford, *Sacred Subdivisions*, 72.

relevant in culture these churches attempt to control God so as to make him appear more "hip," "cool," and even "homeboyish," or like a "superhero." In repeated attempts to control God the biggest loser remains the gospel and its intoxicating aroma of transformation, which in turn leads to the world losing in the end. In fact, in its displacement of God, the church has reoriented the meaning of the biblical reality thereby transforming it into a mere product of the church; a product marketed and advertised so as to draw in larger numbers of converts. This commodification of the once revered teaching of Christ has seemingly become a marketing tool to develop "therapeutic and easily applicable sermons" that are accompanied by "high-quality, upbeat, and cutting-edge worship services."[31] Such rhetoric used by the megachurch promotes the consumer driven desire that deepens our human autonomy and divisions. As the late musician Keith Green pointedly wrote, "It's Jesus Christ and what he can do for you! You cannot have more exact opposites than the Bible's Christ-centered gospel, and our modern, cross-less, me-centered gospel."[32]

The church has to question the cast: Does the *me* even see the *we*? Much of the message of the megachurch today is rooted in economic and anthropocentric language and desires of the consumer as opposed to the redeeming (and sometimes hardly relevant) words of Jesus. Language focused on the individual makes it difficult to remember that life is meant to be relational as humanity is created in the image of a relational God. The allowance of marketing the church to push for a comfortable consumer-driven production can boast of its size but has little to say in regards to breaking down walls of division. If the church today wishes to model herself after a robust biblical-theological approach, it should seek to remain free from a consumer-driven, seeker-sensitive focus. Dan Kimball writes, "Hundreds of thousands of people now attend churches which used the strategy of producing a seeker-sensitive service with great music, and drama .... However, this evangelism strategy will need to be rethought when it comes to reaching emerging generations."[33] While I do not agree fully with the assessment that the church today must concern herself with issues that are simply generational, I do agree with Kimball that the church needs to rethink the ways of reaching out to the community as well as reorienting the ways the church acts within its own walls.

---

31   Wilford, *Sacred Subdivisions*, 10.

32   Keith Green, "What's Wrong with the Gospel?" *LDM Magazine* (Last Days Ministries, 1981), 114.

33   Dan Kimball, *The Emerging Church: Vintage Christianity for New Generations* (Grand Rapids: Zondervan, 2003), 197.

Reorienting the Movement of the Stage

The purpose driven church model is an example of a system that subtly promotes division through its allowance of a homogeneous, self-centered foundation. As stated before, "The 'other' does not map onto an urban center-periphery as easily.... PDE megachurches have built their institutions on concerns for the individuated self."[34] Looking at the five purposes of the church as outlined by Warren, one might not become skeptical of them resulting in division or a self-centered focus, as each can be supported biblically.[35] However after a closer look, concerns arise. The second purpose listed by Warren is the call to "Love your neighbor as yourself." In his exposé of this purpose, Warren fails to identify one's neighbor. Without clear instruction as to who our neighbor is in our surroundings, this purpose can promote subtle forms of discrimination and preference that are expressly condemned in the Bible (see James 2).

One example from Warren's book that portrays the subtle form of separation found within the Saddleback model is his talk of cross-cultural churches, or better yet, the lack of talk discussing cross-cultural churches. Why no cross-cultural churches? Because the purpose driven church is not encouraged to be diverse or multi-ethnic for this kind of thing is stated to be uniquely "supernatural." A multi-ethnic or cross-cultural church is not going to be the norm as the "ability to minister cross-culturally requires a *special gift*, an ability from the Holy Spirit to be able to communicate to people with backgrounds very different from your own."[36] In saying this, Warren never fully develops what he means by "cross-cultural," which seems problematic since if California is anything, it is the crossroads of world civilizations. Warren's idea of loving one's neighbor seems to assume or maybe even prescribe a kind of homogeneity since without the "special gift" one cannot step outside of one's cultural comfort zone.[37]

---

[34]   Wilford, *Sacred Subdivision*, 72.

[35]   Rick Warren, *The Purpose Driven Church: Growth Without Compromising Your Message and Mission* (Grand Rapids: Zondervan, 1995), 103–7. The five purposes of a purpose driven church are: (1) Love the Lord your God with all your heart: worship; (2) Love your neighbor as yourself: ministry; (3) Go and make disciples: evangelism; (4) Baptize them: fellowship; (5) Teach them to obey: discipleship.

[36]   Warren, *The Purpose Driven Church*, 177 (italics added for emphasis).

[37]   By failing to acknowledge sensitive cultural differences, Warren recently stumbled into a spat with Asian Christians, chronicled in Sarah Pulliam Bailey, "Rick Warren's Offensive Facebook Photo SLAMMED By Asian American Christians," *Huff Post*, September 26, 2013, http://www.huffingtonpost.com/2013/09/26/rick-warren-offensive-photo-facebook_n_3997619.html (accessed November 11, 2013).

Stepping out of our personal cultural comfort zone, however, calls the church and its participants to assess their own depth of faith. It also places a focus on the words of Jesus that discuss the uncomfortable realities of fruit that bears witness.[38] No doubt such teaching is uncomfortable and such discomfort goes against the model of growth propagated by the megachurch. Yet the church should strive for a faith that is Christ-centered, a faith that produces fruit through its faith-filled actions. A life of faith calls one to make choices and carry out actions that are not always popular or comfortable—how then does the intensity of a Christ-centered faith compare to the megachurch model?

The megachurch model is one that "will always attract the masses as they have proven to be so successful at simultaneously providing a sort of 'Christianity lite' entertainment model and making their congregants feel good about their spiritual lives and their participation in these churches and ministries."[39] This model of church growth however, does not seem to build on the principles set forth by Christ who reached out to the downtrodden, prisoners, poor, blind, prostitutes, and the like. And while Saddleback does have forms of ministry to the different people groups in discussion, the point being made is that a "Christian lite" model of ministry does not promote an intentional interest in the marginalized as was advanced in Jesus' ministry. Christ's ministry was and is concerned for the whole of humanity. Christ's disciples are a motley crew. Following Christ's example, the church is to live with congregational integrity. The church should be, as Marva Dawn states:

> without any barriers between peoples, without any segregations based on economics, race, or musical style .... Many of the church marketing gurus advocate churches of homogeneity, appealing to those who are like us so that our churches will grow, but this violates the sacrament of Christ's presence and destroys our testimony to the world that there are no divisions and distinctions among the people of God.[40]

Getting back to Warren's point about the Holy Spirit, I do agree that the church's ability to minister and witness to the world comes from the Holy Spirit. Reaching out to the "other" requires the Holy Spirit as it is a move that is often inconvenient, uncomfortable, and costly. But aren't these essential features of the gospel message, describing what was done by another on behalf of believers? Jesus commands his would-be followers to "Go and do likewise" (Luke 10:25–37).

---

[38]   See Matt. 3:8–10, 7:17–19; 12:33; 13:18–23; John 15:1–8.
[39]   Flory and Miller, *Finding Faith*, 191.
[40]   Marva J. Dawn, *Powers, Weakness, and the Tabernacling of God* (Grand Rapids: Eerdmans, 2001), 98.

Moreover, for any church to exist, the Holy Spirit must be present. The problem with Warren's statement is that it denotes that a cross-cultural church will be the "exception" and not the norm of the purpose driven church paradigm. How is this then consistent with the gospel? What then should the church do with such texts as Galatians 3:26–29, specifically stating that faith in Christ breaks down barriers within the church? As Paul writes, all who by faith are in Christ are also daughters and sons of God. Ultimately, in Christ, there is no distinction for all are God's children. Should not the church think along these same lines?

The promotion of a homogeneous model of church embodies racial and class division through this implicit thought that fosters values, beliefs, and behaviors of separation. Today's continued promotion of individualism and isolation in the church is a mirror of society and this is why it is crucial for the church to focus on Christ rather than seeking to make him relevant by intentionally mirroring society. In his book *The Constitution of Society,* Anthony Giddens notes that, "the structural properties of social systems exist only insofar as forms of social conduct are reproduced chronically across time and space." The concept of analyzing the structural properties or structuration of social systems means studying the modes in which humans, or as Giddens states, actors, partake in the routine activities of life. Giddens's study is insightful as he highlights that "structure is not external to individuals, it is in a certain sense more 'internal' than exterior to their activities."[41] Who we are is not determined by what we do. The church, which is a created reality in and by Christ, humbly and transparently needs to carry out its vocation as the church by reminding humanity of its own created reality (its internal structure) so as to illumine that purpose of the church. This is to say that the church as "a created reality" has an essential divinely-constituted internal structure that resists Warren's ecclesial homogeneity and any of society's unfortunate homogeneity. Resistance to the unfortunate residual effects of a homogeneous church model stems from the church pointing humanity back to the reality of its creation in the image of God. It is our *imago dei* (created reality) that defines our purpose according to the *imago dei* from which Christ-like character is produced. Thus, the divine image becomes visible in our actions. Stanley Grenz writes that "the *imago dei* leads inevitably through the church as the prolepsis of the new humanity, and the relational self is ultimately the ecclesial self. The image of God does not lie in the individual per se, but in the relationality of persons in community."[42]

---

[41]   Anthony Giddens, *The Constitution of Society: Outline of the Theory of Structuration* (Berkeley: University of California Press, 1986), 25.

[42]   Stanley J. Grenz, "The Social God and the Relational Self: Toward a Trinitarian Theology of the *Imago Dei,*" in *Trinitarian Soundings in Systematic Theology,*

Human beings are created for relationship based not on race, color, or creed, but based on need—humans need one another. Yet it is recognized that PDE style churches "which include a majority white membership are overwhelmingly likely to be on the residential fringe of a large metropolis near a freeway. But if the church has a majority African American membership ... it is much more likely to be in an urban cluster or in an older suburb." The homogeneous church propagates a subtle form of division, which is usually based on economics (and race). Wilford continues, "it is obvious that these megachurches are founded on the fast-growing urban fringe because that is where the people—with money and kids, especially— are increasingly located."[43] Thus, one's neighbor then will be someone within your same economic class resulting in the tragic loss of those on the fringes—the outcast, poor, those with disabilities, the downtrodden, the other.

To love one's neighbor as one's self is not a command to deny love to those not like us by definition of color or class, but instead to recognize our neighbor by the means of our true identity: a creation in the image of our triune God. Christians are to identify themselves with their neighbors as God has identified himself with humanity in Christ. As Martin Luther explained:

> I will therefore give myself as Christ to my neighbor, just as Christ offered himself to me; I will do nothing in this life except what I see is necessary, profitable, and salutary to my neighbor ... we ought freely to help our neighbor and each one should become as it were a Christ to the other that we may be Christ to one another and Christ may be the same in all. Thus we see that the Christian man lives not to himself but to Christ and his neighbor through love. By faith he rises above himself to God and from God goes below himself in love and remains always in God and in love.[44]

Our neighbor is not the one who is in the same likeness of ourselves by way of race, gender or class, but is one who (like us at one time) is and was alienated and separated from the Lord through sin. Thus, the picture of the Lord's church should be a mosaic of God's creation, a symphony of difference that delights in the truth that "God demonstrates His own love toward us, in that while we were yet sinners, Christ died for us" (Rom. 5:8).

The church must lead the way in breaking down divisions within society (see Eph. 2:13–18). However, according to Warren, this is difficult and the fact remains that while "a church may be unsuccessful in reaching *certain types* of

---

Paul Louis Metzger (ed.), (New York: T&T Clark, 2005), 96.

    43   Wilford, *Sacred Subdivisions*, 54.

    44   Martin Luther, *On Christian Liberty* (trans. W.A. Lambert) (Minneapolis: Fortress Press, 2003), 52–3.

people," this "isn't a matter of right or wrong, but a matter of simply respecting the wonderful variety of people God has placed in the world."[45] Evangelism for the purpose driven church will be successful when done with those in whom we have something in common. As Warren writes, "the most effective evangelistic strategy is to first try to reach those with whom you already have something in common ... because every church is best in reaching *certain* types of people."[46]

To reach these "certain" types of people the church needs to remain relevant to the changing trends of culture. In order to do this, Saddleback and PDE churches must continuously redefine their religious performances. PDE churches are successful due to their ability to "craft meaningful performances that achieve fusion with an audience from a radically de-fused socio-spatial environment."[47] While I agree that at some level the church is meant to fuse together "de-fused" environments, I am not convinced that feeding into a model that avows an openly homogeneous paradigm is the best or most appropriate from a biblical-theological perspective. Rather than seeking out the lost as a whole (because this would distract from growth), PDE churches focus on "specific audiences," and in so doing experience numerical growth. As Wilford notes, "evangelical church growth has largely resulted from churches seeking out specific audiences and performatively responding to their material and symbolic worlds."[48] What this tends towards though, are churches who allow people to pick and choose their "individualized" church "wants and needs" because they are almost encouraged to be guided by a consumeristic mindset that wants what it wants at the lowest cost possible. The dangerous result of such a church paradigm is the separation of people based on personal choice; the subtle promotion of the law of attraction—like appearances (both racially and economically) attract to like appearances. Religion becomes nothing more than a "specialized and individualized relationship with both Saddleback Church in particular and evangelicalism in general."[49]

Instead, the present essay is arguing that meaningful performances of churches can only occur through intense, Spirit-led hearts that look to Christ for the connection point of our fragmented lives that seek to participate in his incarnational and all-encompassing performance. It is through Christ's incarnational act (self-giving) that the fragmented lives of his followers slowly became defragmented. Jesus did not cater to the domestic needs and comforts

---

[45]   Warren, *The Purpose Driven Church*, 175.
[46]   Warren, *The Purpose Driven Church*, 174 (italics added).
[47]   Wilford, *Sacred Subdivisions*, 56.
[48]   Wilford, *Sacred Subdivisions*, 51.
[49]   Wilford, *Sacred Subdivisions*, 80.

of his followers. Instead, in an act that has become almost the antithesis of the gospel message today, Jesus called people away from their homes, imposed upon some a wandering life, upon others the sacrifice of their property, and endeavored by all means to divorce them from their former connections in order that they might find a new home with him, and subsequently in the life of the church. This seems a stark contrast to the PDE church that has at its center a dreamscape focus on "the residential home of the individual and his or her family."[50] Home life is important and much needed, but what is in question, again, is the heart—it is not that family, friends, and even church are to be discarded, but believers must constantly analyze motives and aims to address the question of whether Jesus is their refuge, or whether the sanctuary is among friends, family, and self.

The Casting Call

(Pseudo)Community

A network of individuals seeking authentic community to defragment our fragmented lives is what appears to be the outcome at Saddleback. And this is a type of community setting; but is it the authentic community so desperately needed? By participating in the life of the church—the body of Christ—such fragmentation can become de-fragmented as believers experience the healing, renewal, and wholeness promised in the gospel. The very recognition for the need of community, however, "suggests that there are many who are seeking a new form of spirituality that goes beyond the individualistic questing that characterizes much of the sociological literature on spirituality."[51] For Saddleback this occurs or is intended to occur through its small group ministry. The intent of small groups at Saddleback is to "recapitulate the fragmented, decentralized, and diverse nature of postsuburbia through performances that allow a realization of postsuburbia's binary other: integration, centralization, and uniformity."[52] However, not everyone involved in a small group at Saddleback even attends Saddleback's weekend services—a phenomena for many Orange County megachurches. So what then builds integration, centralization, and uniformity? For Saddleback's small group ministry, uniformity is based on affinity. That is, contrary to the natural grain of a place as culturally diverse as

---

50   Wilford, *Sacred Subdivisions*, 72.
51   Flory and Miller, *Finding Faith*, 185.
52   Wilford, *Sacred Subdivisions*, 112.

southern California, small groups at Saddleback are made up of "like-minded individuals."[53] It is this outcome that is the problem of a church paradigm that has at its core an individualized, consumer driven mindset.

Much of what is taken as church today and as witnessed from the model of Saddleback is hardly a gathered ecclesial body, flock, or bride, but can easily be designated a voluntary association of religious people. However, far from being a voluntary association of religious individuals, the church is what William Cavanaugh calls the Eucharistic community.[54] It is the community which "participates in the life of the triune God, who is the only good that can be common to all. Its reality is global and eternal, anticipating the heavenly polity on earth."[55] To anticipate heaven on earth means to live out the hope of heaven here and now. This however, cannot occur through isolated lives, nor can it occur through lives bent towards the trajectory of loving only that which is like. Life is meant to be experienced in *authentic* community since it is in and through such community that *authentic* living occurs.

Living by faith, or faith-living, should take place in all settings if it is authentic. Saddleback aims for this, attempting to cultivate a lifestyle of "spiritual action" which "is seen to properly take place in the personalized settings of one's own life: in the small group ... at work, or in the grocery store."[56] But how does one enact and sustain such action or performance without an expectation of commitment? The Saddleback model, despite the stories of members that "suggest communal reintegration" and a stated mission to "deepen the connection of its members to the body of Christ," tends toward a varied amount of commitment. Wilford acknowledged seeing members (both old and new) "take very fluid and variegated approaches to church belonging," such as what allows for anonymity and disconnection; if one were to miss a service, a service will eventually occur at a preferable time. With regards to small groups, Wilford continues: "if she has not attended small group in such a long time that she would feel awkward going back, there are over 3,800 other small groups to choose from." What does this mean for community? Such a lack of commitment detracts from the reality of who people are—relational beings who need each other, yet at Saddleback, the

---

53   Wilford, *Sacred Subdivisions*, 112.

54   See William T. Cavanagh, "The World in a Wafer: A Geography of the Eucharist as Resistance to Globalization," *Modern Theology* 15/2 (April 1999), 181–96, which argues that in the body of Christ, as a performative Eucharistic community, spatial and temporal divisions are collapsed in particular localities, creating catholicity.

55   William T. Cavanaugh, "Killing for the Telephone Company: Why the Nation-State is Not the Keeper of the Common Good," *Modern Theology* 20/2 (April 2004), 269.

56   Wilford, *Sacred Subdivisions*, 164.

community is "no *gemeinschaftlich* (community-like) gathering, bound by ritual, repetition, and homogeneity." But rather, "Like its surrounding postsuburban environment, Saddleback is a dispersed, multi-nodal, multi-scaled network through which individuals link up in varying degrees with other individuals."[57]

Authenticity of the Cast

Former Archbishop of Canterbury Rowan Williams stated, "We have got a fragmented society at the moment, internally fragmented, socially fragmented in our cities and fragmented between communities of different allegiance."[58] What is needed to bring about unity in the being and act of the church is freedom, and this occurs through the church's promotion of its, and thus its actors', participation in Christ's reconciliatory performance.

There is a need in the church for participation in this performance. As observed by Wilford, today's performances, in response to the past, do indeed strive for more authenticity. They are performances "that do not *appear* to be performances. Therefore, effective ritualistic performances must appear to arise naturally from daily life, free of artifice and self-consciousness highlights the performances of the actors."[59] What Wilford's observations reveal is the current trend in Evangelicalism of a desire for the performance and action of the church to arise "naturally" from life. A "natural" performance, however, stems not from a "Christian lite" model that places self at the center, but originates from the one to whom our performances must point. That is, in order for the church to exhibit a faithful performance the central focus must be on the protagonist of God's drama—Jesus Christ. From Christ his fellow actors on the world stage gain a freedom that allows them not only to find their purpose, but more importantly, to understand the depth of what it means to be a player in God's drama.

Authentic community then stems from God's own Being and act. It is through the truth displayed in God's revelatory action that we become aware of human freedom. Through such awareness of our freedom we move further and further into the *truth* of our humanness and thus are able to understand our purpose and mission. Being, notes theologian Hans Urs von Balthasar, "coincides with consciousness of self-consciousness thus becoming its own

---

57   Wilford, *Sacred Subdivisions*, 12–13.

58   Rowan Williams, Interview with Christopher Landau, BBC Radio 4, World at One, Thursday February 7, 2008. Transcript of interview can be found at: http://rowanwilliams. archbishopofcanterbury.org/articles.php/707/archbishop-on-radio-4-uk-law-needs-to-find-accommodation-with-religious-law-codes (accessed November 11, 2013).

59   Wilford, *Sacred Subdivisions*, 165.

object. This is the true meaning of the *cogito ergo sum.*[60] Rather than enacting a performance that *appears* to be a performance, any and all truthful performances will naturally arise from the person when our being coincides with consciousness of self-consciousness such that the truth of who we are is awakened due to our intentional participation in Christ's performance.

The unity of today's fragmentation will come when the church realizes its profound call to performance—a performance that recognizes the need to *be* authentic so as to *become* the voice of hope and the call to community for the entirety of the world's stage. The church must courageously follow the actions and performance of its leading actor (Jesus Christ) for in Christ through the Spirit the church creates space for authentic community enveloped and founded on reconciliation and redemption, thereby giving hope to humanity. Authentic community is Eucharistic community and stems from the church realizing that its purpose is driven from its identity *in* Christ. It is therefore in Christ, through the Spirit, that the church finds its Eucharistic performance.

Curtain Call: The Church's Eucharistic Performance

The life of the church rests in its willingness to participate in Christ's reconciliatory performance. This is a performance founded in the reality of self-giving. That is, it is Eucharistic at its core. God's Being-in-act is the foundation of the church's Eucharistic celebration, and thus, its faithful performance. Han Urs von Balthasar writes that "every Eucharistic sacrifice on the part of the Church always proceeds on the basis of a communion with Christ that he has already initiated and has the effect of creating a new and ever deeper communion." Such a deepening of our communion with Christ manifests itself as the church "primarily joins in and assimilates herself to the work of Christ; it is thus privileged to *act*, taking the place reserved for its by Christ, who *suffers* the action of others."[61] It is from the performance of Christ that the church, and thus humanity, witnesses the ultimate giving of self; a giving that re-humanizes the human, so that it might be able to participate faithfully in God's self-giving act through its own acts of self-giving.

Rick Warren understands this idea of self-giving now. I am sure he had an idea of it when writing *The Purpose Driven Church*, but before undergoing a kind

---

[60]   Hans Urs von Balthasar, *Theo-Logic, Vol. 1: The Truth of the World* (San Francisco: Ignatius Press, 2001), 93.

[61]   Hans Urs von Balthasar, *Theo-Drama: Theological Dramatic Theory, Vol. 4: The Action* (San Francisco: Ignatius Press, 1994), 405.

of personal conversion, Warren maintained the evangelical focus on personal behavior and salvation as represented in his best-selling book. Concern for the well-being of the other was only a salvation issue, which neglected their living and social conditions. However, "As a direct result of his *Purpose-Driven* book selling literally millions of copies and the attendant financial windfall and the dramatic increase in his public influence, Rick Warren and his wife Kay ultimately rethought their ministry strategies and organized three foundations that were oriented toward both extending the Christian message and alleviating various global social problems."[62] This is an exciting transformation that has resulted in such efforts as the "Global P.E.A.C.E. Plan."[63] As Wilford notes, Warren now has a mission of "the global alleviation of poverty, disease, and illiteracy. Warren's story of how this becomes the new passion ... is one that leans heavily on the classic themes of conversion and *re*version."[64] While God's heart has always cared about social issues, it is great to hear of Warren's newfound passion. What then of his previous model built on a type of me-for-me mentality? The suggestion being made is that the megachurch needs to re-reorient itself through an intentional following of the Holy Spirit's leading, becoming the pioneer of the new movement of church with its Eucharistic performance.

It is only when a leader stands up, turns around, and announces that the course they have been on was not the correct one that change can begin to happen; when that leader says to his people, today we turn and follow the path set before us—the one paved by the "two hands" of God, and it is a road paved in self-giving through love.[65] It is then that the church can become who it was created to be, an eternal beacon of hope for a fallen world. The church can be the witness to the world of God's transformative love if and only if it realizes its existence is *in* Christ and that from its being (existence) stems its purpose—to sacrificially give of herself as it participates in Christ's Eucharistic performance through its own Eucharistic performance.

God's self-giving (his Eucharistic performance) is the epitome of divine love and in such a performance the church receives the essence of its being so

---

[62]   Flory and Miller, *Finding Faith*, 176.

[63]   For more information see http://saddleback.com/lakeforest/adults/peace/ (accessed November 11, 2013).

[64]   Wilford, *Sacred Subdivisions*, 121.

[65]   This refers to the concept developed by Irenaeus who spoke of God revealing himself through his two "hands," the Son and the Spirit. See Alexander Roberts, James Donaldson, and A. Cleveland Coxe (trans. and eds), *Against Heresies IV.20.1; The Ante-Nicene Fathers, Vol. I: The Apostolic Fathers with Justin Martyr and Irenaeus*, (Buffalo: Christian Literature Company, 1885), 487–8.

as to determine its role on stage (its purpose). The relationality of God must continually ignite and fuel the church's understanding of being. Through his revelation, invitation and reconciliation the church can step into the performance of a lifetime and live out the truth and reality of "God with us" so as to encourage, develop, and reveal our faithful performances that manifest the truth of "we with God." "We with God" manifests itself in acts of kindness and love, acts of self-giving towards the "other" that not only overcome, but transform the postsuburban mentality that seeks to elevate self over the "other."

The church is the congregation of the faithful who are called by faith to the light of the truth and the knowledge of God whereby in unity of faith, the members of the community, through the Holy Spirit, serves the Head—the Son of God—with their whole heart. This is accomplished through embodied responses that manifest themselves through explicit acts of love: for example, giving money to charity, walking our elderly neighbor's dog, feeding the poor, and others. The church is to perform Christ's love to the world and thereby transcend the ways of society so as to *be* the body of Christ in the midst of society and as a witness to it of God's action in Christ to reconcile the world. In this mission, the church realizes its performance as constituted in the expectation of its proclamation and its action to the world.

Our faith, which is rooted in the Being and act of God, is realized through our action. The church is meant to be a dramatic witness to the world of the living sacrifice made by Christ. Christians are not called to market Christ but to mimic him, to participate in his redeeming act that offers hope to this downtrodden world. Both acts of sacrifice and surrender form parts of the Eucharistic act of Christ, an act of giving and receiving that insists upon a response. The only true response from the church is one of mimesis, in the acceptance of not only sharing in this mission—the self-giving to society and the world—but more importantly, working for the continuation of the mission. As Balthasar points out, "Given the plan to bring about creatures endowed with freedom, the ultimate form of this pouring-forth will be that of the Eucharist, which as we know it, is intimately connected with the Passion, *pro nobis*."[66] God for us means we with God. It is a reality that is meant to be actively performed by the church so as to share in the eternal performance of the Redeemer's life.

It is highly significant that "the God who has reconciled the world to himself has entrusted the Apostles, and in a wider sense the church of Christ, with 'the ministry of reconciliation' (2 Cor. 5:18), 'the message of reconciliation' (2 Cor. 5:19), so that we can 'work with him' (2 Cor. 6:1) in the world in

---

[66]   Balthasar, *Theo-Drama, Vol. 4*, 330.

implementing this reconciliation."[67] And this incorporation into God's reconciliatory act is meant to further enliven today's ecclesial endeavors through the sharing of Christ's performance that is self-sacrificial and for the sake of the "other." Jesus does not expect the performative reality of the church to be determined by the world and he does not expect it to be an empty pursuit. In fact, because Christ's performance can only be understood biblically and theologically, so too must the church's performance be understood.

The pursuit of the crucified crown follows the performance of the crucified King such that both performances go against the power structures of the world that tend to think victory and power come only through aggressive and violent means, or otherwise relentless forms of competition often endemic to the life of the megachurch in California. The curtain call of Christ's church presents to the world a final word of love enacted through the church's faithful performances. Christ's performance insists upon the church giving its own self-sacrificial, self-giving performances while enacting the hope of tomorrow through the performances of today.

---

[67]   Hans Urs von Balthasar, *Theo-Drama: Theological Dramatic Theory, Vol. 3: The Dramatis Personae: Persons in Christ*, 121.

PART III
California's Culture
in Theological Perspective

Chapter 7

From the Beach Boys to Surfer's Chapel: A Theology of California Surf Culture

Robert S. Covolo

A Post-Hawaiian, Post-Colonial Theology

Surfing has a history of trafficking in theology—from the ancient Hawaiian priests whipping the water with vines to bring the surf up for festival to the annual "Blessing of the Waves" inter-faith festival in Huntington Beach, California.[1] Even the British explorer Captain James Cook's initial encounter with surfing Hawaiians in 1777 can be seen in terms of the meeting of two different theological impulses regarding surfing. For these Hawaiians, surfing was inescapably theological; it was associated with the festivals surrounding the worship of the god, Lono, who was one of the four gods who existed before the world. In stark contrast were the Western explorers whose culture drew from the verses in the Old Testament that spoke of the sea as a chaotic and foreboding realm. These first observers of Hawaiian surfing could not comprehend the idea of playing in the sea. In the words of a popular British proverb, "Those who go to sea for pleasure would go to hell for pastime."[2]

These theologies began to clash with the arrival of the first missionaries to the Hawaiian Islands. In 1820, seven New England Calvinists arrived after a five-month trip from Boston Harbor to evangelize and "civilize" the Hawaiian Islands'

---

[1]   Humans as *homo significans* inevitably give meaning to surfing through narrative and speech-acts that propose values and behaviors that resonate with particular cultural and religious narratives. See Nick Ford and David Brown, *Surfing and Social Theory: Experience, Embodiment and Narrative of the Dream Glide* (New York: Routledge, 2006), 22–3. This is evinced by a growing number of recent books that speak of surfing in terms of its application to different religious views. For a book comparing surfing to Buddhist teaching see Jaimal Yogis, *Saltwater Buddha: A Surfer's Quest to Find Zen on the Sea* (Boston: Wisdom Publications, 2009). For a recent work comparing Judaism's teaching with surfing see Nachum Shifren, *Surfing Rabbit: A Kabbalistic Quest for Soul* (Los Angeles: Heaven Ink Publishing, 2001).
[2]   Matt Warshaw, *The History of Surfing* (San Francisco: Chronicle Books, 2010), 29.

inhabitants. At their arrival, surfing was a thriving pastime among all segments of Hawaiian society, seamlessly mixed with not only religion and politics, but also sex and gambling. Although the missionaries never used their growing political power to outlaw surfing, they did tightly hem it in with a series of blue laws. These missionaries viewed surfing's resulting decline as an inevitable outcome of the gospel on Hawaiian society. In the words of one missionary, "The decline and discontinuance of the use of the surfboard, as civilization advances, may be accounted for by the increase in modesty, industry, and religion."[3] By all appearances, the Christian God did not care much for surfing.

This famous conflict between the missionaries and Hawaiian surf culture has served as an etiological myth for the current academic supposition that Western theology—especially evangelical and Calvinist strands—is in tension or even incongruous with the roots of surf culture. Representative of this view is Kristin Lawler, who, in her recent monograph, *The American Surfer: Radical Culture and Capitalism*, states, "Intensely opposed is Calvinism and the Puritan work ethic to surfing and the attitude to time, life, and pleasure of which surfing is emblematic."[4] But as a post-colonial surfer and evangelical who can trace his Reformed sentiments to an epiphany that occurred during a very pleasurable surf session at Huntington Cliffs, I am compelled alongside a host of others to question this thesis.[5] After all, cultures that spring up around the practice of surfing are neither uniform nor stagnant, and therefore need to be assessed on a case-by-case basis. Therefore, the idea that nineteenth-century Hawaiian surf culture should be representative of all surf culture is problematic. In fact, as surf historian Matt Warshaw reminds us, "while Hawaii is the birthplace of surfing, California has for better and worse been at the center of the surfing world since the mid-twentieth century."[6] This suggests a contemporary account of Christian

---

[3]   Ben R. Finney and James D. Houston, *Surfing: A History of the Ancient Hawaiian Sport* (Rohnert Park: Pomegranate Press, 1996), 54.

[4]   Kristin Lawler, *The American Surfer: Radical Culture and Capitalism* (New York: Routledge, 2011), 21.

[5]   For example, Tony Dickson and Hugh McLachlan, "In Search of 'The Spirit of Capitalism': Weber's Misinterpretation of Franklin," *Sociology* 23/1 (1989), 81–9; Amintore Fanfani, *Catholicism, Protestantism, and Capitalism* (Norfolk: IHS Press, 2002); Leland Ryken, "'We *All* Know That the Puritans ...': The Original Protestant Ethic," in *Redeeming the Time* (Grand Rapids, 1995), 95–112; Malcolm H. MacKinnon, "Weber's Exploration of Calvinism: The Undiscovered Provenance of Capitalism," *The British Journal of Sociology* 39/2 (1988), 143–210; Jan Rehmann, "The Radical Reformation and the Protestant Ethic: A Political Critique of Max Weber's Sociology of Religion," *Union Seminary Quarterly Review* 53/1–2 (1999), 71–88.

[6]   Matt Warshaw, *The Encyclopedia of Surfing* (New York: Harcourt, 2005), 100.

theology's relationship with surf culture is best found not in nineteenth-century Hawaiian surf culture, but in the rise of California surf culture since the mid-twentieth century, even as we recognize elements of Hawaiian culture have been transposed into California's situation. In turn, Christian theology is neither uniform nor static and must also be examined in all of its variety to discover resonance and dissonance with surf culture. Thus, this chapter reframes the relationship between surf culture and Christian theology by offering an initial sketch of a theology of California surf culture. To begin, a brief history is in order.

From the Beach Boys to Surfer's Chapel

In the first half of the twentieth century, surfing in California was something of an oddity practiced by small pods of surfers who dotted the California coast. But by the middle of the century, surfing was quickly becoming the new activity of choice for a large number of revved-up bushy-blond teens. This excitement was fueled in no small part by the work of low-budget surf film producers Bud Brown and Greg Knoll, the instrumental "surf music" of Dick Dale, and innovations such as Jack O'Neil's development of the wetsuit, Hobie Alter's polyurethane boards, and Walter Katin's bombproof surf trunks. In the late 1950s, forces in Hollywood sensed surfing was reaching a tipping point in popular culture and responded in 1959 with the movie *Gidget*, the first of a slew of low-budget, surf-themed movies. Although surfing was steadily gaining a foothold in Southern California pop culture, all of these developments would pale in comparison to the cultural force of a rock band that formed in 1961 in Hawthorne, California: the Beach Boys. With a steady flow of chart-topping songs such as "Surfing," "Surfing USA," and "Everybody's Gone Surfing," the Beach Boys ushered surfing into the center of California culture. Taking the surf media craze to new heights, they left California indelibly linked to the vision of surfing.

In national and European tours, the Beach Boys unwittingly became the spokesmen of California surf culture, delivering a version of this that celebrated the care-free, fun-loving, soft-hedonism of the American teen—a life with little more than cars, girls, and catching a good wave to fill one's days. Yet in something of an ironic twist, many Californians who actually surfed were reluctant to embrace the Beach Boys. Like the low-budget, Hollywood surf-themed movies that featured East Coast teens like Annette Funicello, the Beach Boys' matching outfits on stage and lack of experience in the water left wave riders feeling as though their own experience of surfing had been co-opted. Their instincts were right, for the success of the Beach Boys marked a new age in the commercialization of California surf culture. Far from Brian Wilson's self-described "teenage symphonies to God," the Beach Boys' songs distilled and exported a version of California surf culture freed from social forces challenging America's post-war materialism.

Among those dissatisfied with the commercially sterilized images of California surf culture were the so-called "soul-surfers." These surfers had found in the surfing lifestyle a subversive and powerful form of spirituality, one that was not recognizable in the catchy ditties of the Beach Boys. Moreover, such ballads were out of touch with the spiritual angst prevalent in 1960s California surf culture: a culture seeking non-conventional lifestyles and re-connecting with nature. In spite of surfing's heritage of competing theologies, the Beach Boys made the very idea of a theology of surfing incomprehensible. It would not be until the late 1960s and 1970s that the soul-surfer movement would merge with the Jesus people, creating a powerful Christian impulse to reclaim surfing's theological voice.

Although a number of scholars have gravitated towards tracing the influence of Eastern religion on California surf culture,[7] little attention has been given to the thousands of surfers who converted to Christianity in the late 1960s and 1970s. These "born-again" surfers emphasized the importance of knowing Jesus—the source behind the power and beauty of the waves—in a personal way. They saw their lives as surfers and believers as interconnected, the freedom they found in the surfing lifestyle and its counter-cultural motifs echoing their freedom in Christ and call to counter the destructive spiritual forces that were at work in the world. This movement would eventually bear fruit in the 1980s and 1990s, resulting in the genesis of a number of Christian ministries drawing on the Golden State's Christian heritage. Included here are the ministries of Calvary Chapel Surfing Association, Christian Surfers International, Walking on Water, and the Surfer's Chapel.

Motifs in California Surf Culture

Anyone who has traveled a significant length of the Pacific Coast Highway knows that to speak of California surf culture in the singular is a mistake. There are a variety of surfing sub-cultures throughout the various communities that share the

---

    [7]   For example, see Bron Taylor, *Dark Green Religion: Nature Spirituality and the Planetary Future* (Berkley: University of California Press, 2010); Drew Kampion, *Stoked! A History of Surf Culture* (Layton: Gibbs Smith, 2003); and Yogis, *Saltwater Buddha*.

California coast—from the Tijuana Sloughs to the stark wilderness of Humboldt. When attempting to define California surf culture, it is fair to ask: What does Santa Cruz have to do with the Orange County, shortboarders with longboarders?[8]

These differences notwithstanding, it is possible to find common features that link these various sub-cultures. Those who examine surfing in California have returned to recurrent themes in California surf culture, such as a love for play, free expression, risk taking, embodied existence, and a fascination with the sea. These themes are pregnant with theologically rich motifs. Because this chapter seeks to provide a broad sketch of a theology of California surf culture, our engagement with its various motifs shall be limited to addressing the significance of leisure for this study.

The Significance of Leisure

California surf culture places a high premium on leisure. After all, to be serious about pursuing good surf requires a flexible lifestyle that can move with the changing swells. But this is also due to an enduring value for freedom that has marked what it means to be a surfer. In its more extreme examples, some forms of California surf culture produce what have been dubbed "beach bums": free spirits who have dropped out of mainstream society to construct their lives around an unhindered pursuit of waves.

Scholars have suggested that to fully apprehend the role leisure plays in California surf culture, one must recognize the influence of Hawaiian culture's non-Western view of "island time."[9] Unlike Western conceptions of time that are organized around a rationally objectified measurement, island time is measured according to nature's rhythms. The Western approach has been an important part of creating a powerful economy; it is a view of time by which our lives can be measured according to productivity and efficiency. In contrast, island time understands work on an as-needed basis. In short, the Western approach views the moments of one's life instrumentally as something to be used or even (in our service society) sold, whereas island time thinks of the moments of time as ends in themselves to be experienced within the moment.

---

[8]   Santa Cruz is a smaller city on the central coast, nestled in the redwood-forested mountains and known for its liberal political views. The surf in Santa Cruz is cold and the coastline predominantly rocky. Orange County is part of the greater LA metropolitan sprawl, geographically within the LA basin and known for its conservative political views. The surf in Orange County is relatively warm and the coastline consists mostly of beaches.

[9]   Lawler, *The American Surfer*, 25–6.

California's dominant culture lives on an instrumental view of time. Yet many Californians sense that this view of time so crucial to our fast-paced lives and prosperity ends up making people little more than instruments for larger commercial powers and consumptive practices. In this way, the surfing lifestyle has drawn both the attention and fascination of the dominant culture—tapping into a collective sense that our lives could, or even should, be different. For most immersed in instrumental time, the leisure time surfing offers remains an elusive ideal of which one can only dream, something that might be attained in retirement after years on the treadmill of instrumental time.

The 2007 documentary *Surfwise*[10] retraces one man's attempt to break out of the confines of his conventional existence within instrumental time. In this movie, Dorian Paskowitz leaves his medical practice and, accompanied by his free-spirited wife Juliette, pursues an alternative lifestyle living out of a camper and attending surf competitions. All is going well until they start having children. With the added strains of child rearing, the idyllic lifestyle begins to look more like a hardship. As the film progresses, the attention shifts to the irony of Dorian's legacy. In his quest for freedom and desire to raise his family in a free-spirited lifestyle, he has unknowingly saddled his adult children with hurdles that have made them unable to function in the broader culture. The film leaves viewers wondering how to navigate the vision surfing offers in light of the dominant culture's view of instrumental time.

Although California surf cultures sense various dangers inherent within instrumental time, they find themselves conflicted with how to live in light of this problem. This predicament, however, is not insurmountable. Christian theology can offer a unique resolution to surf culture's problem with time in the Golden State.

In recent years a host of Christian theologians have addressed the issue of the relationship between work and leisure.[11] The general consensus among these theologians is that there is a pressing need to value *both* leisure and work without pitting one against the other. Instead of being stuck on the horns of a

---

[10] Written and directed by Doug Pray, http://www.imdb.com/title/tt0479547/ (accessed December 14, 2013).

[11] See Robert K. Johnston, *The Christian at Play* (Eugene: Wipf and Stock, 1997); Miroslav Volf, *Work in the Spirit: Toward a Theology of Work* (Eugene: Wipf and Stock, 2001); Leland Ryken, *Work and Leisure in Christian Perspective* (Eugene: Wipf and Stock, 2002); Darrell Cosden, *A Theology of Work: Work and the New Creation* (Eugene: Wipf and Stock, 2006); Robert Banks, *God The Worker: Journeys into the Mind, Heart and Imagination of God* (Eugene: Wipf and Stock, 2008); and Ben Witherington, *Work: A Kingdom Perspective* (Grand Rapids: Eerdmans, 2011).

dilemma—island time versus instrumental time—both must be assessed within the larger framework of the biblical narrative. Only then can the value of both be embraced. In short, Christian theologians have argued that only by living within the biblical narrative can we subsume both the Greek model of leisure and the (so-called) Protestant model of work into a life that has the flexibility and resources to engage both wholeheartedly.[12]

These attempts among Christian theologians to reclaim a more positive theology of leisure and play are refreshing. However, as helpful as they are, they still fail to address the heart of the issue. For in its disclosure of the West's inadequate view of the role of leisure, California surf culture has also revealed the larger problem of our culture's understanding of temporality itself. Island time's quest is, at its heart, an attempt to live "outside the linear march of time."[13] It is to seek a state where "past, present [and] future are unified."[14] In arranging our lives according to the rhythms of nature, it seeks to alleviate our alienation from time itself.

Surfing and the Distended Self

If indeed we see California surf culture as attempting to cope with fallen time— seeking to mend the break between "lived time" and "objective time," we might well ask how Christian theology addresses this problem.[15] Here, St Augustine comes to mind. It was Augustine who first drew attention to the problem of the *distentio* of the self: the inability to find fullness in the past, the present, or the future.

In *Confessions* 11.11–13, Augustine contrasts our experience in time with eternity. While in eternity "nothing moves into the past," in time "the past is always driven on by the future, the future always follows on the heels of the past, and both the past and future have their beginning and their end in the

---

[12] See Johnston, *The Christian at Play*, 83–5.

[13] Full quote: "A surf session is, then, a small occurrence outside the linear march of time." See Phil Edwards, "You Should Have Been Here An Hour Ago," in *Zero Break: An Illustrated Collection of Surf Writing 1777–2004*, Matt Warshaw (ed.), (New York: Harcourt Books, 2004), 339.

[14] Mark Stranger, *Surfing Life: Surface, Substructure and the Commodification of the Sublime* (Surrey, UK; Burlington, US: Ashgate, 2011), 151.

[15] For "lived time" vs "objective time," see Charles Taylor, *A Secular Age* (Cambridge: Harvard University Press, 2008), 56. Also see Charles Taylor, *Sources of the Self: The Making of Modern Identity* (Cambridge: Harvard University Press, 1987), 131.

eternal present."[16] Whereas God stands in an eternal never-ending present with "no future to anticipate and no past to remember," and the heavenly creatures experience temporal mutability without "lapse" (*sine ullo lapsu*), fallen humanity must forever be before the future and after the past in the ever-disappearing present (*Conf.* 12.9).

This three-fold present is constantly mapped, according to Augustine, by the soul continually extending itself (*distentio animi*) and thereby being "divided between time gone by and time to come." It is to be "torn this way and that in the havoc of change" (*Conf.* 11.29). Augustine recognizes that our experience of distention can be mitigated through certain actions (Augustine gives the example of the mental focus involved in reciting a Psalm). This is not a way of overcoming distension, but is instead a way of offering a less fractured experience of temporality.[17] Therefore, *intentio* works against *distentio,* but only for periods of time and as a way to cope with the feelings of being scattered and torn. Augustine's ultimate solution to our experience of being scattered in time is described as creation's Sabbath day, the day when humankind reposes in the contemplation of the very source of all beautiful things, God himself (*Conf.* 12.11). It is only then that humankind can finally feel at home in temporality—when we will find that there is no slippage between the experience of being in time and embracing existence as containing past, present, and future.

There is a striking similarity between the solution surfers have to fallen time and Augustine's own account. Both claim that temporality is inescapably part of the world and that we must share this feature of our existence with the natural world (temporality as intrinsic to creation). Both seek a solution through an aesthetic engagement with what captivates us. Surfing calls us to engage the pleasure, beauty, and sublime glory of the sea; Augustine calls us to reorient our hearts around their true desires—pleasure, beauty, and a glorious God. But the unique element that Augustine adds is the conviction that the natural world—indeed, time itself—has a direction. And therefore fallen time is only redeemed when through *intentio* we move in the direction temporality itself moves.[18] In other words, temporal things can only embrace their temporality when they

---

[16]   Unless noted otherwise, my quotes from Augustine are drawn from Augustine, *Confessions*, R.S. Pine-Coffin (trans.) (New York: Barnes & Noble Books, 1992).

[17]   My reading of the Augustine's relationship between *intentio* and *distentio* here follows Andrea Nightingale, *Once Out of Nature: Augustine on Time and the Body* (Chicago: The University of Chicago Press, 2011), 99.

[18]   I am indebted here to Matthew A. Wilcoxen, "Reading Lolita in Hippo: Augustine and Nabokov on Temporality and Desire," unpublished paper delivered at the Augustine and Augustinianisms Unit of the *American Academy of Religion*, Chicago, November 17, 2012.

are directed *beyond* their temporality. It is then that, in Augustine's own words, "[The Soul] by continually and unfailingly clinging unto Thee, suffers no vicissitude of times" (*Conf.* 12.11.13).[19]

If this analysis is correct, California surf culture's stopgap measure to cope with the alienation of time in our fast-paced culture merely flirts with pre-fallen temporality. While surfing is capable of briefly "emptying your mind of past and future,"[20] Augustine's *dénouement* reminds California surf culture that the quest for "the perfect wave" is ongoing; surfing will never provide the final solution to fallen time.[21]

The Poetics of Surf

Culture involves more than people merely *doing* something (*praxis*) in the world; people *make* something of the world in their doing (*poetics*). Because cultural *praxis* informs and reinforces a given *poetic*—that is, supports a given internal logic of practice[22]—theologians must make sense of cultural arenas not merely as outside observers and theorists, but (to the degree it is possible) as the cultural practitioners they are.[23] As a native Californian who has spent his life surfing, I cannot help but recognize how deeply my own theology has been

---

[19] Here I rely on Pilkington's translation found in Augustine, "The Confessions of St. Augustin," in *A Select Library of the Nicene and Post-Nicene Fathers of the Christian Church, First Series, Vol. I*, Philip Schaff (ed.), (Buffalo: Christian Literature Company, 1886).

[20] Warshaw, *Zero Break*, 339.

[21] Christian philosopher Peter Kreeft suggests surfing holds a window into pre-fallen temporality when he writes, "surfing brings us back to the timelessness of Eden. Maybe Adam and Eve felt that way all the time: exactly the way a surfer feels atop a wave." See Peter Kreeft, *I Surf Therefore I am: A Philosophy of Surfing* (South Bend: St Augustine's Press, 2008), 20.

[22] As Richard Grimes explores at length, there is a knowledge that comes to us in the very act of a practice that is not possible apart from the form and style of that particular practice. Richard Grimes, *Beginnings in Ritual Studies* (Waterloo, Canada: Ritual Studies International, 2010), 4. This has implications for what it means to be a Christian theologian. For example, it may be that to be a Christian theologian who does not engage in worship is to put oneself at an epistemic disadvantage.

[23] Here I follow Graham Ward, *Cultural Transformation and Religious Practice* (Cambridge: Cambridge University Press, 2005), 37–60. Ward argues that theology is never free from the poetics of cultural practice ("the discursive practices of its cultural context"), showing by example how deeply Barth's *habitus* was marked by the poetics of German *Kulturprotestantismus*. Similarly, in Philip Stoltzfus, *Theology as Performance: Music, Aesthetics and God in Western Thought* (New York: T&T Clark, 2006), Stoltzfus claims that Barth's theology was significantly shaped by his sustained sessions of listening to Mozart.

informed by this cultural practice.[24] Therefore, I would like to begin sketching the contours of a theology of California surf culture in a constructive sense—that is, a theology that is informed by the actual *poetics* of surfing.

To develop a theology of surf culture from the inside requires returning to the experience of surfing. Stated simply, surfing involves gliding along a wave of energy passing through water. This practice is the *sine qua non* of all surf cultures, Californian or otherwise. And it is the *poetics* attached to and surrounding this act—the embodied aesthetic engagement of the glide—that is at the center of the language, artifacts, images, meanings, and narratives that surf cultures create. So to better understand California surf culture, we must take a closer look at the act of surfing itself.

The Power of the Glide

Although "stoke," in surfing parlance, typically refers to the reflective afterglow following riding a wave, it can also be used to express any of the aesthetically oriented experiences of surfing that create what has been referred to as a "peak" experience. These include not only the thrill of vertigo that takes place while gliding along the wave, but also the visual and tactile surroundings, as well as the surfer's sense of performance. Social scientists have tried hard to quantify the components of these phenomena through a universalizing language. So, for example, drawing on Abraham Maslow's categories, a surfer's glide on the wave is described as registering a combination of "object unification (total harmony), total attention (complete absorption in the experience), rich perception (lost in the experience), awe and reverence (the most blissful moment, ecstasy) and the fusion of dichotomies (the person and the experience merge)."[25] In this regard,

---

[24]   Among these are the central role the doctrine of creation plays in my theology, particularly an enchanted view nature of the world; its excess being a display of what John Calvin referred to as "a theater of God's glory." See Susan E. Schreiner, *The Theater of His Glory: Nature & Natural Order in the Thought of John Calvin* (Grand Rapids: Baker Academic, 1995). Additionally, I credit the poetics of surf to my heightened sense of the created world as organic, and thereby have been drawn to Herman Bavinck's central theological motif of organism. See James Eglinton: *Trinity and Organism: Towards a New Reading of Herman Bavinck's Organic Motif* (New York: T&T Clark, 2012).

[25]   Ford and Brown, *Surfing and Social Theory*, 158. Maslow's observations are valuable, but the temptation to reduce religious impulses to peak experiences has led to many a Jamesian relativizing of religion as little more than "over-beliefs." On the contrary, as William Dyrness rightly points out, reducing religious goals to such experiences is problematic on (among others) three counts. First, in universalizing such experiences it relativizes that which is not relative—the historically and culturally determinative role in such experiences. Second, this

surfers' lingo can be characterized as an attempt to verbalize these experiences. And given the tacit nature of these experiences, one can understand why surfers often resort to primitive and redundant expressions as a way to vocalize this apophatic encounter of eccentric or transcendent experience.

What are we to make of this? Does surfing offer a tacit religion? Bron Taylor has argued that surfing not only resembles religion in important ways, but also offers a legitimate religious path he characterizes as a form of "dark green religion."[26] To be sure, Taylor is not speaking of religion as a formal institution. Instead, he is referring to those engaging surfing in a way that captures various features commonly associated with religion, including an origin myth (idyllic pre-Western Hawaii), a fall (Western repression of surfing), a prophet (Duke Kahanamoku), an apostle (Tom Blake), religious media (surf magazines, films, and other media), ritual practices (the act of surfing), pilgrimages (surf trips), and an object of worship (Mother Ocean). Regardless of the specifics, Taylor is certainly on solid ground in describing a growing number of surfers who merge their religious sensibilities with their surfing. Yet there is a tension in Taylor's thesis. The more clearly the components of surfing's "dark green religion" are identified and expounded, the more ambiguous the fusing of other faiths with surfing. Aware of this tension, Taylor ends his analysis by affirming every surfer's religious (or non-religious) spiritual impulses. Such affirmations aside, Taylor's treatment leaves the impression that the more deeply one's spirituality is influenced by surfing per se, the more likely one will move toward an Eastern religious outlook.

In spite of how often Eastern mysticism is invoked ("becoming one with the wave"), an alternative understanding is provided by Roman Catholic philosopher Charles Taylor. In his book, A *Secular Age*, Taylor describes a vast gulf that exists between the "porous self" of pre-Enlightenment societies and the post-Enlightenment "buffered self."[27] In pre-Enlightenment societies, the self is vulnerable to forces outside of it, whether God, spirits, demons, or forces in nature. But with the Enlightenment comes the buffered self, creating a rupture between the self and the outside world (be it God, nature, or others). For Taylor,

---

underestimates the crucial role our bodies play in such experiences. Finally, Maslow's optimism that such encounters produce altruism ignores how individuals can become narcissistic and hedonistic in pursuits of such experiences. See William Dyrness, *Poetic Theology: God and the Poetics of Everyday Life* (Grand Rapids: Eerdmans, 2010), 29–30.

[26] Bron Taylor, *Dark Green Religion: Nature, Spirituality and the Planetary Future* (Berkeley: University of California Press, 2010).

[27] See Taylor, *A Secular Age*, 27–30. Taylor's analysis of the alienated modern self is part of a larger discussion on the rupture between the modern self and nature. Included here would be Karl Marx's discussion on alienation, George Simmel on reification and Max Weber on rationalization.

certain aesthetic practices challenge the buffered self. In line with Taylor's argument, I would suggest surfing provides a unique *détente* for the buffered self—from a position over and outside the forces in the natural world to one within and dynamically related to these forces. In other words, the self that is in control of the world as an object to be manipulated becomes, briefly, responsive to a world that has an inescapable power and enchantment.

This dynamic is exhibited in Susan Casey's *The Wave: In Pursuit of the Rogues, the Freaks and the Giants of the Ocean.* Casey follows a group of big-wave riders as they globetrot from one harrowing big wave to the next. When asking a big-wave rider why this band was willing to risk their lives to surf these giants, the surfer responds, "Ecstasy beyond words. Mentally, physically, spiritually, it's the highest place I can imagine being."[28] Casey is astounded that the sheer feeling and prospect of connection to nature at the apex of its power would be something these men were willing to die for. Yet this seems understandable given the way these surfers, who are not formally religious, turn to religious language to speak of what they encounter in surfing big waves. Laird Hamilton, for example, tells Casey, "If you can look at one of these waves and you don't believe that there's something greater than we are, then you've got some serious analyzing to do."[29] Here, Hamilton's appeal to the waves as demonstrating "something greater" comes suspiciously close to Psalm 93:4: "Mightier than the thunders of many waters, mightier than the waves of the sea, the Lord on high is mighty!"[30]

Los Angeleno Steve Kotler is another example of a non-believer who cannot help but be theological when he experiences surfing. In *West of Jesus: Surfing, Science and the Origins of Belief*, Kotler recounts his story as an avowed agnostic who cannot shake the powerful spiritual experience he has while surfing. Having sampled plenty of religions (Eastern and Western) and having never gotten anything out of it, Kotler figured religion was not his thing. But that all changed in his second year of a debilitating case of Lyme disease that left him 25 pounds lighter and barely able to walk. Kotler, deliberating between committing suicide and taking his friend up on his offer to go surfing, chose the latter. And for the first time, Kotler felt like an insider to religion. He writes, "At a time when everything else was gone, when nothing made sense and nothing worked, when

---

[28]   Susan Casey, *The Wave: In Pursuit of the Rogues, the Freaks and the Giants of the Ocean* (New York: Doubleday, 2010), 175.

[29]   Casey, *The Wave*, 184.

[30]   All Scripture references in this chapter are from the English Standard Version unless noted otherwise.

suicide seemed a viable option, surfing saved my life—and I wanted to know why."[31] For Kotler, surfing succeeded when formal religion failed.

Christian Theology and Surf Culture

The merging of religious impulses and lifestyle activities such as surfing are explored in Dyrness's *Poetic Theology*. Dyrness believes those engaged in the aesthetic pursuits of lifestyle sports such as surfing—though they have given up the formal institution of religion—sometimes turn to its practices and social structures to provide the kind of aesthetic formation and satisfaction that religion has traditionally supplied. What is more, Dyrness is interested in understanding this religious impulse in light of Christian theology. Drawing on an Augustinian anthropology that places the desiring self as foundational to the knowing self, Dyrness argues that the idea that everyday aesthetic practices can carry religious import is not only a leftover of nineteenth-century Romanticism, but is related to Christian theology. Here he takes his lead from theologians who have informed the Reformed tradition, such as Augustine and Calvin. Because I am sympathetic to Dyrness's project, I would like to offer my own suggestions on how resources from the Reformed tradition give insight into the poetics of surfing.

In this regard, Calvin's understanding of the *sensus divinitatis*, or *semen religionis*, provides a way to understand the "religious" nature of the experiences of surfers such as Hamilton and Kotler. As Calvin states in the *Institutes*, creation is a "theater of God's glory," whose "exquisite" and "abundant furnishings" display the "immense riches of his wisdom, justice, goodness, and power" (1.6.2; 1.14.20).[32] Humanity was placed in this temple to delight in the beauty and glory of God's majesty. Importantly, Calvin believed that even after the fall, humanity retained its status as *humanity* and therefore could not shake its religious impulse to worship.[33] Furthermore, although humanity's perception of the temple of creation was compromised by the fall, Calvin also held that even those lacking eyes enabled by Scripture and Spirit continued to receive a "witness of God," something "borne in upon the eyes of all" (1.5.13; 1.6.1).

Of course, Calvin's doctrine of the *sensus divinitatis* and understanding of the book of nature is equally informed by his teaching that apart from Scripture

---

[31]   Steven Kotler, *West of Jesus: Surfing, Science and the Origins of Belief* (New York: Bloomsbury, 2006), 53.

[32]   All Calvin quotes are taken from John Calvin, *Institutes of the Christian Religion*, John T. McNeill (ed.) and Ford Lewis Battles (trans.), (Philadelphia: Westminster Press, 1960).

[33]   Schreiner, *The Theater of His Glory*, 71.

and the illuminating work of God's Spirit, people's worship remains idolatrous (2.2.19). Nowhere does Calvin posit a steady or static noetic source by which the unregenerate might climb to new levels of spiritual understanding. To the contrary, he viewed the unregenerate noetic capacity for divinity like "a momentary lightning flash" upon a person stumbling in a field at night, for whom "the sight vanishes so swiftly that he is plunged again into the darkness of the night before he can take even a step" (2.2.18). Clearly, Calvin was not optimistic about the power of the *sensus divinitatis* and the book of nature to produce true worship (1.5.14). That said, we must not miss Calvin's assumption that people are not merely idolatrous *outsiders* to a true knowledge of God; they are also haunted *insiders* to a God-initiated display. Calvin tells us this display, although not capable of starting a fire, "surely strikes some sparks." Moreover, even if apart from regenerating grace the fallen is unable to love God, fallen humanity still cannot shake its need to worship—grounding the self in various liturgies of desire, resplendence, and awe. For Calvin, such "flashes" of nature, whether in a field at night or in the barrel of a wave at Huntington Beach, continue to shape the inescapably religious nature of human poetics.

Calvin's view of humanity as simultaneously insider and outsider also offers a nuanced treatment of the religious role of risk-taking among surfers. On the one hand, Calvin's approach calls theologians to take serious the growing empirical data that risk-taking in surfing has the potential to create ecstatic experiences of self-transcendence.[34] On the other hand, Calvin's approach safeguards Christian theologians from the danger of such experiences absorbing Christian theology. The danger of the latter can be illustrated by the approach found in liturgical theologian, Graham Hughes. In *Worship as Meaning*, Hughes describes sports endangering life and limb as providing "limit experiences" which upon being "thematized," can serve as a basis ("prolegomena") to the Christian faith.[35] But here a question emerges. If the experience is an inchoate form of genuine Christian experience, how does Christian theology escape being merely an add-on or embellishment of the religious kernel surfing provides?

In contrast, Calvin's insider/outsider model assumes there are no neutral observers in such instances; for such sparks rely on divine intervention to take flame, not the qualitative depth of any said cultural practice or the availability of

---

[34]   Matt Stranger, "The Aesthetics of Risk: A Study of Surfing," *International Review for the Sociology of Sport* 34 (1999), 265–76; Nick Ford and David Brown, *Surfing and Social Theory: Experience, Embodiment and Narrative of the Dream Glide* (New York: Routledge, 2006).

[35]   Graham Hughes, *Worship as Meaning: A Liturgical Theology for Late Modernity* (Cambridge: Cambridge University Press, 2003), 260.

Christian themes. This amendment is helpful on two fronts. First, it explains how a practice that creates "ecstatic self-transcendence" could be beset with the vices for which surf culture is notorious: narcissism, localism, hedonism, and the like. Secondly, this approach avoids the twin dangers of an implicit secularization of culture and, conversely, a naive baptism of a given cultural practice. For, recalling Calvin's language, the divine display that produces sparks is not the same as the divine flame.

Positively speaking, Calvin's view implies God is already at work within the frameworks of creation and culture. Thus, Christian theology can speak not only by virtue of its own grammar, but also simultaneously *within* the grammars of cultural texts. In this regard, George Lindbeck's argument that Christianity speaks only within its own grammar—though helpful in many ways—is insufficient.[36] For if the entire world is the place where God continues to display his "brightness," then surely the church's conversation should be brought to bear on the broader dialogues regarding this display.[37] Moreover, Calvin's notion that *all of creation* continues to be a source of revelation means the triune God continues to "strike some sparks" *within* the world of human experience and practice throughout history. Therefore, the church should be concerned with addressing not only its own questions and experiences, but also the questions and experiences of non-Christians (such as Kotler's and Hamilton's), acknowledging that the latter may very well be, through the work of the living and written Word, the beginning of sparks being fanned into flames.

Surfing and the Biblical Narrative

The above notwithstanding, Postliberals like Lindbeck are right that for the church to speak as the church, the grammar of Scripture must enter the dialogue. But how can the church speak faithfully from Scripture regarding a cultural practice that Scripture does not address? Rather than abstracting a set of "timeless truths" that are then applied to all practices or, conversely, establishing a universal "limit experience" that then is read back into both the text and the cultural practice, a more promising method is found within the

---

[36]   George Lindbeck, *The Nature of Doctrine: Religion and Theology in a Postliberal Age* (Louisville: Westminster John Knox, 2009).

[37]   See Richard Crane, "Postliberals, Truth, *Ad Hoc* Apologetics, and (Something Like) General Revelation," *Perspectives in Religious Studies* 30/1 (Spring 2003), 29–53.

canonical-linguistic approach of Kevin Vanhoozer.[38] As Vanhoozer argues at
length, the rich imaginative narrative of Scripture can be read as an open script
from which we are invited to fuse the horizons of the Bible with narratives in
our contemporary world. This fusion is possible because subjects taken up in the
biblical narrative (like father, king, salvation, and others) have fuzzy edges, and
therefore communicate more, not less. (As Gadamer reminded us there is "an
excess of meaning.") Moreover, if the biblical text is always meant to be part of
an ongoing communicative action, a faithful performance *requires* responding
to this communicative action by fusing the horizon of the biblical narrative
with the narratives found in one's culture and/or subculture. Given this
understanding, a number of subjects in the Bible—the sea, waves, sea creatures,
and watercraft—offer an important resource for a theology of California surf
culture. These subjects create the synapses for joining the biblical narrative with
the world of surfing. Furthermore, as we shall see, they form the background
to one of the most common biblical texts appealed to regarding surfing: the
miracle of Christ walking upon water. Therefore we round out this chapter by
taking up themes within the biblical narrative that find overlap with surf culture.
The first of these is the sea.

The Sea and Scripture

The preponderance of the sea informs not only the imagination of California
surf culture but also the biblical narrative. The story of the sea in the Bible begins
with a description of the primeval world as a murky, watery mass: *darkness was
over the face of the deep* (Gen. 1:2). While many have been quick to connect this
pre-creation "deep" with the role of primeval waters in other ancient sources,[39]
of first exegetical importance is the immediate context.[40] The text tells us these
waters were characterized as תֹהוּ וָבֹהוּ (*tohu wa-bohu*): a groundless formless
watery mass inhospitable to life. As the text proceeds, we read a phrase sure to
strike a chord with surfers: *and the Spirit of God was moving over the surface of
the waters*. The term used to describe the Spirit's activity (מְרַחֶפֶת, *merahepet)* is
typically translated as "moving" (KJV, RSV, AV) or "hovering" (NIV, ESV, JB).
The image here is that of the Spirit gliding over the primordial waters to prepare

---

[38]   Kevin J. Vanhoozer, *The Drama of Doctrine: A Canonical-Linguistic Approach to
Christian Theology* (Louisville: Westminster John Knox, 2007).

[39]   Terence E. Fretheim, *God and World in the Old Testament: A Relational Theology of
Creation* (Nashville: Abingdon, 2005).

[40]   Victor Hamilton, *The Book of Genesis: Chapters 1–17* (Grand Rapids: Eerdmans,
1990), 110–11.

them for habitation. With the giving of God's word ("then God said"), darkness is removed from the watery abyss, the watery mass is formed into sea and cloud, and the dry land emerges. As the dark, lifeless waters are given form and filled with creatures, they are transformed into vibrant seas: elements of God's "very good" creation (Gen. 1:31). As such, the sea joins creation's chorus of praise (Ps. 96:11), her bridled power being a testimony to God's omnipotence (Pss 93:4; 107:25).

Although redeemed from watery chaos, the story of the sea does not end there. For it still has within it a "proud" spirit and, therefore, must remain under God's strong power (Job 38:11; Pss 65:7; 89:9). As surfers know firsthand, the sea is not to be trifled with. Likewise, the biblical testimony tells us that apart from God's constraining providence the sea would once again dissolve the world into lifeless, watery chaos. This is, in fact, what we see in the flood narrative of Genesis 7:17–23. When God removes his providential hand, the atmospheric waters and the "fountains of the deep" are let loose and reunited, returning the world to a watery grave (Gen. 7:11). The flood narrative tells the reader the sea is not only a symbol of God's redemptive power and providence, but is also a source of God's judgment. This is most pronounced in the Exodus account (Ex. 14). Here the sea operates simultaneously as a vehicle of judgment and grace: Pharaoh's death-dealing ways meet the watery chaos they deserve even as the sea is bound by God's hand, thereby providing Israel her salvation.

The above suggests the Bible's picture of the sea is complex. On one hand, the sea is included within the creation account as a good gift of God, a reminder of God's providence and a sign of God's redemptive purposes. Yet Scripture also presents another side to the sea. For the sea is also a harbinger of death and judgment; it is a realm that, apart from God's grace and providence, can become a chaotic force for evil that threatens the life-giving order of creation.

The Things that Lurk in the Deep

The waters off California are not only home to a beautiful array of sea creatures; they are also the hunting grounds for a substantial population of white sharks. This two-fold picture is also found in the Bible's depiction of the things that fill the sea. God creates not only fish and other diminutive sea-creatures to invigorate the waters, but also the larger aquatic creatures that lurk in the recesses of the deep (Gen. 1:21). Much discussion has focused on identifying these larger creatures, some of which scholars have claimed to be saltwater crocodiles (Ezek. 29:3; 32:3), serpents (Ex. 7:9–12; Deut. 32:33; Ps. 91:13), and possibly whales (Ps. 148:7). But scripture also references dragon-like mythical creatures inhabiting the seas of the Ancient Near East. Characterized as untamable, fierce, proud, and aggressive, these monsters of the deep serve as a source of fear for humankind, even as they remain subject to God (Ps. 74:13–14; Isa. 27:1, 51:9).

The Bible's most extensive treatment of these monsters of the deep is found in the book of Job's discussion of the creature Leviathan (41:2–26). Leviathan is described as a fearsome creature beyond the pale of human control—a beast capable of making "the deep boil like a pot" (41:3). Safe in her watery depths (38:16), Leviathan laughs at human defenses, making her "over all that are proud" (Ps. 41:34). Standing in stark contrast to Job's domestic livestock at the beginning of the book, Leviathan is untamable and refuses to serve human aims–whether as a source of food, a beast of burden, an object of sport, or as a pet. As such, Leviathan plays an important role in Job's theology. She is not there for human beings, but to serve God's bidding (Ps. 104:26). Thus, she is a symbol of the Bible's non-anthropocentric view of the world. The world is God's, not ours. As Schifferdecker summarizes regarding Leviathan's role in Job's theology: "Humanity has a place in God's creation. It is a place, however, not of dominion, but of humility and of wonder. Job is invited to reorient himself, to understand that he is not the center of the cosmos."[41]

Israel and Watercraft

A third thematic cognate linking the biblical narrative to surfing is that of watercraft. It comes as little surprise that surfers are captivated by the ability to navigate the ocean. However, the biblical material dealing with navigation of watercraft is often overlooked. In part, this is due to the common characterization of ancient Israelites as landlubbers. Yet Berlyn has made the case that ancient Israelites "were familiar with the sea and the creatures that dwell therein and the ships that sailed upon it."[42] One recognizes this awareness in Israel's sages' great respect for navigational skills (Prov. 31:14; Ps. 8:8–9). For these sages, movements that lacked visual cues, such as birds soaring through the air or a snake moving on a rock, were considered to involve great expertise. In a similar way, the sages considered a ship navigating the seas a source of wonder (Prov. 30:18). More than merely "technique," the insight and mystery of navigation were associated with the wisdom of the Creator. If God is the master of the sea, those who demonstrate a relative control of the sea do so by virtue of God's gift.

---

[41]   Kathryn Schifferdecker, "Of Stars and Sea Monsters: Creation Theology in the Whirlwind Speeches," *Word and World* 31/4 (2011), 365.

[42]   Patricia Berlyn, "Down to the Sea in Ships," *Jewish Bible Quarterly* 37/2 (2009), 79.

The wisdom and wonder of God's work is also associated with navigation in Psalm 104. In the midst of extolling the Lord for his innumerable works, the Psalmist praises God not only for the vast sea and its various forms of life, but also for *the ships that pass through the sea*. Some scholars have claimed that the Psalmist is offering praise for both the navigation and design of the watercraft: "it was precisely the human-made nature of the ship which so impressed the ancients and which made it a suitable metonym for divine power and rule in the ongoing religious polemic concerning God's dominion."[43] Thus, God's mastery of the sea is reflected in both those with a gift for navigation and insight into watercraft design.

However, the comparison between God's and humankind's mastery of the seas quickly falls away during harrowing storms. When the sea becomes a raging tempest, even the most skilled sailor is helpless to control it. Psalm 107:33–43 depicts just such a situation. In the midst of a storm, sailors once accustomed to using their wisdom to harness the sea "reeled and staggered like drunken men and were at their wits end" (Ps. 107:27). In contrast, the sea lives in fear of God (Ps. 77:16). Only God controls the sea. He alone can traverse the waters at will (Ps. 77:19). He alone can "make the storm be still and the waves be hushed" (Ps. 107:29; Job 9:8; 38:16). And he alone possesses the ultimate control over the efficacy of human navigational skill, initiative, and watercraft expertise (Ezek. 27; Job 1:4–15).

Walking on Water

Our discussion of the Old Testament view of the sea forms the backdrop to what is consider by many both within and outside the Christian surf community as the *locus classicus* for a biblical engagement with surfing: Jesus walking on the sea. The story is recounted in Matthew 14:22–33, Mark 6:45–52, and John 6: 16–21. Whereas John supplies a terse summary of the miracle described in Mark's narrative, Matthew adds to his account a description of Peter joining Jesus.

Upon studying this account, a complication quickly surfaces in connecting Christ walking on water to the popular practice of surfing. The purpose of this story is to emphasize the absolute uniqueness of Christ. This is highlighted at the end of Matthew's pericope, "those who were in the boat bowed down before him and said, 'Truly you are the Son of God'" (Matt. 14:33). This radical otherness

---

[43] Tova Forti, "Of Ships and Seas, and Fish and Beasts: Viewing the Concept of Universal Providence in the Book of Jonah through the Prism of Psalms," *Journal for the Study of the Old Testament* 35/3 (2011), 365.

of Christ is also underscored by the disciples' initial response upon witnessing Christ walking on water. Because the appearance of a mere *person* walking on water was beyond the pale of credibility, the disciples conclude they are not viewing a human but, rather, an apparition. This question of Christ's identity invites reader to consider a similar question: What sort of human can walk on water? Jesus himself provides the answer to this question with his simple statement, "It is I." This Greek phrase *egō eimi* employs an expression used at times in the LXX when God reveals himself: "I am who I am" (see Ex. 3:14). R.T. France summarizes the implications of this miracle: The event was "a spectacular instance of his supernatural power, which evokes a suitable awed and theologically loaded response from the disciples (v. 33)."[44] This is supported by what both the disciples and Matthew's Jewish audience knew from the Old Testament: God alone commands power over the waters; he alone "treads on the waves of the sea" (Job 9:8; Ps. 77:19; Isa. 43:16). Christ's treading upon the waves echoes the Old Testament "warrior" theme of God's conquest of the sea, the waves, and the things that lurk deep within.[45] In light of these themes, to see Christ as the first surfer would be to miss the thrust of these passages. Christ is not the first of many "dudes"; he is the one and only God-man.

But Matthew's Gospel adds another interesting dimension to the account. Unlike Mark and John, Matthew records that Peter *also* walked on water. In fact, Jesus invites Peter to participate with him in his water-walking feat (Matt. 14:28–29). Jesus' inclusion of Peter re-opens the possibility that others are to follow Jesus in this activity. It reintroduces the question of what (if anything) this might imply for those comparing Peter's water-walking with the modern practice of surfing.

We must be careful here. As stated before, the goal is not to anachronistically read the biblical account as if the modern practice of surfing was in the minds of the Gospel writers. Quite the contrary, a survey of exegetes confirms that Matthew's addition of Peter in the narrative aims to introduce the role of faith in the face of fear-producing evil, not water-walking.[46] And far from thinking about any particular practice or sub-culture, Matthew's Gospel addresses *all* in the community of faith. Like the story of the feeding of the 5,000 that precedes the water walking account, Matthew desires to show his audience that the same

---

[44]   R.T. France, *The Gospel of Matthew* (Grand Rapids: Eerdmans, 2007), 566.

[45]   See A.R. Angel, "Crucifixus Vincens: The Son of God as Divine Warrior in Matthew," *The Catholic Biblical Quarterly* 73/2 (2011), 299–317.

[46]   France, *The Gospel of Matthew*; D.A. Hagner, *Matthew 14–28*, B.M. Metzger (ed.), (Dallas: Word, 1995); Leon Morris, *The Gospel According to Matthew* (Grand Rapids: Eerdmans, 1992); Ben Witherington, *Matthew* (Macon: Smyth & Helwys, 2006); C.S. Keener, *A Commentary on the Gospel of Matthew* (Grand Raids: Eerdmans, 1999).

Jesus who performed these miracles stands today to meet his people, saving them from the storms that beset them and providing for them even when they are in doubt. These are Matthew's primary concern for his readers.

However, we must not forget that Matthew is writing with the larger scope of the Old Testament narrative in the background. Thus, the sea in this story symbolizes the chaotic waters that threaten to undo God's order. Additionally, Peter's fragile condition apart from God's help resonates with the Old Testament witness that human beings, though able to reflect God's ability to traverse the sea, only do so by God's help. Matthew's account draws additional connections between the disciples experience on the Sea of Galilee and Israel's on the Sea of Reeds.

Pushing the hermeneutical circle even further beyond Matthew's immediate Gospel and the larger canon of Scripture, we might also ask if the idea of walking on water was part of first-century culture. Is it possible that the broader culture informed the background of the Gospel's water walking? In response to this question, Luz has identified a number of sources in the ancient world of the Mediterranean Sea that spoke of people walking on water. As Luz summarizes, "walking on water was of great interest to people—not only and not primarily the Jews. It was a dream, a fascinating idea."[47] If Matthew was writing with this cultural value in his purview, then it should come as little surprise that modern day surfers might likewise find a similar water-walking fascination with Matthew's account of Peter joining Jesus. But we must not make too much of this. Although the idea of walking on the sea existed in other ancient cultures, Angel suggests that there are cues in Matthew's text that require the reader to maintain a specifically Jewish perspective while engaging the story.[48] Luz's argument that Matthew's account of Peter walking on water should be read within other "limit experiences" in the history of religions is at odds with the text's emphasis on the uniqueness and necessity of Christ. Rather than focusing on the universal need to embrace one's limitations and overcome fear and despair, Matthew emphasizes humanity's inescapable need for Jesus. Making strong connections between Matthew and other ancient cultures significantly removes the reader from the immediate concerns of Matthew's Gospel and the broader Jewish context in which he operates. At most, we are left to speculate the link between Peter's water walking, the first century imagination ... and contemporary surfers.

---

[47] Ulrich Luz, *Matthew 8–20: A Commentary* (Minneapolis: Augsburg Fortress, 2001), 320.

[48] Angel, "Crucifixus Vincens," 306.

Making Connections

Still, the above discussion evinces a number of places where the horizon of the text meets the horizon of the contemporary world of surfing. In contrast to a facile romanticism or, conversely, a nihilistic fatalism, the biblical narrative views the sea through a complex lens as both a vehicle of judgment and grace—a foreboding *and* providential realm. Emulating the Bible's complex understanding of the sea, surfers speak of the sea as both terrible and beautiful—a means of both revelation and judgment: "You are simultaneously propelled by the wave and pursed by it. The best position is the worst; the greatest power is closest to the curl. Apotheosis and annihilation are separate by the narrowest margins."[49] Surf culture's description of the sea's capacity to elevate and destroy, like the biblical description of the sea as a vehicle for grace and judgment, goes beyond a post-Kantian view of the sea as merely sublime.[50]

Additionally, California surfers are all too aware of their own Leviathan—the white shark. Here again, the narrative world of the Bible converges with contemporary surf culture. Although white shark attacks among surfers in California are relatively rare, they are widely publicized (one might even say "mythologized" in their numerous retellings) among various surf communities. As those who regularly enter into the realm "where the wild things are," surfers must make sense of regularly immersing themselves (both literally and figuratively) into an environment in which they are not master. Such encounters call to mind the book of Job's non-anthropocentric view of the natural world. Arguably, such regular "humblings" help contribute to the strong environmental impulse among California surfers—an impulse responsible for the establishment of national and international environmental organizations such as the Surfrider Foundation (based in San Clemente) and the Surfer's Environmental Alliance (based in Santa Cruz). A constructive theology of California surf culture would do well to draw out this connection between the biblical treatment of "the things that lurk in the deep" and the non-anthropocentrism in California surf culture.

In like measure, the admiration of navigation and elevated status of watercraft design in Israel finds resonance with surfing. Part of the "stoke" that surfers speak of revolves around rejecting a purely technical or empirical description of navigating the sea as one finds within the Enlightenment's rational order. Instead, surfers are lost in the wonder of being carried along a wave of energy passing through the water. California surfers in particular are famous for their

---

49   Stranger, *Surfing Life*, 165.
50   Stranger, *Surfing Life*, 172.

quasi-apophatic expressions of the magic they feel in navigating a surfboard in and out of the barrel of a wave. The practice of surfing invites participants into this state of wonder, and in so doing the participants echo the biblical sages' own wonder regarding watercraft. This capacity among surfers to elevate "the mundane, routine and taken for granted experiences" (what sociologists refer to as the "aestheticization") reaches toward the social imaginary of the biblical sages' enchanted world. One wonders, is it possible to recognize the inadequacy of language among contemporary surfers as betraying the shortcomings of a post-Kantian appeal to the non-descript "sublime"?

Conclusion: Surfing and Cultural Theology

Theology refers not only in the narrow sense to accounts of Scripture's teachings on God, Christ, and the church, but can also in a broader sense refer to a "God-centered understanding" of any subject, of things in relation to God, or *sub ratione dei*. In this chapter, we have attempted this kind of God-centered understanding of California surf culture by analyzing it from three different angles. First, we examined a central motif found in the subculture of surfers and surfing, and then responded with an analysis of how this motif related to the Christian faith. This approach can be called a "kerygmatic" theology of culture: bringing theological categories to bear on the sub-culture. Although this approach is important, one cannot stop here. Theologians must make sense of cultural arenas not merely from the outside, but from within the inner logics of the culture's practices. This second approach is "apologetic," working within the frameworks of the culture. In light of this, we also examined surfing from within the established grammars of the cultural practice—a practice that contains its own questions. With this move, we have affirmed the need for a post-colonial theology; for it was entering into the cultural practice that eluded the New England Calvinist missionaries who came to evangelize Hawaii in the nineteenth century. Finally, we have taken up the two horizons of the biblical narrative and contemporary surf culture to find the features they hold in common. We might call this third approach a "narrative" theology of culture. Here, the rich imaginative world of Scripture is brought into dialogue with the imaginative world of surf culture.

The growing discussion of surfing and the international influence of California surf culture has led us to believe a theology of California surf culture is of consequence. As the current interest in both the academy and popular literature has indicated, competing views are vying for a compelling account of this powerful cultural practice and the sub-culture that it has spawned. If Christianity is the world's *true* story, Christian theologians must take seriously their role in addressing these real cultural worlds. In other words, Christian theology must not restrict the conversation to safe topics within intramural bounds. When it does move outside her comfort zone, theology's refractions, such as those found in this chapter, provide not only fresh terrain for theological reflection, but serve the Christian ministries working within this cultural world as well as the thousands of people in California and elsewhere who surf.

Chapter 8

Silicon Valley and the Spirit of Innovation: How California's Entrepreneurial Ethos Bears Witness to Spiritual Reality

Bruce Baker

"It wasn't a quest for fame and fortune that drove us in those early years of isolation and struggle. It was passion—a passion to develop, proliferate, and evangelize technology to empower people everywhere to lead more productive lives."

– Jerry Sanders, CEO, Advanced Micro Devices

Silicon Valley, the world-renowned birthplace of technology start-up companies, stands alone as the quintessential image of entrepreneurial spirit. What is it about Silicon Valley that has created such phenomenal success? How did this agriculturally gifted valley give birth to so many world-class technology companies—Hewlett-Packard, Intel, AMD, Sun Microsystems, Apple, Cisco and Google, to name but a few—and manage to create the world's most admired culture of entrepreneurial spirit?

It seems as if there must be something special in the water, or in the air. Many scholars and journalists have sought to trace the roots and parse the mechanisms of the Silicon Valley's phenomenal entrepreneurial accomplishments. They have traced the history of Silicon Valley,[1] examined its unique competitive advantages,[2] and interpreted the stories and cultural heritage that have emerged

---

[1]   Kevin Starr, *Coast of Dreams: California on the Edge, 1990–2003* (New York: Knopf, 2004), 271–8; Arun Rao and Piero Scaruffi, *A History of Silicon Valley: The Largest Creation of Wealth in the History of the Planet: A Moral Tale* (Palo Alto: Omniware Group, 2011).

[2]   AnnaLee Saxenian, *Regional Advantage: Culture and Competition in Silicon Valley and Route 128* (Cambridge: Harvard University Press, 1994); AnnaLee Saxenian, *The New Argonauts: Regional Advantage in a Global Economy* (Cambridge: Harvard University Press, 2006); Martin Kenney (ed.), *Understanding Silicon Valley: The Anatomy of an Entrepreneurial Region* (Stanford: Stanford University Press, 2000).

from the most amazing collection of technology start-up companies the world has ever seen.[3]

But for all the efforts to glean lessons from the fruit of Silicon Valley, scant attention has been paid to theological interpretation of the Silicon Valley phenomena. That is the impetus of this chapter—to explore the entrepreneurial spirit of Silicon Valley from a theological perspective in order to gather theological insights into the phenomena of the Valley's ethos and spirit. This exploration shall proceed along two principal arcs of inquiry: first, to "exegete the culture," that is, to understand from within a theological perspective how the ethos of the Valley has engendered entrepreneurial efforts; and second, to gain insights based in theological anthropology to better understand the cultural microcosm of the Silicon Valley ethos. My thesis is that by viewing the entrepreneurial ethos of Silicon Valley through a biblical lens, we shall gain insights into the business climate which has produced such remarkable entrepreneurial success. Through this study I hope to offer fresh insight into the social, cultural, and moral conditions which have contributed to the ethos of Silicon Valley, and I hope also to gain wisdom capable of contributing to the cultivation of productive and soul-enriching work in modern society in general.

This is admittedly a speculative endeavor. There is an experimental character to this sort of theological inquiry as we ask open-ended questions about the meaning of secular culture displayed through the lifestyles and history of actors and events in a particular place and time.[4] We might even have titled this chapter, "What hath Silicon Valley to do with Jerusalem?" echoing Tertullian's riposte, "What hath Athens to do with Jerusalem?" The concern, of course, is to avoid the errors and pitfalls of turning to secular culture as a source of theological truth. Without distracting ourselves by rehashing that question, I offer this reminder merely to recognize the risk inherent in apologetics, and to explain my intent to steer clear of those pitfalls. My aim is to hold true to divine revelation as the one source for theological truth, as revealed in Christ and the witness of the Bible via the illumination of the Holy Spirit. The better question (better

---

3   Everett M. Rogers and Judith K. Larsen, *Silicon Valley Fever: Growth of High-Technology Culture* (New York: Basic Books, 1984); Michael S. Malone, *Betting It All: The Entrepreneurs of Technology* (New York: Wiley, 2002); Michael S. Malone, *Bill and Dave: How Hewlett and Packard Built the World's Greatest Company* (New York: Portfolio, 2007); W. Isaacson, *Steve Jobs* (New York: Simon and Schuster, 2011).

4   This experimental approach to theological investigation corresponds to the *theologia experimentalis* endorsed by Jürgen Moltmann as a path to discovery of theological wisdom through dialogical engagement with modern culture and science: Jürgen Moltmann, *Science and Wisdom*, Margaret Kohl (trans.) (London: SCM, 2003), 7.

than Tertullian's) would be this: when we look with eyes of faith, what do we see in the story of Silicon Valley which might quicken our understanding and enrich our faith? My thesis is that we can indeed discover worthy theological lessons through the sort of experimental theology entailed in this exploration. Wisdom is also available from these lessons, as we learn to apply them faithfully to the real-world challenges of cultivating healthy communities of work and building shalom into our civil economy.[5]

In short, this chapter hopes to gain theological insights through this study of the entrepreneurial ethos displayed in Silicon Valley which could provide practical lessons for society and business enterprise, and to help the church exegete the culture for the sake of faithful preaching of the gospel and ministry effectiveness.[6]

A Pisgah View of the "Valley of the Heart's Delight"

When the ancient Israelites heard about God's promise of a land flowing with milk and honey they might well have imagined something like the Santa Clara Valley as it was in the late nineteenth century and into the early decades of the twentieth century. This scenic valley stretching from the Stanford land tract down to San Jose was gifted with such a pleasing climate and fertile land that it became an agricultural paradise known during the early 1900s as, "Valley of the Heart's Delight." The nickname has stuck to the present day, although the apricot, cherry and almond blossoms have been largely replaced by industrial parks producing a very different kind of fruit—silicon microchips at first, and then also the computers and software that utilize them.

The story of the microchip has been well told by others and it does not need repeating here. The one historical theme I would like to consider however is the extent to which the establishment of Silicon Valley parallels the narrative of the Israelites as they crested Mount Pisgah and entered the Promised Land. This is a precarious comparison, of course, because the technology entrepreneurs were set on a decidedly mundane and irreligious quest. The most poignant similarities

---

    5   For a rich theological discussion of the idea of civil economy, see Luigino Bruni and Stefano Zamagni, *Civil Economy: Efficiency, Equity, and Public Happiness* (New York: Peter Lang, 2007). See also Steven Garber, *Visions of Vocation: Common Grace for the Common Good* (Downers Grove: InterVarsity Press, 2014).

    6   See a similar emphasis in Alister E. McGrath, "The Cultivation of Theological Vision: Theological Attentiveness and the Practice of Ministry," in *Perspectives on Ecclesiology and Ethnography*, Pete Ward (ed.), (Grand Rapids: Eerdmans, 2012), 107–23.

between the two stories are likely to be found in roots of their failure, rather than in the conditions which led to their flourishing; nonetheless, we can see interesting correlations in the settings of their entry into new lands. There is an "exodus" theme here common to many people who migrated into California in search of a fresh start in a fertile land. In the case of the technology pioneers, they occupied the beautiful agricultural landscape of the Santa Clara Valley, thereby driving out most of the extant farming communities. This harkens back to the manner of the Israelites dispossessing the extant peoples of Canaan. The similarities continue with the Deuteronomic themes of blessing and curse. Just as the Israelites forgot to honor God as the source of their material wealth and blessings (Deut. 8:17), the success of the technology pioneers fosters a culture of wealth-seeking techno-idolatry in which many ventures have collapsed in hubris. The culture instilled by the pioneering founders of Fairchild Semiconductor and its spinoffs—the so-called "Fairchildren"[7]—thus are rich in lessons which can be traced to the Torah, especially Deuteronomy.

Let's consider the parallels. Both the Israelites and the Silicon Valley founders were refugees—the former from enslavement under Pharaoh in Egypt, and the latter from more hospitable but nonetheless hierarchical corporate powers of East Coast capitalists. These modern-day refugees hailed largely from the Midwest. They were leaving behind the dominant business culture of corporate America and setting off to create a new type of company—a community of work organized around a mission. They were not beholden to the hierarchies and customs of established corporations headquartered "back East." They were risk-takers. They were entering a new geography, a new fruit-bearing land, in fact, with a clear directive to establish a new type of community which had never before been seen on the face of the earth. They needed a new type of leadership also—a humble leader styled in the form of a shepherd, a servant leader rather than a feudal land-owning king. They had to establish new norms of behavior also: rules and customs, and methods of sharing responsibility in their collaborative work in new forms of business organizations. In all these ways the adventures of the "Fairchildren" parallel the adventures, opportunities and risks facing the children of Israel as they entered the valley viewed from Mount Pisgah.

In making these comparisons, I choose to focus on the example of the entrepreneurs who founded Fairchild Semiconductor in 1957 and later abandoned it in the process of begetting the family tree of Silicon Valley

---

7   "Thirty-one semiconductor firms were started in Silicon Valley in the 1960s, and the majority traced their lineage to Fairchild." Saxenian, *Regional Advantage*, 26; and see Saxenian, *The New Argonauts*, 28.

technology companies. Fairchild itself was founded in precisely such an exodus of engineer-entrepreneurs who revolted against the domineering style and lack of management skill demonstrated by their previous boss, William Shockley, Nobel laureate and founder of Shockley Semiconductor—the first company in the Santa Clara Valley aimed at capitalizing on the newly discovered properties of the materials known as "semiconductors." Shockley's core team of young PhDs resigned en masse in order to set out on their own, and thus earned their nickname as the "Traitorous Eight."[8] They invested $3,500 of their own money in the risky venture of developing a new transistor technology based on unproven but promising properties of silicon. In a matter of months they managed to raise an additional $1.5 million investment from the tycoon Sherman Fairchild, and thus Fairchild Semiconductor was born on October 1, 1957.

Fairchild Semiconductor and its offspring, the "Fairchildren," were not the first technology startups in the region. That history begins more properly in 1912, when Cyril Elwell, a Stanford graduate, joined the Federal Telegraph Corporation (FTC) based in Palo Alto, and developed new radio transmission technologies.[9] Then in the 1930s Bill Hewlett and David Packard founded the company that bears their name. Hewlett-Packard has earned the status of being the most famous garage startup of them all. From their humble beginnings in a garage, Hewlett and Packard grew their company to become a multibillion-dollar global leader in computers and instrumentation. Perhaps their most admirable legacy is the corporate culture they brought to life in the form of the "HP Way"—widely known throughout the industry as an "enlightened model of doing business built on trust."[10] Bill and Dave (as they were affectionately known) espoused a purpose for their corporation which transcended the profit motive. Packard explained the higher motive of their corporation in terms of a desire "to make a contribution to society."[11] By word and deed they dedicated themselves to creating a corporate culture that placed supreme value in the dignity of employees and customer relationships.

---

[8]　The "Traitorous Eight" were Gordon E. Moore, C. Sheldon Roberts, Eugene Kleiner, Robert N. Noyce, Victor H. Grinich, Julius Blank, Jean A. Hoerni and Jay T. Last (http://www.fairchildsemi.com/company/history/# [accessed November 23, 2013]).

[9]　T.J. Sturgeon, "How Silicon Valley came to Be," in *Understanding Silicon: The Anatomy of an Entrepreneurial Region*, Martin Kenny (ed.), (Stanford: Stanford University Press, 2000), 19–20; and see Rogers and Larsen, *Silicon Valley Fever*, 30–1.

[10]　Michael S. Malone, *The Valley of Heart's Delight: a Silicon Valley Notebook, 1963–2001* (New York: John Wiley & Sons, 2002), 21.

[11]　Charles Handy, *The Hungry Spirit: Beyond Capitalism: a Quest for Purpose in the Modern World* (New York: Broadway Books, 1998), 71.

In many ways, HP embodies those qualities which are most admirable within the spirit and culture of Silicon Valley, and they have done so in an enduring and remarkably successful fashion.[12] They also have pride of place, having preceded Fairchild by almost 20 years. Why then should this study choose to focus our attention on the "Traitorous Eight" and the more tumultuous history of Fairchild and the Fairchildren, rather than on the culture of Hewlett-Packard? Because the singular item that grabs the immediate attention with laser-sharp focus is the *entrepreneurial energy and spirit of Silicon Valley*. This energy shines most incandescently in the adventures of the "Traitorous Eight" and the many entrepreneurs who have adopted their ethos and followed in their footsteps. Fairchild Semiconductor and the companies spawned from its success stand out as the prime exemplars and progenitors of the industry's entrepreneurial ethos. I agree with the assessment of Rogers and Larsen who point out "the most pronounced characteristic of Silicon Valley: its freewheeling high-energy entrepreneurial drive."[13] This energy created 31 semiconductor firms in Silicon Valley in the 1960s, and the majority of these trace their lineage to Fairchild.[14]

Reflections of the *Imago Dei*

The creative aspect of entrepreneurial activity may be considered a mark of the *imago Dei* in human nature. Human creativity corresponds analogically to God's creative energy and acts. From the earliest artwork of cave dwellers, artistry is seen to lie very close to the heart and origins of human nature. Art, music, poetry, and ingenuity are distinctive capabilities of humanity made in God's image. These creative talents point to that ineffable source of willful creative inspiration within the *humanum*—the essential character which makes humans *human*. Following gardening and animal husbandry, the artistic crafts are the first occupations named in the Bible. In Exodus, the Spirit of God fills Oholiab and Bezalel with intelligence, knowledge and craftsmanship (Ex. 31:1–11) and calls them to create beautiful works for worship. Scripture links God's Spirit directly to the creative arts in craftsmanship. The inspiration of craftsmanship here is directed explicitly for production of the tabernacle and objects for use in worship. While the focus here is on worship, the workmanship is applicable to all trades—"all manner of

---

12   For an extended discussion of this see: Michael S. Malone, *Bill and Dave*, (New York: Portfolio, 2007); David Packard, David Kirby, and Karen R. Lewis, *The HP Way: How Bill Hewlett and I Built our Company* (New York: Harper, 1995).

13   Rogers and Larsen, *Silicon Valley Fever*, 41.

14   Saxenian, *Regional Advantage*, 26.

workmanship" (Ex. 31:5)—and thus suggests that the source and inspiration of all kinds of creative workmanship are by the Spirit of God.

We may presume that creativity in general points to God as the ultimate and primordial Creator and as the source of all creativity.[15] The arts and crafts are the most obvious expression of this creative element in human nature, yet these are by no means the only forms of creativity attributable to the *imago Dei*. Creativity is required to the daily functions of life—decision-making and adaptation to each new circumstance demands some sort of creative response. By no means then do I mean to suggest that an entrepreneurial spirit of the Silicon Valley sort is somehow a superior or more relevant expression of the creative component of the *imago Dei*. Neither is entrepreneurial creativity to be equated with divine creativity or the fulfillment of human potential. The Silicon Valley flavor of creativity which here occupies our attention is merely one sort of potential witness to the gifts and talents engendered by the *imago Dei* in humankind.

Although the creative aspect of the *imago Dei* may be discerned in all sorts of activities, there remains something particularly interesting about the sort of entrepreneurial creativity on display in the Silicon Valley ethos, for no other reason than the far-reaching influence it has upon society at large through business and technological developments, leadership styles, corporate cultures, and aspirations for wealth and success. Theological interpretation of the Silicon Valley ethos thus may be presumed to offer edifying insights into human nature, the spirituality of work and organizational behavior.

What makes this inquiry more than a simple observation on the connection between human ingenuity and the glory of creativity reflected in the *imago Dei*? My thesis is that there is more on display here than a merely generic creativity. The distinctiveness of the innovative spirit of Silicon Valley, as compared to artistic endeavors in general, is *the focused investment of creative energy into inventive problem-solving for the good of the broader community*. This is the distinctive contribution which entrepreneurial activity gives to human flourishing, and this gift of creative energy is conveyed in four specific traits:

1. Innovation: there is an element of clever inventiveness in the application of technology.
2. Intentionality: there is a concern to provide something, a product or service, which makes a desirable contribution to society.

---

[15]   For a recent discussion of this, see Steven R. Guthrie, *Creator Spirit: The Holy Spirit and the Art of Becoming Human* (Grand Rapids: Baker, 2011).

3. Pragmatism: these innovations must be delivered in an economically feasible business model that yields tangible benefits for society. Mere creativity and inventiveness, no matter how artistic or original, are not enough.
4. Newness: these businesses offer benefits that in many cases are so new that they open up unforeseen opportunities for customers and society in general, occasionally offering solutions to problems previously unrecognized.

These four traits are not unique to Silicon Valley entrepreneurs. These are generally found to some degree in most entrepreneurial businesses. Nonetheless, the accumulated momentum and singular excellence of Silicon Valley in displaying these directions calls for interpretation. There seems to be lessons that can be learned from focused attention to the Valley's ethos.

By highlighting these four traits I do not mean to imply that they are normative or sufficient to yield beneficial or virtuous outcomes. Indeed, the creation of new products and the commercialization of new technologies is a two-edged sword, leading frequently to new problems and potentially creating desires for products which make dubious contributions to the quality of human life.[16] The silicon chip, for example, has generated countless boons to society, such as online libraries and life-saving medical devices, yet it has also engendered violent video games and addictive behaviors. Furthermore, newness for newness sake is a bland and meaningless sort of creativity that can hardly be considered a witness to divine creativity. God creates with divine intentionality to bring goodness into existence. Human creativity inevitably falls short of this ultimate good. We can however see that the human creativity on display in entrepreneurial activity may be aligned with God's intentionality when it is aimed at bringing genuine benefit to the broader society.

The ultimate goodness of God's creation extends beyond beauty and artistry—as conveyed in the praises of Psalm 19, for example—and are revealed in the overarching purposes and intentionality for which God creates. Covenantal relationships of God with humankind, and humans with one another provide the source, direction and context of divine creativity. Relationships which bear witness to the love and covenantal community that flow from the trinitarian God are the basis for recognition of the deep beauty inherent in creation.

---

[16]   J.K. Galbraith articulated this trend in the free market and called it "the dependence effect." His analysis anticipated many of the deleterious effects of consumer society. John Kenneth Galbraith, *The Affluent Society* (Boston: Houghton Mifflin, 1958).

Barth's treatment of this topic in his exploration of human nature is helpful for our purpose: "Covenant is the internal basis of creation" and creation is the "external basis of the covenant."[17] Thus Wolf Krötke concludes: "Creation is structured by God in such a way that it is suitable for the accomplishment of the covenant."[18] This implicit aspect of covenantal intention within creation also finds an analog in the creative spirit of entrepreneurship. We may even say that human creativity corresponds to divine creativity to the extent which it bears witness to God's purposes as the context in which to behold beauty. Since this context includes the intentional invigoration of covenantal relationship, we may suppose that entrepreneurial creativity may also bear witness to the dominion given humankind to serve as co-creators through stewardship of the Garden (Gen. 2). To the extent which creative works are aimed at bringing a boon to humanity or to the world in general, we may say they point to the divine source of creativity bestowed through the *imago Dei*. How fitting then that the Santa Clara Valley earned the nickname "Valley of the Heart's Delight" based on its garden of agricultural delights! Agriculture and entrepreneurial culture each cultivate products to delight the heart, provide sustenance, and reveal the beauty inherent in God's creativity and covenantal intentions. Perhaps the very prolificacy of the Santa Clara Valley, a place where nature seems to collaborate with every gardener's efforts to grow any fruit, contributes in some fashion to the business climate which nurtures the creative impulses entrepreneurs need to attempt to grow every new idea.

Alongside the witness to the *imago Dei* and covenantal community, of consideration is also the deleterious aspects of Silicon Valley culture, and there are several: the unwholesome pursuit of mammon, the frenzied culture of attainment and fleeting success, the pursuit of goals built of hubris, and the confusion of spirituality with ego-driven philosophies. Before offering some theological reflection on these issues, there is value in continuing to probe the potential correspondence between the innovative spirit of the Silicon Valley and aspects of creativity and relationality which bear witness to the *imago Dei* and covenantal community.

---

[17] Karl Barth, *Church Dogmatics*, G.W. Bromiley (trans.) (London: T&T Clark, 1936–1977), III/1, 94ff.

[18] Wolf Krötke, "The humanity of the human person in Karl Barth's anthropology," in *The Cambridge Companion to Karl Barth*, John Webster (ed.), (Cambridge: Cambridge University Press, 2000), 167.

Homo Innovaticus

It seems an easy step to connect human creativity with the *imago Dei*. Indeed, the Bible begins with a straightforward depiction of God as a creative worker. To describe human nature in similar terms seems obvious enough. But what is more subtly on display in the ethos of Silicon Valley, and also more poignant with respect to the *imago Dei*, is that God's creative acts are to be understood as being *creatio ex nihilo*. To speak of *creatio ex nihilo* is to declare a supernatural reality; it is to declare a discontinuity with everything that has come before. There is a radical newness here. For *creatio ex nihilo* to occur it is necessary and essential to think a thought that has never been thought before. Furthermore, this creativity is displayed not in the application of power or might to manipulate nature, but rather in a mere speech-act. The only identifiable "event" in the history of the creative act is that the Creator spoke it, and therefore willed it to be so. This understanding of the creation story of Genesis 1 serves quite well to describe also the special nuances of the essence of the Silicon Valley's innovative spirit.

Of course human productivity of every kind is categorically different from God's *creatio ex nihilo*. Human inventions are produced within history, and with extant materials, and are thus certainly not *ex nihilo*. Nonetheless, there can be a certain correspondence to the creative speech-acts of entrepreneurial creation and God's creation. This correspondence can be seen most easily in the intangible speech-act component of innovation—innovation in the realm of ideas, and not just any sort of ideas, but ideas which generate new material blessings which seem to spring from sheer inventiveness. Innovators delight in conceiving a new idea, or designing a new computer chip, or coding a new algorithm, or delivering a new networking opportunity, when no such thing existed before they thought of it. Is there not some freshness mimicking God's acts of *ex nihilo* creation here in the sheer inventiveness of such innovation? And is there not some meaningful (although creaturely) correspondence to the divine *creatio ex nihilo*? I would suggest that there is something to be learned here about the essence of the *imago Dei* by studying ordinary creaturely sorts of creativity.

We might say the same for creative crafts and fine arts also. Here too there is an aspect of newness and discontinuity with what has gone before. And here too there is a transcendent component to the creative act itself in the souls of both the artist and the admirer. As much as art reflects and depends upon the beauty of God's creation, the creative acts of entrepreneurship correspond to God's creativity in a way that art does not—they fulfill a willful purpose of tangible function, and that tangibility exists for the sake of God's purposes for human flourishing. This combination of radical newness and tangible contribution to human flourishing distinguishes the innovative spirit of entrepreneurism as a remarkably vivid demonstration of the ways in which human creativity can be seen to conform to God's creativity.

The pragmatic aspect of this activity aimed at delivering tangible benefits to society through economic exchange differentiates it from the fine arts, and herein we find a correspondence between divine creativity and the spirit of innovation—both are aimed intentionally at the creation of tangible value. Of course the fine arts also yield values which can be measured by economics, but the difference in entrepreneurial activity is that products themselves have tangible, material, functional benefits, and these benefits are reproducible via business activity that transcends the inventor and exceeds the personal expression of the entrepreneur.

This value is recognized via economic exchange. The free market is an "instrument whose purpose is to deliver social benefits," and it is from within the economic sphere of the market that the innovative spirit of Silicon Valley shines a light on "the better part of human nature," in the words of Edmund Phelps, Nobel laureate in Economics.[19] Phelps approaches the topic of human nature through the lens of economics, and comes to the conclusion that at the core of human nature, at the heart of the *imago*, there lives an innovator, a Creator of radically new, useful and tangible benefits for humankind and for all nature. To speak of the *humanum* therefore requires discussion of the innovative spirit: "[T]he positive moral content of economics [is] to realize an anthropology that starts with innovative human nature: *homo innovaticus*, not *homo economicus*."[20]

This conception of *homo innovaticus* as the better part of human nature surely conveys a more theologically useful notion than the idea of *homo economicus*, an idea popularized in twentieth-century economics based on the idea that human nature can be reduced to consciously utilitarian decisions that aim to maximize happiness. The overwhelming flaw in that idea of human nature is that the quintessential *humanness* of human kind *cannot be reduced* to economic functions but rather has to be understood in a larger context of spirituality expressed in and through relationships with one another and with God.

We would be hard-pressed to find more noteworthy specimens of *homo innovaticus* than the "Traitorous Eight" who left Fairchild Semiconductor with the dream and passion to develop products of tangible value in precisely the

---

[19] Edmund Phelps, "Economic Justice and the Spirit of Innovation," *First Things* (October 2009), 27–31.

[20] Phelps cites Silicon Valley as an exemplary model of this sort of innovation, and concludes that "capitalism's dynamism offers to human experience and human benefit the true moral dimension of economics ... [and] it allows human beings to realize their true nature as creators and innovators" ("Economic Justice and the Spirit of Innovation," 31).

sort of creative act that shines a light on the better part of human nature. Their creativity is conveyed through the shared ethos of a community of work, and their efforts are impelled by a shared dream of achieving something never done before in order to deliver valuable products to society.

The dream-like aspirations of their enterprise is iconic; it echoes through the dreams of so many others who arrived in California dreaming of adventures and financial rewards. Their attempts to do what had never been done before epitomize the culture. Their visionary dreams seem to be a crucial feature of the Silicon Valley mystique. Kevin Starr finds that "the communal belief in a fast and lavish future, together with a dream of perpetual youth, was at the core of Silicon Valley, where there thrived an abiding sense that it had all first happened here and that it had changed the world." He describes it as

> an enchanted, transformed place, another part of the forest, Shakespearean in magic, resistant to replication. Here, in this crowded portion of the coast of dreams, its housing prices soaring and its Porsche dealerships out of stock, had been nurtured not only the technology of the globe but also a dream of endless youth and creativity. It was not about the money, nor was it about the fame. It was about the thing itself—the dream, the thrill, the rush of being wired.[21]

In addition to the above observations concerning the *imago Dei* and the spirit of innovation, there are also theological insights concerning community to be gleaned from the story of these tech pioneers. Perhaps the most significant of these is to see how their work relationships display traits of covenantal and missional community. There is a component of spirituality in their organizational behavior. This is the next topic to be examined in the case of the Traitorous Eight.

Covenantal and Missional Community

"There are a lot of people who come to work in the morning believing that they work for Silicon Valley."[22] From the outset, the founders of Silicon Valley recognized that their mission was entirely dependent upon their interdependence. It was a team effort, which sounds trite today when language of teamwork has become commonplace in business vernacular. But the Fairchild

---

21   Starr, *Coast of Dreams*, 32.

22   Wilfred Corrigan, founder of LSI Logic, quoted by John Markoff, "Silicon Valley Faces a Midlife Crisis," *New York Times*, September 28, 1992, C1, C5. See also Saxenian, *Regional Advantage*, 37.

entrepreneurs created a style and culture of teamwork that had hitherto been exceedingly rare in their industry. They intentionally broke down the hierarchy of their predecessors and emphasized the horizontal management style that has become a pattern admired in Silicon Valley. By examining the way in which they created a new style of work, new structures and new management practices for their organizations, we can discover how the biblical concept and embodiment of covenantal community yields valuable lessons for all sorts of enterprise.

Perhaps no one has written more poetically of this matter of "covenantal community" than Tom Wolfe in his tribute to Bob Noyce and the dawn of Silicon Valley.[23] In Wolfe's telling the story begins with Josiah Grinnell, the young pastor to whom Horace Greeley uttered the famous words, "Go West young man, go West." And so he did—to Iowa, where he founded a congregational community which went on to become the town of Grinnell, hometown of Bob Noyce. In Wolfe's lyrical telling, Grinnell's congregants "opened up the virgin land in a common struggle out on the frontier. They had given up the comforts of the East ... in order to create a City of Light in the name of the Lord." These people trusted not only in the strengths of their faith, but also in the value of education, especially engineering. The values near to the hearts of these pioneers—congregational community, piety, education and ingenuity—became the fertile soil from which Bob Noyce emerged. The cultural values of Grinnell, Iowa, carried forth in the ethos of Bob Noyce and his fellow engineer-entrepreneurs, proved to be a key ingredient in the formation of Silicon Valley. This ethos contributed a form of spiritual capital that has shaped the new communities of work they established. Wolfe finds more than a hint of "Dissenting Protestantism" in the spirit of Silicon Valley:

> Oh yes! What a treasure, indeed, was the moral capital of the nineteenth century? Noyce happened to grow up in a family in which the long-forgotten light of Dissenting Protestantism still burned brightly. The light, the light at the apex of every human soul! Ironically, it was that long-forgotten light ... from out of the churchy, blue-nosed sticks ... that led the world into the twenty-first century, across the electric grid and into space .... [Noyce's] is the last generation to have grown up in families where the light existed in anything approaching a pure state. And yet out in the Silicon Valley *some* sort of light shines still.[24]

---

23   Tom Wolfe, "The Tinkerings of Robert Noyce: How the Sun Rose on the Silicon Valley," *Esquire Magazine* (December 1983), 346–74; see http://www.stanford.edu/class/e140/e140a/content/noyce.html (accessed November 24, 2013).

24   Wolfe, "The Tinkerings of Robert Noyce."

Wolfe describes the "spiritual ecstasy" Grinnell and his friends must have felt as they "bought up five thousand acres of land in order to start a new congregational community the way he thought it should be done. A City of Light!"[25] This language is high and fanciful, but how else can one describe the exhilaration of making a fresh start and planting community roots in religious faith with a sense of gathering greatness in joining a divine appointment in a new fertile land?

Writing in the 1980s, when the semiconductor firms founded by the Fairchildren still dominated the economics and power of the Silicon Valley, Wolfe marveled at how the leaders of these young companies would "talk about the soul and spiritual vision as if it were the most natural subject in the world for a well-run company to be concerned about."[26]

Admittedly, Noyce was not a religious man. In this also he is an archetype for the entrepreneurs and engineers of Silicon Valley who followed him—few have ever acknowledged religious faith in any significant way as a factor in their success or as a foundation for their corporate cultures. Nonetheless, they are apt to appreciate the willful creativity of the human soul that shines in their management philosophies. Their corporate cultures likewise bear witness to innovation and the importance of creating work environments conducive to the relational and creative aspects of human nature. Even though most of these leaders might deny the religious connotations of the word "soul," they speak proudly of the "soul" of their companies using transcendent language which invokes biblical meanings. The nurture of employee spirituality has even become an explicit goal and responsibility in some firms. Google is a prime example of this trend. One of the most popular classes offered at the Googleplex is a course in spirituality taught by Chade-Meng Tan, a brilliant engineer, practitioner of Zen-like disciplines, and Google employee number 107.[27] His class is aimed at the care of soul. Even though the precepts taught are distinctly Buddhist, there is a witness here of some sort to the ineluctable connections between the human spirit, entrepreneurship and corporate responsibility.

It is safe to say that the Valley's links to Dissenting Protestantism have become obscured during the past 50 years, but they were still present in the 1980s when Intel Corporation still seemed to embody everything good about Silicon Valley's culture of innovation. Times have changed, putting some distance between the Fairchildren and the new generation of start-ups. Silicon Valley has continued to

---

25   Wolfe, "The Tinkerings of Robert Noyce."
26   Wolfe, "The Tinkerings of Robert Noyce."
27   Caitlin Kelly, "O.K., Google, Take a Deep Breath," *New York Times*, April 28, 2012, http://www.nytimes.com/2012/04/29/technology/google-course-asks-employees-to-take-a-deep-breath.html?pagewanted=all (accessed August 13, 2013).

grow geometrically as new waves of immigrants have brought fresh energy and new cultural interpretations to California. Nonetheless, there lingers a distinct remnant of the original ethos established by Noyce and his generation.

Before turning to explore the ways in which Silicon Valley corporate cultures display these spiritual realities, I will offer a closing observation on the parallel between the story of the Israelites and the story of Fairchild and the "Traitorous Eight." If we were to compare the early Silicon Valley entrepreneurs to the Israelites, it seems safe to say Robert Noyce would best fit the role of Moses. Noyce displayed the heart of a servant-leader. He is remembered as much for his self-effacing character and the egalitarian, participatory culture that he left behind as his legacy at Intel, as for his technological achievements and patents. Noyce and his business partners established a new corporate culture unlike any seen before. They left behind the hierarchical power structures of corporate America favored in the East, and deliberately established a new way of doing business—a new admixture of meritocracy and democracy, in which exemplary leaders did not lord power over their underlings, but rather emphasized communal responsibility to corporate mission. And that corporate mission was measured not so much in terms of profit as in terms of creating valuable products and building a company with shared values. This culture became for them a kind of moral or spiritual capital to be invested in building organizations as a worthy legacy.

Now we ought not to over-spiritualize the Silicon Valley culture. Neither is there any justification here (or anywhere) for hagiography. As previously noted, Noyce and his colleagues espoused no explicitly religious purpose or belief. The entrepreneurs and their supporting cast of lawyers, venture capitalists, recruiters, and other specialists have always thrived on the fast pace of aggressive competition. Nonetheless, there was something new in the management style of the silicon pioneers, and the parallel to Moses is instructive because of his archetypal example of the humble servant-leader. We can see these qualities clearly in Noyce, along with his idiosyncrasies and frailties. Michael Malone has spent his professional life in journalism chronicling the culture of Silicon Valley and he sums up Noyce in these terms:

> In person, Noyce was not a commanding figure. He was a relatively small man, with a rumbling voice and the compact build of aging athlete. He was genial and unaffected, swore with care, and had a keen sense of irony that would result in a chuckle and crooked grin like that of a mischievous schoolboy.[28]

---

[28] Malone, *Betting It All*, 73.

Noyce is famous for eschewing any trappings of positional power or affluence. He insisted on using the same old beat-up secondhand metal desk throughout his time at Intel and he eliminated the pretense of fancy offices.[29] From the top down, everyone at Intel worked in a maze of cubicles built from movable partitions. These temporary structures symbolically resemble the nomadic tents and tabernacle of the Exodus tribe. This lack of permanence keeps people in a perpetual state of openness to new ideas, new structures, and the changes which are surely coming. These symbols are also sincere expressions of equality. There was no false modesty in them. The unpretentious furniture and open architecture were matched by the democratic and participatory spirit of the organization. The resulting ethos of shared values and community spirit combined with a fast-paced innovative climate are the enduring legacy of Robert Noyce, Bill Hewlett, David Packard and so many other Silicon Valley pioneers. "Fairchild, thanks to Noyce, would become the most democratic company of its generation," says Mike Malone in his summation of a lifetime of observing the Silicon Valley culture. "It is difficult now, when the Silicon Valley management style is so firmly incorporated into our culture, to fully appreciate the courage of Noyce's decision [to start a new company]"[30]

Since the 1980s the number of startups founded by immigrants from overseas has increased dramatically. Entrepreneurs from India and China have become a significant factor in the Valley's growth, as seen in the establishment of more than 30 immigrant professional and technical associations by 2004.[31] These immigrant entrepreneurs bring cultures far different from that of the Midwesterners of Noyce's generation, but they share the commonality of being newcomers in a new region, and they take on similar characteristics in terms of the innovative style that has become rooted in Silicon Valley. There is a common aspect of shared commitment to the corporation as a mission-oriented community of work.

There is also a shared commitment to the overall community—a culture of collaboration "in a process of mutually beneficial bootstrapping, which some refer to as 'growing up together.'"[32] In contrast to the industrial models of previous generations, this new culture of work established at Fairchild and Intel was "collegial, entrepreneurial, nonhierarchical, with long hours and no frills,"

---

29 Wolfe, "The Tinkerings of Robert Noyce."
30 Malone, *Betting It All*, 71.
31 Saxenian, *The New Argonauts*, 59.
32 Saxenian, *The New Argonauts*, 42.

having a distinctive ambience and ethos reminiscent of a university research laboratory.[33]

Tom Wolfe notices the critically important role this new form of community plays in nurturing the innovative spirit of entrepreneurs working to bring a boon to humankind. Bob Noyce leads his people into this new community of work and together they set in motion a new form of society, in stark contrast to the "feudal approach to organization" seen in the East.[34]

> Corporations in the East adopted the feudal approach to organization .... There were kings and lords, and there were vassals, soldiers, yeoman, and serfs, with layers of protocol and perquisites, such as the car and driver, to symbolize superiority and establish the boundary lines .... Noyce ... [r]ejected the idea of a social hierarchy at Fairchild .... Everywhere the Fairchild émigrés went, they took the Noyce approach with them. It wasn't enough to start up a company; you had to start a community, a community in which there were no social distinctions, and it was first-come, first-served in the parking lot, and everyone was supposed to internalize the common goals. The atmosphere of the new companies was so democratic, it startled businessmen from the East.[35]

In her ground-breaking study of the differences between the East Coast ways of Boston's Route 128 high-tech corridor and Silicon Valley, Saxenian sums up the unique ethos cultivated by Noyce and Hewlett and Packard:

> Long before it was fashionable, William Hewlett and David Packard, and later Intel's Robert Noyce, pioneered management styles based on teamwork, openness, and participation. Even as their firms grew large, they strove to preserve the openness, intensity, and sense of purpose that had characterized working life in early Silicon Valley start-ups.[36]

The HP Way is described as "a participative management style that supports, even demands, individual freedom and initiative while emphasizing commonness of purpose and teamwork." While Intel's culture was notably less paternalistic than HP's was in the lifetimes of their founders, both companies were similar in their disdain for hierarchical power, and in their commitment to egalitarian teamwork. The distinctive characteristics on display in these cultures

---

[33] Starr, *Coast of Dreams*, 273.
[34] Saxenian, *Regional Advantage*, 29.
[35] Wolfe, "The Tinkerings of Robert Noyce."
[36] Saxenian, *Regional Advantage*, 50.

are directly attributable to the personal styles and values of their founders. While it might be tempting to explain away these nuances of the Silicon Valley ethos as merely pragmatic necessities forced upon them by the demands of developing complex new technologies, that explanation fails to account for the persistent differences with other high-technology companies elsewhere in America and around the world.

> But the differences between these economies ran deeper than variations of style and attire. While Silicon Valley and Route 128 companies advanced similar technologies and competed in similar markets, the organization of production in the two regions diverged from the earliest days. Initial differences in social structures and industrial practices laid the foundation for the creation of two distinct industrial systems.[37]

There is no simple explanation for the Silicon Valley success story. Every plausible factor has been considered as an explanation for the Valley's remarkable competitive advantage—economics, history, politics, legal, investment, educational and social infrastructure. None of these offers a robust explanation. Each attempt to identify and codify the ingredients which have made the "Valley of the Heart's Delight" the world's most productive "maternity ward" for innovative companies fails to account for its giftedness in birthing and nurturing the next generation.[38] Analysis based in the quantifiable variables comes off as insufficient.[39] Neither are explanations based on the special charms of California—say, climate, beauty, or the real possibility of being able to sun-bathe, surf and snow ski in a single day—sufficient to explain why so many entrepreneurs thrive there. Nor does the earlier leadership of California in several other technologies account for the Valley's difference.[40] Every attempt

---

[37]   Saxenian, *Regional Advantage*, 29.

[38]   Albert Bruno, professor of marketing at Santa Clara University, has studied Silicon Valley business for decades. He describes the Valley's infrastructure in these terms. Rogers and Larsen, *Silicon Valley Fever*, 47–8.

[39]   For a helpful collection of essays considering many of the key factors in Silicon Valley infrastructure, see Kenney (ed.), *Understanding Silicon Valley*. A notable essay within this volume concludes that Silicon Valley represents "a vastly different kind of social capital than that popularized by the civic engagement theorists" (Stephen S. Cohen and Gary Fields, "Social Capital and Capital Gains: An Examination of Social Capital in Silicon Valley," 191).

[40]   Kevin Starr surveys the remarkable technological prowess of the state, and puts the "scientific and technological virtuosity" of Silicon Valley within the context of California's earlier world-class success in geology, mining, astronomy and aviation. Kevin Starr, *California: A History* (New York: Random House, 2005), 259.

to formulate the "secret ingredient" of the Silicon Valley's success falls into reductionism.[41]

Critical Theological Assessments

The innovative and entrepreneurial spirit of Silicon Valley embodies a living history which bears witness to the ineffable yet recognizable presence of a special sort of creative activity and a special form of community in which this activity takes place. The very ineffability of its ethos points to spiritual reality. The innovative spirit of this ethos models both the creative aspect of the *imago Dei* as well as a biblical understanding of covenantal community.

This witness to spiritual reality does not present a totally positive picture, however. Side by side with the many favorable and laudable aspects of Silicon Valley spirituality and culture, there are also many unfavorable and unattractive characteristics which bear the stain of sin in humanity.

The Cult of Mammon

The obvious style of fallen-ness specific to Silicon Valley is observed in the cult of mammon. The allure of wealth is a temptation common to all financial endeavors. This is the distasteful fruit of avarice. The newfound wealth of Silicon Valley propagates the gold-driven dreams of the Golden State. These dreams have survived successive waves of upheaval and disruption in technology and global markets, and the Silicon Valley has demonstrated a surprising robustness in its ability to produce millionaires from scratch. "During the heady days of glory prior to the collapse of internet and computer company fortunes in the so-called 'dot-com' bust at the turn of the millennium, Silicon Valley was generating about sixty millionaires per week."[42]

The tragic story of Dennis Barnhart is an iconic reminder that worldly riches are fleeting and empty pursuits. The 40-year old president of Eagle Computer was made a millionaire by his company's IPO on June 8, 1983, but Barnhart died a few hours after the his stock went public, as he drove his red Ferrari through

---

[41] The essays in Kenney (ed.), *Understanding Silicon Valley*, are helpful in explicating the wide range of special ingredients to be considered—historical factors, legal infrastructure, access to venture capital, defense contracts, university Research and Development, and various conflicting concepts of "social capital"—as well as the insufficiency of any formulaic approach as a recipe to explain the essential source of the Silicon Valley's spirit of innovation.

[42] Starr, *Coast of Dreams*, 274.

a guard rail and into a ravine a block away from his company headquarters in Los Gatos.[43] His story is legendary in the Valley. Yet for every sad reminder that the pursuit of worldly riches is ultimately void significance, the perennial siren song of mammon continues to inspire California dreams.

Even so, we should avoid drawing hasty conclusions that equate mammon with the spirit of innovation. At its core, there is a more worthy motive which beats in the hearts of most entrepreneurs. It is not cash which inspires them, but achievement. This too can become a form of idolatry by paying undue homage to human skill, placing worship at the altar of egoism. But the idea that the money drives the entrepreneurial spirit is a myth. At root, the innovative spirit is not driven by money. Of course money is essential for business, and "cash is king" is a popular aphorism among venture capitalists and entrepreneurs. This is a nuts-and-bolts common-sense pertaining to the challenge of getting a business off the ground. But it's not the root of the entrepreneurial spirit. More important than money is simply *the entrepreneurial spirit*. Entrepreneurship is the secret ingredient, the chief asset, and singular advantage of Silicon Valley. Leading venture capitalist and founder of Sequoia Capital, Donald Valentine debunks the myth that money drives the Silicon Valley: "Too many people think that the criticality in the environment is the money. For me the criticality in the environment are the entrepreneurs."[44]

In addition to the availability of money there are many factors necessary for the success of the Silicon Valley's enterprises—technological talent, of course, and a bevy of helpers including lawyers, recruiters, and a whole infrastructure of consultants and suppliers. But it's the entrepreneurial spirit that makes everything happen here. In response to the question of how to explain the amazing capacity of Silicon Valley to conjure up new products and create new market opportunities in abundance, the best answers point to the entrepreneurs and their passion. The most important single factor is that spirit which Rogers and Larsen call "entrepreneurial fever."[45]

---

[43]   Isadore Barmash, "Corporate Triumph, Then Death in a Ferrari," *New York Time*, June 10, 1983, http://www.nytimes.com/1983/06/10/business/corporate-triumph-then-death-in-a-ferrari.html (accessed August 13 2013).

[44]   Kenney (ed.), *Understanding Silicon Valley*, 28. For further assessment of this idea, see Richard Florida and Martin Kenney, "Silicon Valley and Route 128 Won't Save Us," *California Management Review* 33/1 (Fall 1990), 68–88, esp. 83.

[45]   Rogers and Larsen, *Silicon Valley Fever*, 234; Michael Lewis, *The New New Thing: A Silicon Valley Story* (New York: W.W. Norton, 2000) similarly documents a Silicon Valley story full of avarice.

Of course this entrepreneurial spirit is not anti-materialistic. Entrepreneurs are not generally driven by an entirely spiritual sort of altruism or the outpouring of self-sacrificing *agape* love described in the New Testament. Certainly not. William Shockley is a case in point—"he wanted to make a million dollars," and he made no effort to conceal his desire to become rich.[46]

But money does not seem to have been the force that drove the "Traitorous Eight" to abandon Shockley and head out on their own at great risk to their careers. There is no good case to be made that they abandoned Shockley in pursuit of personal wealth. Their risky step in abandoning secure employment to dream up a new way of doing things, a new type of company, was an outright rejection of the conventional wisdom about work and business. They sought a new opportunity for their creative and productive instinct to flourish. They sought to do a new thing, to build a new type of company. Indeed, at the spiritual level it was not even technology that was the heart of the matter, but rather the passion of freedom to collaborate in new development. This was their driving motive: to escape from the onerous and frustratingly authoritarian control of Shockley and venture out as a team with freedom to create.

There is a paradox here in the pursuit of material accomplishments which are not moved by entirely materialistic motives. The motivational driving force demonstrates a missionary zeal that is captured well by Jerry Sanders, one of the Fairchild émigrés who went on to become the CEO of AMD: "It wasn't a quest for fame and fortune that drove us in those early years of isolation and struggle. It was passion—a passion to develop, proliferate, and evangelize technology to empower people everywhere to lead more productive lives."[47] The entrepreneur's quest is paradoxical. It is motivated by spiritual as well as worldly aims. Both intentions are real, and this paradox points to spiritual reality because the expansive longings of the heart to create beauty, steward one's gifts and build covenantal community bear witness to the transcendent source and aims of human motives.

Failure

The risk inherent in this entrepreneurial activity is another pointer to its spirituality. Risk-taking is so integral to the experience of Silicon Valley entrepreneurs that failure has become almost a badge of honor, in sharp distinction to the demerits which it brought in the previous models of business culture. Failure is seen as a source of wisdom and learning. Many venture

---

[46]   Rogers and Larsen, *Silicon Valley Fever*, 37.
[47]   Malone, *Betting It All*, vi.

capitalists will not even consider investing in an entrepreneur who has not experienced some sort of failure. From a spiritual point of view we can see how failure serves also as an antidote to pride and hubris.

This positive regard for failure refutes a common idea in business ethics, which suggests that business failure is an indication of unrighteousness putting one's salvation in doubt, rather than an open door to wisdom and the grace of being given a second chance in new economic opportunities. This thesis paints a picture of the businessperson as an anxious striver who seeks financial gain as a bulwark against the judgment of an angry God. This then becomes a kind of "iron cage" that the soldiers of capitalism build for themselves. They are trapped in their anxious toil, as it were, needing to be successful in order to vindicate their belief in their own salvation. This thesis depends so heavily upon a distorted work ethic which is historically said to be laid at the feet of the Protestant Calvinists.[48] In the spirit of Silicon Valley, however, failure is not the last word on these matters; rather, it is a step on a path toward redemption. It becomes a source of capital in its own right, which is an entirely paradoxical way to think of capital. In the conventional sense of economics, failure would be exactly the opposite of a capital asset; it would be a liability marked against an asset, a debit against a credit. But in the spiritual realm failure can take on value as a source of discipline and learning. The fact that failure can be favored within the culture of innovation points to a greater reality and a higher purpose transcending immediate material success.

Idealism and the Tower of Babel

Spirituality slides effortlessly into idealism in the absence of a defining narrative which grounds faith in relationship with God. For this reason the spirit of Silicon Valley is frequently seen to lead in the direction of idealism—a recognizable theme of the dreams carried into California by generations of newcomers. The spiritual quality of dreams, when disconnected from the greater reality of God, feeds into the idolization of human accomplishment. This sort of idealism has been abundantly apparent in the outsized ambitions of some of the most successful entrepreneurs the world has ever seen. It's a two-edged sword—both a strength and a weakness for the visionary leaders whose companies make headline news in business and technology.

---

[48]   Max Weber, *The Protestant Ethic and the Spirit of Capitalism*, Talcott Parsons (trans.) (London: G. Allen and Unwin, 1930).

In his own words, which comprise a sort of autobiographical epitaph at the conclusion of the masterful biography by Walter Isaacson, Steve Jobs describes his personal vision for Apple in uplifting idealistic terms:

> My passion has been to build an enduring company where people were motivated to make great products. Everything else was secondary. Sure, it was great to make a profit, because that was what allowed you to make great products. But the products, not the profits, were the motivation.[49]

Jobs displays here the non-materialistic idealism of accomplishment that expresses the ethos of Silicon Valley. He placed an overarching significance on creating things of beauty and value. In no small way, Jobs's spiritual ideals led to the creation of this: "Apple itself, which Jobs considered his greatest creation, a place where imagination was nurtured, applied, and executed in ways so creative that it became the most valuable company on earth."[50] Jobs goes on to explain his passion for building a great company, and how this transcends monetary gains:

> I hate it when people call themselves "entrepreneurs" when what they're really trying to do is launch a startup and then sell or go public, so they can cash in and move on. They're unwilling to do the work it takes to build a real company, which is the hardest work in business. That's how you really make a contribution and add to the legacy of those who went before. You build a company that will still stand for something a generation or two from now. That's what Walt Disney did, and Hewlett and Packard, and the people who built Intel. They created a company to last, not just to make money. That's what I want Apple to be.[51]

As admirable as this idealism is, by virtue of disregard for financial gain, and its passion for beauty and meaning, and full contributions to society, there is a dark side lurking. The idealistic focus on a single company's products has more than once been played out in modern versions of the story of the Tower of Babel (Gen. 11). Steve Jobs's vociferous defense of his belief system regarding Apple's product strategy conveys an element of the attempt to construct a monolithic edifice. In the case of Apple, this is based upon Jobs's stance on "the great debate of the digital age: closed versus open, or as Jobs framed it, integrated versus

---

49 Walter Isaacson, *Steve Jobs*, (New York: Simon and Schuster, 2011), 567.
50 Isaacson, *Steve Jobs*, 566.
51 Isaacson, *Steve Jobs*, 569.

fragmented."[52] Jobs was known for his passionate articulation of this belief, and for his perfectionism in driving Apple to stick to it.

There is another name in the headlines now espousing his vision for a monolithic structure of towering proportions—Mark Zuckerberg. The founder/CEO of Facebook sees his company as the eventual and ultimate pipeline for the entire stream of human consciousness. It is hard to imagine a more powerful business parallel to the idea of the Tower of Babel. In Zuckerberg's own words, the mission of Facebook is to capitalize on the "massive stream of information" from Facebook users:

> It's almost the stream of all human consciousness and communication, and the products we build are just different views of that. The concept of the social graph has been a very useful construct, but I think increasingly this concept of the social stream—the aggregate stream for everyone—will be as important .... People are going to have to have a device with them at all times that's [automatically] sharing. You can predict that.[53]

What grander vision could there be than to gain access to "the stream of all human consciousness and communication," and to have it all coursing through the veins of Facebook's network? This is the dark side of the Silicon Valley spirit—the tendency toward fresh visions of Babel, and the idolatry which accompanies the unholy worship of human creativity. In the isolated heights of human spirit and achievement, that siren song continues to waft from the tower of Babel. The architects of entrepreneurial genius can also become unwittingly architects of Babel dreams. California and Silicon Valley have had their share of these dreamers, who dream the kind of dreams which ceaselessly seem to resonate in the California psyche.

Conclusion

This chapter has explored briefly the parallels between the story of Silicon Valley and the biblical story of the Exodus. Along the way we have seen how these parallels bear present-day witness to biblical understanding of the *imago Dei*

---

52   Isaacson, *Steve Jobs*, 513.

53   David Kirkpatrick, *The Facebook Effect: The Inside Story of the Company that is Connecting the World* (New York: Simon and Schuster, 2010), 313–14. For a synopsis of the ethical issues pertaining to the rise of digital society, see David Bollier, *The Promise and Peril of Big Data* (Washington, DC: Aspen Institute, 2010).

and covenantal community. We have encountered also some of the paradoxes observable within the spirit of innovation that thrive in this place, the world's most famous and prolific maternity ward for start-up companies. With theological lenses, we can see how these paradoxes point to the greater spiritual reality which empowers them. At the same time, we can see how this same spiritual energy, when severed from its true source in God, provides a temptation towards sin and idolatry. Yet for all this there remains something winsome in the ethos of the Silicon Valley—something admirable that speaks of an assured beauty in human character, something brave and virtuous in taking risks for to sake of the greater good, something even bordering on love, in giving one's all to create a better world. And although each accomplishment wrought by the innovative spirit "wears man's smudge," as Hopkins would remind us, there is also a portion of glory to be seen in those who bear God's image and receive blessings of creativity:

> And all is seared with trade; bleared, smeared with toil;
> And wears man's smudge and shares man's smell: the soil
> Is bare now, nor can foot feel, being shod.
> And for all this, nature is never spent;
> There lives the dearest freshness deep down things.[54]

The glory of the Silicon Valley is praiseworthy to the extent it reveals the glory of God who made humankind male and female in his image. Signs of this glory do appear in the accomplishments, visions, innovative spirit and missionary zeal of Silicon Valley entrepreneurs, if we can look beneath the smudge that blemishes the *imago Dei* with the stains of ego and the idolatry of human constructs. Lessons learned from this exploration may help inspire more thought on how to nurture the Silicon Valley virtue, and all the other pockets of innovation around the world where people strive to create value and beauty in marketable products and culture in general. New things are always on the horizon. A new generation of entrepreneurs is now once again fallen into fortune with the in the intangible datasets of information and the commodities of personal information. How will these new pioneers adopt the characteristics of covenantal community that inspired the earlier generation who made fortunes out of silicon, the most common element in the very ordinary material of sand? My hope is that the *imago Dei* will continue to shine through and that the Silicon Valley will continue to serve the world as a reflection of the higher virtues.

---

[54]   Excerpt from Gerard Manley Hopkins's poem, "God's Grandeur," in *Poems of Gerard Manley Hopkins* (London: Humphrey Milford, 1918).

Chapter 9

Drive-By Evangelism, the Growth in Gang Violence and Community Development[1]

Paul Louis Metzger

In the spring of 2011, I was invited to the San Francisco Bay Area in my role as Director of The Institute for the Theology of Culture: New Wine, New Wineskins of Multnomah Biblical Seminary in Portland, Oregon.[2] I met with church leaders of diverse ethnic backgrounds during my visit. Themes that surfaced repeatedly were isolation and fragmentation.

We discussed the isolation of churches from one another, especially along ethnic lines, and the fragmentation that is occurring in the region as reflected in increasing violence as the result of gang activity. I believe that the two problems are related. Whenever there is isolation and fragmentation as well as objectification, conflict and confrontation will inevitably result as the isolated parties cross paths.

Churches from across the city and the region must come together in solidarity to address the problem of social fragmentation and what it entails for gang violence. It will not do to engage in drive-by evangelism, where affluent churches in well-to-do sections of town, the suburbs or outlying areas engage in charity events and quick-fix solutions and make inner city ministries victims of their charity or worse. A holistic response is required.

---

[1]   This chapter develops further claims made in an earlier version published at the following domain and titled "Taking Focus on the Family to a Whole New Level: the Church as Family and Gang Violence," *Fathers and Families Coalition of America*: http://fathersandfamiliescoalition. org/wp-content/uploads/2012/01/TAKING-FOCUS.pdf (accessed January 5, 2013). A similar version of that piece also appeared in *Great Commission News*.

[2]   I wish to express thanks to Revs Leroy and Leversie Johnson and Ms Gloria Young of San Francisco for their hospitality and initiative. Not only were they responsible for making possible this venture, but also they have modeled long-suffering leadership in the face of the challenges noted in this chapter as pastors at Greater Life Foursquare Church in the city (the Johnsons) and as a leader in city government and as a lay leader in churches over the years (Young). I dedicate this article to them. For more on New Wine's work at large, see www.new-wineskins.org.

In what follows, we will first discuss the need to come to terms with the lack of widespread social solidarity in cities like San Francisco and Portland, in large part shaped by their involvement and responses to racialization. We will then address the subject of passive racism and what that entails for social fragmentation. Then consideration will turn to a reflection on church growth patterns, church identity and outreach, and how we need to expand our sense of family and community as the body of Christ in order to contend against such forces as fatherlessness that lead to gang violence.

LA Car Crashes and San Francisco Cool

The situation described by church leaders in the San Francisco Bay Area reminded me in certain respects of the movie *Crash*, which focuses on racism and the underlying problems of isolation and fragmentation as well as objectification in Los Angeles. In the movie, people of diverse ethnicities crash into one another at the busy traffic intersections of life as a result of social isolation and fragmentation. As the detective played by Don Cheadle remarks, people in LA live behind glass and metal and crash into one another so that they can experience the feeling of touch.[3]

It is not always the case that people of diverse ethnic backgrounds crash into one another in violent ways. While they may crash into one another in places like LA, according to *Crash*, in Minnesota, where people are seemingly nice, self-deprecating and averse to confrontation, conflict might manifest itself in other ways. For example, while one might slow down to let another driver into one's lane, it might show in passive aggressive behavior such as procrastination and resistance to changing lanes when needed on the highways and byways of life.[4]

In Portland, where I teach, we prize tolerance. A friend of mine, Emily Rice, calls it "Portland Cool." Unfortunately, Portland Cool often masks indifference. In this regard, it is worth noting that according to a statement attributed to Dr Martin Luther King, Jr, in the South, white people don't care how close African Americans get, but how high they get; in the North, white people don't

---

[3]   *Crash*, directed by Paul Haggis (Santa Monica: Lions Gate Films, 2004), http://www.crashfilm.com/ (accessed February 17, 2013).

[4]   See Annette Atkins, *Creating Minnesota: A History from the Inside Out* St Paul: Minnesota Historical Society, 2008, 242–3, 248; Syl Jones, "The Unwritten Rules That Tell Minnesotans How To Be Nice," St Paul: Minnesota Public Radio, December 14, 2009 (accessed December 2009); "Wobegonics" on *A Prairie Home Companion*, Saturday, April 19, 1997 (accessed December 14, 2009).

care how high African Americans get, but how close they get. In other words, racism shows up in different ways in different places. People may leave LA for Portland to relive the 1990s as in the show *Portlandia*;[5] however, there has been a lack of interest and intentionality there and elsewhere to relive or better live out the Civil Rights movement in the 1960s, which was likely the church's and nation's finest hour in confronting racism.[6] Urban renewal still often means Negro removal in Portland due to the far-reaching and negative impact of gentrification in the city and region. While white people don't usually crash into African Americans in Portland in cars, displacement through gentrification in historic African American neighborhoods now brings with it bike lane tensions.[7] In many situations, the African American community has not been consulted and included as a key stakeholder in an ongoing conversation; if they are approached on a subject bearing on them, it is often too late. The city is known for being green, not black. In fact, North Portland, which for several decades was predominantly black, is now increasingly white, calling to mind an

---

5 *Portlandia*, directed by Jonathan Krisel (Portland: Broadway Video Television and IFC Original Productions, 2011–present), http://www.ifc.com/shows/portlandia (accessed March 23, 2013). See the following clip: http://www.youtube.com/watch?v=FE_9CzLCbkY (accessed February 16, 2013). See my discussion of Portland with reference to *Portlandia* and the themes of racialization and negative forms of gentrification in this city in "What the Gospel Means for Portland: What Christ Might Say to the City of Roses," for This Is Our City project, *Christianity Today*, October 20, 2011, http://www.christianitytoday.com/thisisourcity/portland/meansportland.html (accessed February 16, 2013).

6 According to James Cone, the problem is widespread. In a 2006 interview with *America: The National Catholic Review*, Cone exhorted white Protestant and Catholic theologians to speak out against white supremacy, asserting that white theologians remain largely silent on the topic. Cone argued that "white supremacy is more deeply entrenched now than it was in the 1960s and early 1970s." People were more cognizant of it then due to the work of Dr King and others. The church's finest hour in addressing racism was at that time. Cone goes on to claim, "But now, having confronted it years ago, they think they have made the racial situation better, whereas in some ways it is worse. It is like a new form of racism, in that it accepts the tokenism of a few blacks in churches, educational institutions and government in order to make people think everything is fine on the racial front. But just look at the statistics about the African-American community with regard to imprisonment, health care, education and employment. We are worse off today in areas like these. So I want to challenge white theologians and their churches to speak out in a sustained and prophetic way about racial injustice." George M. Anderson, "Theologians and White Supremacy: An Interview with James H. Cone," in *America: The National Catholic Review*, November 20, 2006, http://americamagazine.org/node/147942 (accessed February 16, 2013).

7 Sarah Goodyear, "Bike Lane Backlash, Even in Portland," *The Atlantic*, Cities—Place Matters, September 20, 2011, http://www.theatlanticcities.com/neighborhoods/2011/09/portland-bike-lanes-open-racial-wounds/138/ (accessed March 10, 2013).

earlier displacement of African American homes and businesses from the area now known as the Rose Quarter.[8]

Portland is similar to San Francisco in certain respects. I have actually heard it claimed that San Francisco is Portland on steroids. Regardless of what one makes of that claim, it is true that both cities pride themselves on tolerance and being cool on matters of diversity. However, as already noted, tolerance can also serve to mask indifference. Still, one cannot mask racialization, no matter how subtle its entrenchment. Racialization, which manifests itself in terms of variables rather than constants, influences life in a variety of ways. Racialization refers to race's impact on such matters as employment, education, health care, place of residence, and social relationships and networking.[9]

Concerning social relationships and networking, it is worth noting here that some African American pastors in San Francisco shared with me how they are often excluded from a vital place at the table of fellowship with other Christian leaders in the Bay Area. One Chinese American pastor responded to their statement by saying that "We Chinese have not been invited to the table either, so we simply made our own table." These diverse leaders were saying to me that there is not sufficient intentionality toward the development of community involving equality, mutuality and solidarity in ministry among people of diverse ethnic backgrounds. As is often true in the Greater Portland area, it seems that Christian ministries in the Bay Area often struggle with doing their own thing—whether Anglo American, Asian American, African American, or other.

When we do our own thing, it negatively impacts others around us. Generally speaking, those whose indifference has the most negative impact are majority culture individuals and communities (often white) given their influence and power. However, these individuals and communities are often unaware of how they benefit from a system that often caters to race, in this case, whites like me.

---

[8]   For a discussion of the history of gentrification and displacement of the African American community in Portland and the present day impact, see Aaron Scott, "By the Grace of God," *Portland Monthly*, February 17, 2012, http://www.portlandmonthlymag.com/news-and-profiles/culture/articles/african-american-churches-north-portland-march-2012 (accessed March 10, 2012).

[9]   Michael Emerson and Christian Smith speak of how racialization manifests itself not according to constants but according to variables. They define a racialized society in the following terms: "[A] racialized society is *a society wherein race matters profoundly for differences in life experiences, life opportunities, and social relationships.*" They add that "a racialized society can also be said to be 'a society that allocates different economic, political, social, and even psychological rewards to groups along racial lines, lines that are socially constructed.'" See Michael O. Emerson and Christian Smith, *Divided by Faith: Evangelical Religion and the Problem of Race in America* (New York: Oxford University Press, 2000), 7–8.

Given the negative impact of such privilege and how white people are often unaware of it, it is important that we pause at this point and consider the subject of passive racism.

Passive Racism, Immovability and Negro Removal

We all struggle with racism. However, those of us who are whites, especially white men like me, have to be especially alert to our struggle with being passive racists, or perhaps more accurately, passive racialists. When one speaks of being a racist, one often has in mind matters of intentionality. I am not intentionally attacking people of diverse ethnicities. I am not targeting or profiling them in any active sense. I have friendships with many people of diverse ethnic backgrounds. I want to cultivate healthy relationships with them. Thus, I would not say I am an active racist. But am I doing enough to change the structures that still inhibit equality and mutuality in the church and society surrounding matters of ethnic diversity? I do not think so. This is why I refer to myself as a passive racialist.

When I speak of being a "passive racialist" as a white person, I am speaking of passively benefiting from living in a racialized society that caters to people of my ethnic background. As stated above, we live in a society shaped by race on matters pertaining to education, health care, home ownership and where we live, employment, and the like. I benefit from a system that favors whites like me much of the time.

Whenever I say that I am a passive racist (or more accurately passive racialist), people of my ethnic background—white Euro-Americans like myself—are a bit stupefied or puzzled. They often—rightly and understandably—ask for clarification. Further to what was said above, I inform them that I do not claim to be an active racist. I do not intentionally favor myself or "my kind of people" over others. This is why I say that I am a passive participant in the problem. I unintentionally benefit from a system that has historically and even presently in various ways favored the white Euro-American heritage. Interesting fact: while Caucasians are still the largest group if framed in terms of ethnic categories, minority births now outnumber white births.[10] Still, the Caucasian population is the majority culture in terms of influence. While one cannot change history's past, one can change how history shapes us today. While I am not trying to do

---

[10]   Michael Muskal, "Minority Births Outnumber Whites for First Time," *Standard Examiner* (originally published in the *Los Angeles Times*) May 17, 2012, http://www.standard.net/stories/2012/05/17/minority-births-outnumber-whites-first-time (accessed March 10, 2013).

away with white people like myself shaping our culture, I want to make sure that I am intentionally collaborating with fellow white Euro-Americans *and others of diverse ethnic backgrounds* in shaping our country's and church's future. This has to happen in places like San Francisco with great intentionality.[11]

Some will take this as a move to foster a sense of white guilt. I am not looking to lay a guilt trip on people. I do not intend these remarks to be deconstructive, but rather constructive. While the situation is complex and the reasons multiple, I want us to acknowledge our guilt in not actively addressing structures that cater to the white majority and move forward toward true freedom beyond guilt where everyone has equal access to employment, education, health care, and the like. I want to be free from guilt, and I want all of us to be free, too. I cannot be free if I do not know I am guilty, and to not know I am guilty does not mean I am innocent. Thinking and knowing are not enough, though. If I am not responding constructively to turn away from my participation in structures that inhibit others' full expression in terms of owning and shaping our country's as well as the church's future, I am actually intensifying my guilt. I am actually guilty in terms of benefiting from white privilege and not doing enough to level the playing field. Instead, I am often in danger of blaming the victim.[12]

---

[11]   One cannot speak enough of the need for intentionality, including tenacity. One white Christian leader in San Francisco indicated to me that he and his community are trying to make inroads into the African American community to build relationships and ministry connections. He indicated that it has been quite difficult. Perhaps, as in my context in the Greater Portland area, there is a level of *weariness* and *wariness*: *weariness* in that some African American leaders have experienced the good though short-lived intentions of white Christian leaders to engage them; *wariness* in that some African American leaders are afraid that the white Christian leaders will come in and try and take control (playing the white Messiah card). Having always struggled to survive in a white man's world and carve out a space for themselves, there is the fear perhaps of the loss of the limited amount of "turf" they have worked so hard to gain. It will require white Christian leaders demonstrating that they are there for the long haul and that they are positioning themselves to be partners who will place themselves under the authority of the African American leadership and their communities if they are to build trust and bridges of partnership so as to make the table welcoming to all and to equal the playing field. This is the way Lesslie Newbigin approached his work in Madras. While quite radical at the time, especially for an Englishman in India, it stands as a sound practice today. See a brief account of this in Geoffrey Wainwright, *Lesslie Newbigin: A Theological Life* (Oxford: Oxford University Press, 2000), 162–4.

[12]   William Ryan, *Blaming the Victim* (rev., New York: Vintage Books, 1976). Even in the movie *Crash*, the young police officer who thought he was beyond racism and who judged his partner as being beneath him for a heinous incident of racism is ominously told by his partner as he transfers to work with someone else: "You think you know who you are. You have no idea who you are." Before the movie ends, this same young police officer misjudges an

I know I am not alone, nor are whites generally. I believe all people of every ethnic background are guilty in various ways, and in need of God's grace. Moreover, the victim in one system can and often does become the victimizer in another system.[13] Jesus alone is truly innocent, and yet he bears our guilt and blame in his work as God's spotless moral agent in reconciling the world to himself. Still, while Jesus alone is innocent, that does not mean all cats are gray or that two wrongs make a right. In other words, the moral culpability of all does not excuse my passive involvement in this system and with it my responsibility and need to level the playing field and bring everyone as equal participants to the table of reconciliation. These reflections should make clear that simply acknowledging one's need and culpability is not enough; active repentance is also necessary for forgiveness to be effective. So, I need to be involved in shaping the culture of my community at large, and church community, to reflect multifaceted representation in a variety of ways pertaining to ethnic diversity. Cultivation of diverse representation in leadership roles in the local church and in other spheres in our society is vitally important in this regard, along with other initiatives.

Others will think that I am catering to people of diverse backgrounds. I beg to differ. There is a difference between *catering* to people of diverse ethnic backgrounds (a form of political correctness) and *cultivating* community that fosters ownership of the community by people of diverse ethnicities. If a system caters to one kind of people, it is important to counter this move and make sure that everyone has a place at the table. The desired outcome is for us to reach a place where those of diverse ethnic backgrounds feel welcomed and appreciated, sense that they are being heard, and find that they are also able to shape the

---

African American man and shoots him dead. His lack of self-awareness and blindness to his own prejudice leads once again to making the victim of white prejudice bear the blame.

[13]   Rowan Williams puts it this way: "I am, willy-nilly, involved in 'structural violence,' in economic, political, religious and private systems of relationship which diminish the other (and I must repeat once more that the victim in one system is liable to be the oppressor in another: the polarity runs through each individual). Yet I find, through the resurrection gospel, that I have a choice about colluding with these systems, a possibility of belonging to another 'system' in which gift rather than diminution is constitutive. I am thus equipped to understand that structural violence is not an unshakeable monolith: critical action, constructive protest, is possible. My involvement in violence is most destructive when least self-aware, and simply understanding that involvement is a crucial first step. But to understand it in the presence of the Easter Jesus is to understand that violence is not omnipotent, and that my involvement in it does not rule out the possibility of transformation of my relations." Rowan Williams, *Resurrection: Interpreting the Easter Gospel* (rev., Cleveland: The Pilgrim Press, 2002), 73.

conversation around the table, making certain that ownership of the table is shared by all.[14]

Some will no doubt claim: "Don't fix what's not broken." Or, "There's no problem. So, don't make it a problem." It is easy to say these things when you are benefiting from, or no longer hurt by, the system. And just because people of diverse ethnicities might not always say there is a problem, it does not mean that all of them think the system is fine or that there is no problem. They might not wish to rock the boat. If change is to occur, those of us who benefit most need to be the ones who change the structures most. We are responsible. Still, we will need the involvement of those of diverse ethnic backgrounds to help us find our way.

So, I need to continue moving forward in becoming an active ethnic relationalizer rather than a passive racist/racialist. In place of political correctness, I want to foster ethnic relational awareness and equality/mutuality. This requires a desire for collaboration. In a collaborative system, everyone benefits, not just one kind of people or one or two people. The desire is to make sure that everyone benefits and everyone belongs. What might such active ethnic relationalization (over against passive racism and racialization) look like? How might it shape the conversation in a place like San Francisco? We will offer the answer in the context of discussing the rise of gang violence in the San Francisco Bay Area.

We need to understand we live in a racialized world and sense our need to move beyond it through relational solidarity that breaks through racial divisions, if we are going to destroy the structures that foster gang violence. Our immovability or failure to move beyond these divisions is often covered over by our drive-by movement through vulnerable communities. However, our drive-by evangelism does not keep the people there or help those left behind and who are experiencing increasing marginalization become vital participants in shaping the community. As a result of racialization, many African Americans have been forced to move elsewhere. We need to see that the economic, educational and employment structures in place bound up with racialization led to the migration of African Americans away from our cities and the increasing marginalization of those African Americans left behind in urban areas. This is a pertinent problem in cities like San Francisco and Portland. Some African Americans in Portland call urban renewal "Negro removal." Portland's central city is increasingly white and decreasingly black.[15] San Francisco and neighboring city Oakland, like

---

14   See John M. Perkins, *Beyond Charity: The Call to Christian Community Development* (Grand Rapids: Baker, 1993).

15   Nikole Hannah Jones, "In Portland's Heart, 2010 Census Shows Diversity Dwindling," *The Oregonian*, April 30, 2011, http://www.oregonlive.com/pacific-northwest-news/index.

California as a whole, have witnessed the migration of thousands of African Americans elsewhere.[16] Whereas we used to witness white flight from the cities because blacks and others were moving in, now we are witnessing black flight from the cities as whites and Asians are returning,[17] which inevitably raises the prices on property and other costs of living.

We need to realize that this migration brings with it vulnerability and instability,[18] which inevitably leads to unpredictable behavior and negative reactions. Communities where such migrations occur have a void to fill, including advocacy and support for school improvements and expansion of housing opportunities. How can the rest of us step in and build the infrastructure necessary to bring them back and support those who are still there? How can

---

ssf/2011/04/in_portlands_heart_diversity_dwindles.html (accessed March 23, 2013).

[16]   For example, Oakland has a rich and vibrant African American history. Nonetheless, thousands of African American residents left Oakland from 2000 to 2010. The San Francisco-Oakland metropolitan region witnessed a decline of 33,003 or 8 percent of its black population, leaving Oakland with 106,637 African Americans. Hans Johnson, a demographer for the Public Policy Institute of California, claims that California's overall black population has also experienced decline. See Judy Keen, "Blacks' Exodus Reshapes Cities," *USA Today*, May 19, 2011, http://usatoday30.usatoday.com/news/nation/census/2011-05-20-chicago-blacks-exodus_n.htm (accessed February 16, 2013).

[17]   According to one report based on the census, San Francisco and Oakland "saw an exodus of African-Americans, but this was more than offset by growth in the city's Asian population—which rose by more than 30,000 even as the numbers of blacks dropped .... Overall, the city's population grew by 3.7 percent to 805,235 residents between 2000 and 2010 .... The number of whites in the city rose by a modest 5,000." Aaron Glantz, "What the Census Says about the Bay Area," *The Bay Citizen*, March 8, 2011, https://www.baycitizen.org/news/census-2010/what-census-tells-us-about-bay-area/ (accessed February 16, 2013).

[18]   Cedric Brown moved from San Francisco to Oakland in 2009. Brown, an African American, who is the CEO of the Mitchell Kapor Foundation, which works with low-income minority communities, "believes the city can sustain its black cultural institutions, but he says the African American community's "political strength and base has eroded because of this out-migration." One of the dangers of the departures, he says, is that "the folks who remain behind because they can't move are increasingly isolated and marginalized." Brown served on a task force created in 2007 to study the decline of San Francisco's black population. The task force called for improving the schools and expanding housing opportunities. Amos Brown, who is the Pastor of Third Baptist Church and the President of San Francisco's NAACP chapter, served with Brown on the task force. Pastor Brown says San Francisco "has become a city of the rich, the immigrant poor, and that's it—no black middle class." The effects can be seen in black congregations, including his own: "For the past five years, no major church has put down (extra) chairs for Easter, Mother's Day or Christmas," he says. The discussion is taken from Keen's article, "Blacks' Exodus Reshapes Cities," which was referenced previously in this chapter: http://usatoday30.usatoday.com/news/nation/census/2011-05-20-chicago-blacks-exodus_n.htm (accessed February 16 2013).

we work with those who are still there, as they combat gang violence? For the church, the solution begins in the church. It must speak and live as a prophetic witness to a better, more inclusive way of life, where everyone has a place at the table in San Francisco and beyond. However, given church growth dynamics, it is difficult to operate in a strategic, comprehensive and inclusive way. If we ever wish to address adequately as the church the problem of fatherlessness and the resulting gang violence that occurs, we will need to expand our sense of community and engage in rigorous community development.[19] To this subject, we now turn.

---

[19]   An important study put out by the Center for Religion and Civic Culture, University of Southern California titled "Opening the Gates: L.A. Congregations Confronting Gang Violence" highlights several factors that must be accounted for in addressing gang violence in LA. Three items that stand out to me are the need for research on place-based religion; the need for a theology that addresses social ills, safeguarding against the escapism of individualistic, overly-spiritualized theology, otherworldly religion and prosperity gospel spirituality; and the need for multi-ethnic ecclesial solidarity, as the ecclesial ethnic tensions so often mirror the ethnic tensions found in the community at large, and which bears upon gang violence. Here are three quotations from the document that reflect these items respectively. First, on place-based religion: "Historically, religion scholars have been focused on religious beliefs—how they develop, are influenced by, and in turn influence culture, and, how beliefs may influence social action. In contrast, a place-based religion approach seeks to discern how religious organizations operate as community actors within a network of other community resources. This approach promotes a scholarly understanding of how religion and community relate to each other, but it also can aid communities as they seek out religious organizations as partners in improving the lives of its members, and for congregations as they perform important roles within the community: socializing children and imparting values that enable them to be responsible members of the human community; being a prophetic voice for justice; nurturing, consoling, and inspiring people in need; and being an important location for a variety of community-based activities" (10). Second, on the need for a more robust theology that addresses social ills: "For many congregations, their theology is a significant barrier to community engagement. Some congregations simply spiritualize issues and believe the answers can only be found in praying, Bible reading and relying on 'God's will.' For other congregations, the internally focused and purely spiritual nature of their religious belief limits their activity. Still others remain focused on material gain, spreading the 'prosperity gospel' that inspires many to view economic gain as a sign of God's blessing" (21). Third, on the connection between ecclesial ethnic tensions and those in the communities where congregations are based, and the need to break through the ecclesial divisions for the sake of the broader community: "An additional community issue that limits the role of congregations is the tension in the community around the issue of ethnic and cultural differences, especially between Latinos and African Americans. The churches mirror these tensions. Despite the demographic shift that has taken place, there are few multi-ethnic congregations within these neighborhoods. While this is not necessarily a surprising result— multi-ethnic congregations are inherently fragile organizations—faith leaders in these

Home Communities, Community Development and Fatherlessness

One of the things that we need to address in the church is how affinities so often dictate to us how we minister. Niche-based affinities keep us from building inclusive communities. For example, home communities often bring people of similar life experiences together. Certainly, small groups have their place, as they can help one cope with the negative forces of individualism,[20] among other things. Moreover, small groups where there are cultural affinities often make it easier to connect initially, since there is a certain level of trust and rapport based on those affinities. Still, we must take note of the fact that biblical community always makes space for the diverse other. Henri Nouwen goes so far as to say that true community is the place where the person one least likes always lives.[21] Making such space for the diverse other will require great intentionality. In fact, making space is not sufficient. One must celebrate and cultivate diverse unity in the body of Christ at all levels. Such intentionality will entail cultivating staff and leadership networks in one's church that are increasingly diverse ethnically and experientially, reaching out to diverse peoples in one's evangelistic and discipleship initiatives, and developing partnerships with churches of diverse ethnicities in one's region. After all, in the biblical world, there was really only one church in a given city. As with Ephesus, Corinth and Philippi, we must come to see our various ecclesial communities as one.

Moving on, we must expand our social networks, including our church growth initiatives, no matter how difficult and time consuming, if we want to become part of the solution (rather than simply part of the problem) in transforming our cities' churches. Doing so will help us to grow in our awareness of other people's experiences and make us more attentive to the struggles and difficulties they face, including those involving racialization.

---

communities need to understand the potential that their respective congregations represent if they can figure out ways to work together, if not worship together" (23). See http://crcc. usc.edu/docs/Opening_the_gates.pdf (accessed March 21, 2013). See also the Institute for Violence Prevention at USC: http://crcc.usc.edu/initiatives/ivp/ (accessed March 21, 2013). In one way or another, this chapter bears upon each of these items noted here.

20   Robert Wuthnow speaks of how small groups help people cope with problems associated with the individualism and instability that are so rampant in our culture today: Wuthnow, *Sharing the Journey: Support Groups and the Quest for a New Community* (New York: The Free Press, 1996), 317–66.

21   "Community is not easy. Somebody once said, 'Community is the place where the person you least want to live with always lives.'" Henri Nouwen, "Moving from Solitude to Community to Ministry," *Leadership Journal* 16/2 (Spring 1995), 83.

It is worth noting here what J.I. Packer argues concerning the complexities and dynamics of my own heritage, Evangelicalism, in terms of its predominant church growth patterns:

> Evangelical Christianity starts with the individual person: the Lord gets hold of the individual; the individual comes to appreciate certain circles—the smaller circle of the small group, the larger circle of the congregation. These circles are where the person is nurtured and fed and expanded as a Christian. So, we evangelicals are conditioned to think of social structures in terms of what they do for us as individuals. That's all right, but it does lead us to settle too soon for certain self-serving social structures. And we are slow to pick up the fact that some of the social units that we appreciate for that reason can have unhappy spinoff effects on other groups.[22]

As a result of such limited social conditioning, we are often unaware of what goes on in other ethnic communities. To illustrate this point, I remember addressing the subject of urban renewal and Negro removal in the Greater Portland area several years ago for a missional leadership event at a megachurch in a Portland suburb. One lay leader in a group of around 250 people stood up to challenge me based on my claims about key initiatives in urban planning in Portland over the years leading to the displacement of the African American community.[23] After finishing his heated remarks, I informed him that the reason why he probably did not see these patterns that continue on to the present is because he likely lacked the social network that would expose him to situations of historic and ongoing red-lining and negative forces in gentrification. Not everyone at that meeting shared his angst. They experienced a different form of concern: they had come to realize that their church, which had so often been known for a form of Field of Dreams outreach model ("If you build it, they will come"), was not connecting well with its increasingly diverse surroundings. Since that time, this church has slowly and gradually moved forward to be more intentional and inclusive in its outreach and church growth initiatives, though it has come at a cost.

The emphasis on the individual in evangelical circles has a bearing on how we view the church in relation to other institutions and the community at

---

[22]   J.I. Packer, quoted in "We Can Overcome," *Christianity Today,* October 2, 2000, 43.

[23]   For a discussion of this and related themes, see the following video of the panel discussion I moderated in 2012 at The Justice Conference in Portland, Oregon. The panel session was titled "Justice, Race, Gentrification and the Land." The panelists in the video are Dr John M. Perkins, Ms Jeri Williams, Dr Randy S. Woodley, Mr John G. Canda, Rev Dr LeRoy Haynes, Jr, and Mr Steve Hanamura. Their reflections are very instructive and beneficial, http://vimeo.com/40019975 (accessed February 17, 2013).

large. For example, we must also account for how often American Christianity approaches the church as a voluntary association of religious individuals, whose true allegiance lies with the state, the market, and the nuclear family.[24] Generally speaking, in my experience, Roman Catholics and African American Protestants understand my claim much better than white evangelicals, since Catholics have a rich tradition of public theology and the African American Christian community has itself often been an extended family to its parishioners while experiencing marginalization as a result of the political and economic powers/ structures in place in their cities.

White evangelicals tend to cultivate church growth programs, including home communities, which often cater to nuclear families. While such programs help build a church's membership base, such catering often comes at a cost in terms of viewing the church as God's ultimate family.[25] Moreover, as Rodney Clapp argues, what many conservative Christians take to be the traditional family owes more to middle class values of the nineteenth century than to Scripture.[26] This being the case, it proves very difficult to mobilize such churches to address systemic issues of injustice that impact communities outside their immediate social networks, injustices from which their social networks might benefit. All too often, they limit their outreach to charitable endeavors that have no lasting impact, revealing their blindness to structures that keep people poor and communities in disrepair.

In the book titled *The Evangelicals You Don't Know*, *USA Today* religion columnist Tom Krattenmaker praises what he takes to be a new breed of evangelicals who are more compassionate in their approach to the poor. Nonetheless, Krattenmaker highlights the concern of many critics of

---

[24] For a prior discussion of this issue, see Brad Harper and Paul Louis Metzger, *Exploring Ecclesiology: An Evangelical and Ecumenical Introduction* (Grand Rapids: Brazos, 2009), Chapter 7.

[25] We must come to see our immediate families as part of our churches' extended family.

[26] See Rodney Clapp, *Families at the Crossroads: Beyond Tradition & Modern Options* (Downers Grove: InterVarsity Press, 1993). See also my article, "Downward Mobility and Trickle-Up Economics: A Trinitarian Reflection on Money and Power," delivered at The Carl F.H. Henry Center at Trinity Evangelical Divinity School, http://henrycenter.tiu.edu/wp-content/uploads/2013/11/Paul-Louis-Metzger_Trinity-Symposium_Downward-Mobility-and-Trickle-Up-Economics.pdf (accessed December 11, 2013), where I address how free market values rather than Scripture often shape evangelicals. In this regard, see also my blog posts at Patheos prefaced with the title "Jesus, Darwin and Donald Trump": http://www.patheos.com/blogs/uncommongodcommongood/2013/02/jesus-darwin-and-donald-trump/; http://www.patheos.com/blogs/uncommongodcommongood/2013/02/jesus-darwin-and-donald-trump-part-ii/ (accessed March 10, 2013). Such blindness to these other values shaping us impact negatively our engagement of racialized structures.

Evangelicalism that while these evangelicals are involved increasingly in charitable endeavors in service to the poor, as a whole, they are not supporting political policies that would contend against those structures that lead people, including families, into poverty and keep them there.[27] For all our talk as evangelical Christians on focusing on the family, we the church need to take the focus on family cohesion to a whole new level as local ecclesial families that come together as church bodies to care for families and communities in disrepair and the fatherless in our communities.[28] After all, Scripture prioritizes the church as a family over what we have come to call 'nuclear family' allegiances.

Further to what was said above, if and when our allegiance as evangelicals is to middle class values concerning the nuclear family, we will not be able to provide a prophetic critique and constructive response to the oppressive forces at work in our society, including gang violence. Instead, congregants will often wonder how issues in our society bear upon their own nuclear families and those in their immediate social networks, leaving it there. For example, churches that cater to affluent white populations through children and family programs developed just

---

[27]   Tom Krattenmaker, *The Evangelicals You Don't Know: Introducing the Next Generation of Christians* (Lanham: Rowman and Littlefield, 2013). In view of this claim, it is worth drawing attention to a 2012 article in *The Economist*: "The vast majority of evangelicals oppose gay marriage. They are more likely than non-evangelicals to oppose extra funding for public education, unemployment benefits and aid to the poor, both within and outside America. And a poll taken by the Public Religion Research Institute in 2010 showed that nearly half of all white evangelicals favour deporting illegal immigrants." "Lift Every Voice," *The Economist*, May 5, 2012, http://www.economist.com/node/21554201 (accessed January 20, 2013). See also The Pew Forum on Religion and Public Life's analysis of the connection between the Tea Party and white evangelicals. "The Tea Party and Religion," February 23, 2011 (*analysis written by Scott Clement and John C. Green*). "They draw disproportionate support from the ranks of white evangelical Protestants." "Americans who support the conservative Christian movement, sometimes known as the religious right, also overwhelmingly support the Tea Party. In the Pew Research Center's August 2010 poll, 69 percent of registered voters who agreed with the religious right also said they agreed with the Tea Party. Moreover, both the religious right and the Tea Party count a higher percentage of white evangelical Protestants in their ranks (45 percent among the religious right, 34 percent among the Tea Party and 22 percent among all registered voters in the August 2010 survey). Religiously unaffiliated people are less common among Tea Party or religious right supporters than among the public at-large (3 percent among the religious right, 10 percent among the Tea Party and 15 percent among all registered voters in the August poll)." See http://www.pewforum.org/politics-and-elections/tea-party-and-religion.aspx (accessed January 21, 2013).

[28]   In his new book, Krattenmaker has also written on the ministry of Focus on the Family and its new President, Jim Daly. Krattenmaker points out how its work beyond politics in Washington has focused increasingly on such important matters as care for foster children and the crisis surrounding children in our communities here and abroad.

for them may very well discount the need to attend to gang violence, seeing it simply as an African American or Hispanic problem. How wrong they are. Gang activity affects the whole of society. Gang activity and violence is no respecter of persons or cities.

We must come to see that God is no respecter of persons or churches or communities, regardless of how economically and educationally sound we are. Those of us who are evangelicals should especially take to heart the words of evangelical leader, the late James Montgomery Boice, who in an article published in 1998, affirmed Martin Marty's assessment that America's most worldly people at the end of the twentieth century would be evangelicals. Boice writes, "We have fulfilled his prophecy, and it is not yet the year 2000." Boice claims that evangelicals have focused their attention on acquiring the kingdom of the world and "have made politics and money our weapons of choice for grasping it." Among other things, Boice laments the evangelical movement's fixation with "success, wonderful marriages and nice children," in addition to being preoccupied with "numerical growth and money." Disturbed that evangelicals care very little for "getting right with an offended God," Boice challenges us to take seriously the prophet Amos, who warned, "Woe to them who are at *ease* in Zion." Boice said that his fellow evangelicals should become uncomfortable with their complacency and comfort. One area where such complacency is clearly evident is in our movement's striking failure in America's inner cities: "I would like us to become uneasy about our failure to establish strong churches in America's inner cities, where the breakdown of American culture is so obvious and the needs of the people are so great."[29]

In addition to the lack of solidarity based on fixation with nuclear family priorities and middle class values, we also must contend with and challenge privatized faith. Otherwise, the church will not be able to address the problem of gang violence extensively and significantly. As Cynthia Moe-Lobeda remarks on privatized faith, "The social construction of human-divine intimacy as private has served the interests of established power structures, for singularly private relationship with God cannot issue in public challenge."[30] We will need to move

---

[29]   James Montgomery Boice, "On My Mind: Our All-Too-Easy Conscience," *Modern Reformation* 7/5 (September/October 1998), 44.

[30]   Cynthia D. Moe-Lobeda, *Healing a Broken World: Globalization and God* (Minneapolis: Fortress Press, 2002), 106. Moe-Lobeda's critique of Reinhold Niebuhr in this context could be made against Evangelicalism, too. She argues that Niebuhr and liberal Christianity espoused two contradictory assertions: on the one hand, "Personal relationship with God" is "the centerpiece of faith" and on the other hand, "Personal relationship with God" is "*not* a centerpiece" of the Christian's political and public life. She claims that these

beyond privatized faith and work together as the church(es) in confronting the established power structures that foster and promote gang violence. Of course, we must also work with other publics in our society, such as the government and business sectors, to effect change. The entire community must be involved, including churches and other religious bodies.

Gang violence poses a very large challenge that has the potential to tear our society apart unless the churches come together along with other institutions to build solidarity and effect constructive and long-term change. Both the Portland region and the San Francisco Bay Area struggle increasingly with gang activity and violence, including domestic violence.[31] The growth of violent gangs reflects an increasing fragmentation in key quarters of our society.[32] While gangs often demonstrate strong social bonds internally, they reflect the dissolution of social

---

two contradictory assertions reflect the theological anthropology of liberal Christianity. Niebuhr held that the individual rather than the community is the primary human agent in relationship with God; the self, while a social entity, is positioned before God as an individual. The outcome of this approach "is a public-private dichotomy in which the moral knowledge and norms that faith offers are understood and enacted by individuals, rather than by social groups" (106).

[31] See for example the following articles on Portland: Susan Harding and Katu.com Web Staff, "Spike in Portland Gang Violence Worries Many," *KATU.com*, January 12, 2009, http://www.katu.com/news/37453054.html (accessed January 5, 2013); Maxine Bernstein, "Portland Gang-Related Killings in 2011 Highest in a Decade," in *The Oregonian*, January 1, 2012, http://www.oregonlive.com/portland/index.ssf/2012/01/portland_gang-related_killings.html (accessed January 5, 2013). See also the following articles on San Francisco and the Bay Area: "Police In East Palo Alto, Menlo Park Partner to Stem Growing Gang Violence," *CBS San Francisco*, November 29, 2012, http://sanfrancisco.cbslocal.com/2012/11/29/police-in-east-palo-alto-menlo-park-partner-to-stem-growing-gang-violence/ (accessed January 5, 2013); "Justice Officials in SJ to Talk about Gang Violence," *ABC Video*, http://abclocal.go.com/kgo/video?id=8773992 (accessed January 5, 2013); Justin Berton, "Jordan Blames Gangs for Oakland's Violence Spike," *San Francisco Chronicle*, February 8, 2012, http://www.sfgate.com/crime/article/Jordan-blames-gangs-for-Oakland-s-violence-spike-3123826.php (accessed January 5, 2013); "String of Violence Prompts Expansion of Anti-Gang Efforts," *KTVU.com*, August 24, 2012, http://www.ktvu.com/news/news/string-violence-prompts-expansion-anti-gang-effort/nRKGn/ (accessed January 5, 2013).

[32] According to Carolyn N. Kinder, there has been a dramatic increase in the recent past in violent deaths among youths in our society: "Over the past quarter of a century, there has been a three hundred percent increase in the number of teenage homicides in the United States. While violence cuts across ethnic and gender lines, females have lower homicide statistics because they are involved in fewer fighting behaviors than males." See her article, "The Roots of Violence in Society" at http://www.yale.edu/ynhti/curriculum/units/2002/6/02.06.02.x.html (accessed January 5, 2012).

bonds across society.[33] Such dissolution of solidarity often reflects ethnic and economic tensions.[34]

One striking instance of a gang network that transcends ethnic divisions is the notorious 18th Street gang, Southern California's largest gang whose reach extends to Oregon and nationwide. For the 18th Street gang, there is great strength in numbers and so the ethnic tensions are overcome for the sake of size and power. The following lines from an *LA Times* article speak to this issue:

> Called Dieciocho by its Spanish-speaking members, the gang is a quintessential Los Angeles phenomenon: sprawling, multiethnic, a product of the region's changing economics and demographics.
>
> "It's the gang of the 21st century ... an anomaly that breaks all traditions of the ethnic gang," says Jose Lopez, a Cal State Long Beach Chicano studies professor who has researched 18th Street.
>
> Although predominantly Latino, the gang has opened its arms to blacks, Samoans, Middle Easterners and whites.
>
> "If you think 10 or 15 years from now ... it ain't gonna be no brown this, black that," says one gang leader. "It'll be about who's got the numbers."[35]

---

[33] It is worth noting what the President of the Society of Catholic Social Scientists, Stephen M. Krason, says about the matter of mass violence in our society in his January 1, 2013 article in *Crisis Magazine* titled "The Causes of Violence in America": "While we can never truly understand evil—the eminent priest-sociologist Paul Hanly Furfey spoke of 'the mystery of iniquity'—it is not difficult to pinpoint the basic, broad causes of outrages such as the one in Connecticut. Five sweeping cultural developments of the past fifty or so years are crucial: the rejection of traditional religion, the subversion of sound morality, the breakdown of the family, the dissolution of solid communities that provided reference points and restraining and helping forces, and the proliferation of destructive, illicit drugs. During that period of time in America, mass murders—although not unknown before that—have become all too frequent occurrences." Such factors likely play into the increase in gang violence as well. Stephen M. Krason, "The Causes of Violence in America," *Crisis Magazine: A Voice for the Faithful Catholic Laity*, January 1, 2013, http://www.crisismagazine. com/2013/the-causes-of-violence-in-america (accessed January 5, 2013).

[34] See for example *The Guardian* discussion of diversifying police forces ethnically to combat social tensions involving gang violence as well as underlying economic tensions that bear upon gang violence in communities. The article features the initiatives of US "Supercop" Bill Bratton who has served as chief crime adviser to the UK's Prime Minister in addition to serving as police chief in Los Angeles and New York; David Batty, "UK Riots: Police Should Tackle Racial Tension, Says 'Supercop' Bill Bratton," *The Guardian*, August 13, 2011, http://www. guardian.co.uk/uk/2011/aug/13/bill-bratton-advice-uk-police (accessed January 5. 2013).

[35] Rich Connell and Robert J. Lopez, "18th STREET: Southern California's Largest Gang Aims for Dominance," first in a three-part series, *LA Times*, November 17, 1996, http://www.streetgangs.com/news/111796-column-one-an (accessed December 18, 2013).

Unlike the 18th Street gang, the church should not pursue ethnic diversity for the sake of wielding the most power, but rather the most love. Churches will have to come together in solidarity, transcending ethnic barriers, if they are to contend against the dissolution of society represented in ethnic gangs as well as multi-ethnic gangs like 18th Street.[36]

The lack of cohesiveness and unity in one part of society has a bearing on other parts of society. There is likely a connection between the lack of unity in the body of Christ and the lack of unity in our society at large. Such disunity may even bear upon gang tensions and rivalries. All too often, we do not engage issues, if we do not think they affect us. But all systemic issues in a society affect every person, directly or at least indirectly. If systemic problems are allowed to fester and grow, the malignancy works its way throughout the society, as a disease often spreads through one's whole body if left untreated.

Today's youth are very vulnerable to gang influence in impoverished inner cities and other communities in disrepair, where there is great fluctuation and instability. Many gangs are made up of youth who come from families and urban communities in crisis; these youth form and join gangs to find some sense of social cohesion and belonging.[37] Having said that, the reality is that gang activity is spreading into the suburbs as well. Think of Santa Rosa, California, and the amount of gang activity there.[38] In these days, it is not just impoverished inner cities but other communities, too, where such problems occur, since families are in disrepair and dysfunction everywhere, leaving the youth most vulnerable. Gangs provide social and familial bonds of a kind, but among other things, they are often missing out on earthly and heavenly father figures. Young people are looking for membership and inclusion in a seemingly fatherless world.

---

[36]   According to this article "Los Angeles-based Gangs—Bloods and Crips" by the Florida Department of Corrections, the LA-based gangs, Crips and Bloods, are themselves "no longer racially specific." See http://www.dc.state.fl.us/pub/gangs/la.html (accessed January 17, 2013).

[37]   This point was brought home to me by Mr John Canda, a community leader in Portland, working to stem the tide of gang violence. See the profile on his work by Cornelia Seigneur, "100 Men Standing Against Portland's Gangs," for This Is Our City project, *Christianity Today*, November 30, 2011, http://www.christianitytoday.com/thisisourcity/portland/portlandsgangs.html (accessed November 3, 2013).

[38]   See the website devoted to gang prevention in Santa Rosa, California: http://ci.santa-rosa.ca.us/departments/recreationandparks/programs/mgptf/Pages/default.aspx (accessed February 18, 2013).

Here I call to mind the movie, *Fight Club*.[39] The story encapsulates the traumatic experiences of a significant number of men in our society. A young unnamed man whom we'll call "Jack" (played by Edward Norton) cannot come to terms with having been raised without a dad. His dad split when he was a child and set up franchises of bedding wives and producing kids in various places, causing the same relational wounds the size of a man wherever he went.

In the effort to come to terms with his pain and the loss of a childhood and failure to become a man, Jack takes to fighting. He starts a fight club that evolves and grows and goes nationwide. In the movie, men like Jack die and rise again every night as they beat on one another. They can identify and locate their pain as it sears their bloodied and bruised bodies. They are not seeking to medicate their pain or eradicate it, but identify with one another in experiencing the pain of the depression that is their purposeless lives. Such men know hedonism will not save them; it is simply the other side of the nihilism that is closing in to write them off. So they fight, thinking perhaps that through chaos comes order. For them, self-improvement gives way to self-destruction.

As the character Tyler Durden (played by Brad Pitt) claims in *Fight Club*, their war as men is ultimately spiritual and their lives are the great depression. Having been raised by TV to think they would be movie gods, rock stars and millionaires, they realize it is all a lie. Some are pumping gas and waiting tables. Some are white collar slaves. They slave at jobs that they hate to get things they do not need. What they were promised is unfulfilled and what they need they cannot have. It makes them angry and they are taking action through fighting to medicate their pain and anger.

As profoundly disturbing as *Fight Club* is, it speaks to the need for people to share their pain with others. While there are no doubt many significant ways that men and also youth can grieve the apparent loss of their manhood and youth rather than pour out violence on others, coming together to listen to one another grieve serves to heal old wounds. Such safe and authentic spaces do exist, though I am sure they are often hard to find.

I know of one such place. A friend of mine is an African American pastor, who is praying and partnering with my African American pastor friends in San Francisco and me. Pastor Clifford Chappell helps African American men come to terms with low self-esteem. He calls this work "Man-Up." Man-Up includes "Huddles" where men form relationships in small groups in safe places

---

[39] *Fight Club*, directed by David Fincher (Los Angeles: 20th Century Fox, 1999), http://www.imdb.com/title/tt0137523/ (accessed March 23, 2013).

where they can share and release their pain. [40] Pastor Chappell says the pain and trauma these men experience go back in many cases to the slave block, where families were divided and where the white masters became lords over the homes of their African American slaves. Many slave owners made sure to indoctrinate their male slaves that they had no worth or dignity other than what their owners allowed them to have. Man-Up would work for all men, irrespective of color. Why? Male rage today, whether white or black or that of another hue, is often bound up with realizing that our futures have been squandered. We deserve more, but all we will ever get is far less. Only as men are healed of their relational wounds will they be able to provide relational healing to children and youths in their midst.

Instead of tapping out, men need to tap in as men as they find their humanity in sharing the loss of it with one another. Maybe they/we can help one another find it again. They should not internalize and suppress it; they will only get ulcers, perhaps even commit suicide. They must not externalize it by beating on others, dehumanizing them, calling other men boys and robbing them of their dignity at the slave block of various forms of seemingly manly competition. Rather, they need to personalize the pain by sharing life with other men, honestly confessing the loss of their innocence and manhood and locating it once again in relationship. They must not go to therapy and addiction groups where they can fake an addiction, like Jack did earlier in the movie. Rather, they need to be honest with their addiction. They must not content themselves with raging against it. Real men do not rage. Real men confess. As unbearable as the disease of lost manhood can be, men will only come to find it in relation to other men and also women, youth, and children—with people of different backgrounds. Together they/we can grieve so that together we can someday rejoice in having discovered and shared in our corporate humanity again.

As the movie *Fight Club* maintains, the crisis or war for men is a spiritual crisis/war. Their fathers' failure to raise them suggests to many men, as for Tyler and Jack, that God has failed them, for their fathers were models for God. As Tyler prompts Jack to consider, God probably does not like him, even hates him, and never wanted him around.

Not only do fathers model God for many people, but also churches model God. If churches do not care about a fatherless generation and do not parent

[40]   The timely and critically important work of Portland Pastor Clifford Chappell called "Man-Up" addresses these issues while attending to how they bear upon domestic violence involving African American men in our community. Pastor Chappell is involved in the New Wine, New Wineskins John 17:23 Network partnership that also includes pastors in San Francisco, http://stjohnsallnationscogic.org/Man-Up.htm (accessed January 5, 2013).

them, what is to keep these men and youth from maintaining that churches also hate them, confirming further that God also hates them? Churches must become fathers to this fatherless generation.[41]

However, churches often function as gangs or fraternities, not as heavenly families who parent a fatherless generation.[42] I have my gang and you have yours. We do our own thing and protect our own people and interests to the neglect of others. Often, our church gangs are ethnic in stripe. While we do not pick up arms to fight with one another in the church, we fight against one another in other ways, even by simply not partnering together as equals.

In John 17:23, our Lord pours out his heart in prayer to his Father, longing for God to make his people one so that the world might know that God has sent his Son. Our Lord longs today for our churches to move beyond gang identities along ethnic and socio-economic lines to partner together to confront the ills that plague all of us, including gang violence.

So, how can we get out of our ethnic ghettos and trenches and partner together as Christ's body? How might such partnerships bear on the gang violence sweeping through our society? As one African American leader in the

---

[41]   Katie Worth, "San Francisco Tops State's Foster Care Rates," September 18, 2011, http://www.sfexaminer.com/local/2011/09/san-francisco-tops-state-s-foster-care-rates (accessed March 10, 2013); Kristina Puga, "First-Time Filmmaker Tells His Story about Growing Up Fatherless and Forgiving," NBCLatino, September 13, 2012, http://nbclatino. com/2012/09/13/first-time-filmmaker-tells-his-story-about-growing-up-fatherless-and-forgiving/ (accessed March 10, 2013). Note also: "Juveniles have become the driving force behind the nation's alarming increases in violent crime, with juvenile arrests for murder, rape, robbery and aggravated assault growing sharply in the past decade as pistols and drugs became more available, and expected to continue at the same alarming rate during the next decade." The following articles are set forth in support: "Justice Dept. Issues Scary Report on Juvenile Crime," *San Francisco Chronicle* (September 8, 1995); "Crime Wave Forecast With Teenager Boom," *San Francisco Chronicle* (February 15, 1995); "Criminal behavior experts and social scientists are finding intriguing evidence that the epidemic of youth violence and gangs is related to the breakdown of the two-parent family." See "New Evidence That Quayle Was Right: Young Offenders Tell What Went Wrong at Home," *San Francisco Chronicle* (December 9, 1994), http://www.fathermag.com/news/2756-suicide.shtml (accessed March 10, 2013).

[42]   John Zizioulas argues that other groups besides the church experienced loving solidarity among its members. Such loving solidarity involved sharing possessions with everyone in the community. However, Zizioulas contends that what distinguished the church or Eucharistic assembly from these other communities was that it crossed ethnic, economic and social lines in the ancient church. John D. Zizioulas, *Being as Communion: Studies in Personhood and the Church* (Crestwood: St Vladimir's Seminary Press, 1985), 150–52. As such, the church was not merely a fraternity, but rather a true heavenly family made up of people of all backgrounds sharing all things in common.

Bay Area told me recently, "We are a fatherless nation which affects our families and communities and even to the place where fathers may be present in the home but the home is still fatherless." The churches must come together to help parent parentless communities.[43] Among other things, this will entail leading the younger people in our churches even now to look to godly elders for wisdom and counsel. So seldom do we inquire of them, when we have so much to gain from them. We are often looking to a future of which we know nothing, and fail to draw insights and perspectives on how to live now in view of history which others have already lived. While attending to the needs and cultural identity of our youth is extremely important, fixation with the youth culture and failure to engage the older generation inside and outside the church can only harm our social fabric inside and outside the church.

The reverse must also be true. The older generation must also be intentional about discipling and mentoring today's youth culture. Church growth must be based on person to person discipleship with consideration also being given to vocational mentoring. David Kinnaman, President of Barna, has claimed that churches must be intentional on drawing from the vocational resources in their own congregations to help youth develop their own passions and skill sets.[44] Extending his claim to the current discussion, I would go so far as to say that pastors and elders must be attentive to helping their youth stay in church and school by transforming their churches from religious gangs in otherworldly ghettos to holy guilds with divinely sanctioned secular callings in our cities. Where possible, mentors from other churches in other locales can assist pastors who have lost congregants with amazing skill sets as a result of forced migrations to help train up the youth in these ways. As such, they build upon the important Christian community development work of Dr John M. Perkins, who speaks

---

[43]   See Mark E. Strong's important new book on the subject of fatherlessness and gang violence and how churches can be involved in confronting the problem and making effective, constructive changes in communities: *Church for the Fatherless: A Ministry Model for Society's Most Pressing Problem* (InterVarsity Press, 2012). See also the work of Harry Louis Williams, who in addition to writing extensively on the subject of gang violence prevention, serves on the board of Shalom of Oakland: Teaching the Way of Jesus to Young People in East Oakland, http://www.shalomofoakland.com/Harry-Louis-Williams- (accessed February 18, 2013). His books include *Straight Outta East Oakland* (Oakland: Soul Shaker Publishing, 2008) and *No Easy Walk: The Dramatic Journey of African-Americans* (Downers Grove: InterVarsity Press, 1999). Williams is working on a new book, *Straight Outta East Oakland 3: Funk Season*. This latest volume is intended to assist young people in reflecting upon the causes and repercussions of street war.

[44]   David Kinnaman, *You Lost Me: Why Young Christians Are Leaving Church ... and Rethinking Faith* (Grand Rapids: Baker, 2011); see, for example, Chapter 1.

of the need to relocate, reconcile and voluntarily redistribute resources for the sake of rebuilding at-risk communities. In this way, we can move beyond that voluntary association of religious individuals' mentality, where regrettably people's true allegiance is to their own economic well-being which revolves exclusively around their nuclear families.[45]

Beyond the important concerns over vocational training and the like, what is the collective wisdom of our elders in the Christian community at large in the San Francisco Bay Area and beyond? Among other things, they teach us respect and the need to take responsibility and develop appropriate boundaries as it concerns honoring laws that promote the common good. Diverse elders must have the opportunity to come together to share their collective wisdom with the community at large for the common good. Will that opportunity be provided, and will we all come together? Pastors have been father figures. Pastors from diverse backgrounds need to come together to help parent their communities and partner with fellow leaders of diverse ethnicities to model for their communities a spirit of collaboration.

White Euro-American Christian leaders like myself have so much to learn from leaders of other ethnic heritages. For instance, we need the help of the Asian American Christian community. The church at large has so much to learn from our Asian American brothers and sisters. Generally speaking, there is so much respect for elders and such strong family ties in the Asian American church context. Moreover, at times, there have been greater inroads toward reconciliation involving Asian Americans and African Americans based on shared experiences of oppression and because of certain relational instincts in having such strong solidarity in their communities. As a result, Asian American Christian leaders are often well-placed to promote reconciliation between African Americans and white Americans like myself. We need the insights and perspectives of Asian American pastors and other leaders to help build these bridges.

It is also important that Asian American and African American leaders work together with other ethnic groups, since their surrounding communities will engage in violent activity more readily with one another than with whites because of power imbalances in our society. The powers that be will often crack down much more readily when white communities experience violence at the hands of minorities. In addition, minority communities of similar economic status tend to compete with one another over scarce land resources. As with domestic

---

[45]   See John M. Perkins, *With Justice for All*, with a foreword by Chuck Colson (Ventura: Regal Books, 1982), especially the section entitled "The Strategy," which includes chapters 6–18.

violence, those who lash out will often lash out violently toward those closest in proximity. So, learning, understanding and respecting one another will build the community at large, moving us beyond fear and hate to beloved community. Such trust and solidarity will build the social fabric and help decrease violence.

We can lament our lack of unity, or look with prayerful expectation to how God might bring us together in solidarity as a collective force to effect good in support of those most marginalized. Unless we sense our need for one another, we will not come together. We will not come together unless we know that we are dependent on God and one another for our ministry to succeed in society. The challenges we face are just too daunting to go it alone.

We must realize that if we do not make headway, further disunity in the body of Christ leading to spiritual death might occur and in turn lead to bloodshed involving members of warring gangs in these communities. We will not be able to make headway if we do not intentionally seek to share life with those who are different from us. Not only must we sense the need to work together, but also we must sense our need for one another. We need to come together as the church and build family and develop community across ethnic and socio-economic lines if we are to address the problems associated with the dissolution of families and increasing gang activity in our society.

Perhaps the church in San Francisco and Portland, among other places, will take to heart what Randy White, the former Executive Director of InterVarsity's Fresno Institute for Urban Leadership, said of the church situation in Fresno, California. It was only when the church leaders sensed that they could not survive in Fresno without one another that they began working together.[46]

The only way to conquer such social problems as ethnic divisions, isolation and fragmentation is to move beyond objectification, where we no longer see the ethnic other and those of similar groupings in oppositional terms. Instead, we must recognize one another's shared humanity, shared values on key issues, and the necessity of working through our differences toward mutual understanding and solidarity. We can learn a thing or two from Atticus Finch in *To Kill a Mockingbird*: "If you can learn a simple trick ... you'll get along a lot better with

---

[46]   Randy White is currently the Director of the Doctor of Ministry Program for Bakke Graduate University. Previously, he served as the National Coordinator for Urban Projects for InterVarsity Christian Fellowship in the US. Prior to that time, he founded the Fresno Institute for Urban Leadership, where he served as Executive Director. His publications include *Journey to the Center of the City: Making a Difference in an Urban Neighborhood* (Downers Grove: InterVarsity Press, 1996) and *Encounter God in the City: Onramps to Personal and Community Transformation*, with a foreword by Ray Bakke (Downers Grove: InterVarsity Press, 2006).

all kinds of folks. You never really understand a person until you consider things from his point of view ... until you climb into his skin and walk around in it."[47] We can learn even more from Jesus who climbed into our skin and walked around in it for his whole earthly life. Jesus did not engage in drive-by evangelism, but moved next door. As Eugene Peterson puts it, "The Word became flesh and blood, and moved into the neighborhood."[48]

Without exposure to one another and building ties with one another where we move beyond stereotypes and prejudgments and move across the tracks, we cannot become one. Did our earthly fathers raise us to view those of different ethnicities as equals? Did the fathers of our churches parent our churches so that for all our churches' rich and beautiful ethnic textures, they also sought to build bridges with those churches of diverse ethnic backgrounds?

Even the founding fathers of this great nation of ours failed to hold true to this country's grand ideals, including the conviction in the Declaration of Independence "that all men are created equal, that they are endowed by their Creator with certain unalienable Rights, that among these are Life, Liberty and the pursuit of Happiness." These founding fathers permitted the slave trade to flourish; and, even though the slave trade has long been abolished, the impact of the slave block with the blatant disregard and destruction of African American families as husbands/fathers and children were torn from their wives/mothers continues to play a role in African American homes and our society as well.

All too often, we blame the victims of those injustices for the fragmentation of African American homes. The Chinese and Japanese faced huge and grievous challenges as immigrant and minority populations in the nineteenth and twentieth centuries with oppressive working conditions and internment camps in some cases, while others who longed to come here fell victim to exclusion acts. No doubt, the descendents of these Asian immigrants can appreciate something of the horror that African Americans have experienced. What about the rest of us?

Each situation is unique, and so the response to each scenario will be different. Still, we must not repeat past sins by failing to care for families and ethnic communities in need.[49] We must also learn to welcome new immigrant

---

[47]   Harper Lee, *To Kill a Mockingbird* (1960; reprint, New York: HarperCollins, 1988), 33.

[48]   Eugene H. Peterson, *The Message: The Bible in Contemporary Language* (Colorado Springs: NavPress, 2007), 209.

[49]   This runs against the grain of California's history. For while technically a free state that offset the balance of slave to free states in 1850 when California was constituted, California has treated various Asian groups especially poorly, known especially for early lynchings of the Chinese, and also the incarceration of Japanese during World War II, with California hosting most of the prison camps. Yet racial tensions of all kinds and amongst

populations, remembering the old saying: "It takes a village to raise a child." Our churches must come together to parent our youth inside and outside the church, even engaging in civic partnerships in increasing measure. While we should never view our churches as babysitters for our children, nonetheless, our church communities must partner with nuclear families to care for the at-risk children and youth.

The church needs to take its focus on the family to a whole new level to care for families in disrepair and the fatherless. James tells us God calls his people to care for orphans and widows in their distress (James 1:27). The San Francisco Bay Area and other regions are experiencing increasing distress. Will we the church come together across the ethnic spectrum to partner to parent our communities? We need the collective resources, including the wisdom of our elders who have fostered solidarity and social cohesiveness for years so that we can be agents of God's healing embrace for these orphans and widows. In the end, we will all be changed through the process.

Beyond *Crash* to *Gran Torino*

In closing, I would like for us to consider the movie *Gran Torino*[50] as a parable of the kind of work that is needed if we are to move beyond *Crash*. In the movie, a cantankerous and racist Korean War veteran and widower named Walt Kowalski played by Clint Eastwood becomes fast friends with his Hmong neighbors. While at first, he expresses disgust and disregard for them, especially the teenage boy named Thao, Walt eventually warms to them based on their warm regard for him and hospitality. He moves beyond objectifying them to sharing life with them. Over the course of time, he teaches Thao various skills and how to carry himself. Not only does he help Thao land a job, but also he helps him in his dating life. In fact, he even gave Thao the keys to his cherished Gran Torino. This is especially striking given that Thao had once tried to steal the car as a result of a gang initiation rite being forced upon him. That initiation event, which led initially to a collision with Walt, propelled them forward toward becoming exceptionally close.

---

many groups have marked California life. See Kevin Starr, *California: A History* (New York: Random House, 2005), 305–7.

50   *Gran Torino* (Burbank: Warner Brothers, 2008). Directed by San Francisco-born Clint Eastwood, who is also the former mayor of Carmel, California, this film could have just as easily been set in California, which boasts the largest number of Hmongs in the US, instead of Michigan.

The relational collision, along with the care of his parish priest, would eventually save Walt relationally. This Hmong family came to know him better than his children. They did not want his stuff or to put him away in an old folks home, as his children did; rather, they simply wanted to share life with him. Walt in turn saved the Hmong family by laying down his life for them in the face of increasing gang violence. Together Walt, Thao, his sister and the rest of their family moved beyond crashing into one another to touching one another's hearts and lives. The story ends with Thao driving down a road in Walt's Gran Torino, which was left to Thao in Walt's will, as Eastwood's voice is heard singing Gran Torino.

It is a great story. What kind of story would we want written on our lives in San Francisco, Portland, and beyond? One like *Crash* or *Gran Torino*?

PART IV
Is There a Theology of California?

Chapter 10

Is There a Theology of California?

Fred Sanders

In a previous chapter,[1] I argued in favor of a localist approach to the work of systematic theology, and in particular to claim that such a thing was desirable in this particular locale, California. That chapter was an exploration of methodological possibilities, and in order to help expand the borders of what was plausible or at least conceivable in the area of California theology, I chose to engage in one extended case study from a parallel discipline: literary regionalism. The concreteness of literary experience and expression, the range and richness of California writing, was a great help in giving "a local habitation and a name" to the notion of a Californian theological imagination.

Now, while presupposing and (I hope) obeying the methodological constraints I put in place before, I would like to take a further step along that path by actually sketching out the broad outlines of a theological project that is recognizably Californian. And instead of enlisting literary studies as a dialogue partner, this time I would like to begin by engaging the field of philosophy.

The Higher Provincialism as a Golden State of Mind

I do not know who the most important California philosopher may be, but one figure does stand out as being both historically significant and self-consciously Californian: Josiah Royce (1855–1916). Indeed, if we are asking how a thinker can be formed by regional loyalties, Royce is the author of a classic, short work on the subject. His 1902 essay, "Provincialism,"[2] takes up this very question. Royce chooses the word "provincialism" for what we might now call "localism" or even, perhaps, "diversity." He admits that in the essay he uses the

---

[1] "California, Localized Theology, and Theological Localism," Chapter 2 of the present volume.

[2] Josiah Royce, "Provincialism," in *Race Questions, Provincialism, and Other American Problems* (New York: Macmillan, 1908), 55–108. Though the book was not published until 1908, the essay itself was first delivered in 1902.

word provincialism "in a somewhat elastic sense," as referring to "any social
disposition, or custom, or form of speech or of civilization, which is especially
characteristic of a province." He puzzles briefly over whether a province can be
precisely defined, but concludes that as long as a region is less than a nation and
has some sense of cohesion, it deserves the name: "For me, then, a province shall
mean any one part of a national domain, which is, geographically and socially,
sufficiently unified to have a true consciousness of its own unity, to feel a pride
in its own ideals and customs, and to possess a sense of its distinction from other
parts of the country."[3]

Royce was not only one of the most important theorists of this emphasis on
the local, but he was also self-consciously Californian. As early as 1886 he wrote
a history of the first few decades of the state of California,[4] and returned to the
theme several times in shorter writings.[5] The same 1908 volume that featured his
essay on provincialism also contained an interpretation of "The Pacific Coast,"
which Royce noted was "that particular form of provincialism to which I, as a
native Californian, personally owe most."[6]

Seeking greater clarity on the nature of this provincialism which he was
commending, Royce gave a fuller definition of it as:

> an abstract term, to name not only the customs or social tendencies themselves,
> but that fondness for them, that pride in them, which may make the inhabitants
> of a province indisposed to conform to the ways of those who come from
> without, and anxious to follow persistently their own local traditions. Thus the
> word 'provincialism' applies both to the social habits of a given region, and to the
> mental interest which inspires and maintains these habits.[7]

Royce freely admitted that in certain phases of cultural development,
provincialism was a negative impulse. In the Civil War, for instance, sectional
loyalties and divisions needed to be subordinated to national, patriotic, and even
federal unity. But by the opening of the twentieth century, according to Royce,
things had changed. America had by this time a spiritual, indeed a metaphysical,
need to cultivate local goods. "My thesis," he argued, "is that, in the present state

---

3   Royce, "Provincialism," 61.

4   Josiah Royce, *California, from the Conquest in 1846 to the Second Vigilance Committee
in San Francisco: A Study of American Character* (Boston: Houghton Mifflin, 1886).

5   For a discussion of all Royce's historical work, see Earl Pomeroy, "Josiah Royce,
Historian in Quest of Community," *The Pacific Historical Review* 40 (1971), 1–20.

6   Royce, in *Race Questions, Provincialism, and Other American Problems*, vi.

7   Royce, "Provincialism," 58.

of the world's civilization, and of the life of our own country, the time has come to emphasize, with a new meaning and intensity, the positive value, the absolute necessity for our welfare, of a wholesome provincialism, as a saving power to which the world in the near future will need more and more to appeal."[8]

It seemed to Royce that American life had already reached such a state of technological and cultural organization that a great, bland uniformity was beginning to set in. "I should say today that our national unities have grown so vast, our forces of social consolidation have become so paramount, the resulting problems, conflicts, evils, have been so intensified, that we ... must flee in the pursuit of the ideal to a new realm."[9] It worried him that "we tend all over the nation, and, in some degree, even throughout the civilized world, to read the same daily news, to share the same general ideas, to submit to the same overmastering social forces, to live in the same external fashions." This was sure to "discourage individuality," he warned, "and to approach a dead level of harassed mediocrity."[10] A nation the size of America was simply too large for individual action to make any difference, or for actual people to feel a part of. Royce used very evocative language to describe the way this outsized leviathan, too vast to be proportioned to any human scale, threatened human values. "The nation by itself, apart from the influence of the province, is in danger of becoming an incomprehensible monster, in whose presence the individual loses his right, his selfconsciousness, and his dignity. The province must save the individual."[11] He called on his readers to embrace and cultivate a sense of local community in order to stave off the generality of a monolithic national or cosmopolitan culture:

> I hope and believe that you all intend to have your community live its own life, and not the life of any other community, nor yet the life of a mere abstraction called humanity in general. I hope that you are fully aware how provincialism, like monogamy, is an essential basis of true civilization. And it is with this presupposition that I undertake to suggest something toward a definition and defence of the higher provincialism and of its office in civilization.[12]

This "higher provincialism" was difficult for a philosopher to articulate in 1902. It is interesting that another powerful voice was calling for it, more imaginatively, at the same time: G.K. Chesterton's short novel on the subject,

---

8   Royce, "Provincialism," 62.
9   Royce, "Provincialism," 97.
10   Royce, "Provincialism," 74.
11   Royce, "Provincialism," 98.
12   Royce, "Provincialism," 67.

The Napoleon of Notting Hill, was published in 1904. Today we have any number of regionalist or localist writers and public philosophers. Much of Royce's description of the higher provincialism sounds like one of Wendell Berry's southern agrarian manifestoes, as when Berry describes a healthy small town as an extended membership that is "the center of its own attention."[13] Here is Royce on the benefits of life in a backwater town:

> A country district may seem to a stranger unduly crude in its ways; but it does not become wiser in case, under the influence of city newspapers and of summer boarders, it begins to follow city fashions merely for the sake of imitating. Other things being equal, it is better in proportion as it remains selfpossessed—proud of its own traditions, not unwilling indeed to learn, but also quite ready to teach the stranger its own wisdom.[14]

There is even a subterranean Royce influence on some of the great movements of social change in the course of America's twentieth century: Martin Luther King Jr related his civil rights ideals explicitly to the Roycean conception of "the beloved community" of mutually-connected interpreters, a kind of modified cosmopolitanism that is only possible as an expression of the higher provincialism.

More could be said about Royce's musings on the higher provincialism, especially as it bears on the actual history of California's self-awareness as a region. But I invoke him here just to suggest one philosophical angle on the value of a regional sensibility in even the most abstract of intellectual undertakings.

As for an application of such a higher provincialism, or a localization, of theology to the subject of California, that task is perhaps best thought of as somewhere between "A Theology of California" and "Theology from California." Those two phrases would encapsulate the two main emphases of such a project. The former, "Theology of California," indicates bringing theological reflection to bear on this entity which is California, to offer a theological account of its existence and character. The latter, "Theology from California," indicates that we're doing theological reflection about the usual subjects (for example, God, creation, providence, humanity, sin, redemption, church, eschatology, and others) in this particular location, intentionally cultivating resources that are Californian.

---

[13]   http://www.newsoutherner.com/Wendell_Berry_interview.htm (accessed December 15, 2013).

[14]   Royce, "Provincialism," 79.

California Accents in the Traditional *Loci* of Systematic Theology

Systematic theologians work with a standard set of topics, *loci communes*, which follow a traditional dogmatic order set more or less by the logical connections among the doctrines. These *loci* are not the peculiar property of any of the denominations or traditions within Christian theology, but are a shared heritage among all the churches and confessions that take up the task of theology. Particular confessional groups have disagreements among themselves regarding the content of some of these *loci*, but the list and its ordering are relatively uncontroversial. A theological mentality or school of thought, if it has the kind of purchase that actually pervades an entire system rather than merely requiring a special consideration of one of the doctrines, can be expected to show up in all or at least most of the *loci* of systematic theology. In the remainder of this chapter, I would like to assemble a few materials for working out California theology in each of these loci.

The Doctrine of Revelation

The question of how God takes the initiative to make himself known to human creatures is fundamental for any theology. The doctrine of revelation is sometimes subdivided between general revelation and special revelation. General revelation is said to be the way God reveals himself in universally-available structures of creation. California, with its exaggerated consciousness of the natural world, is sometimes inclined to hear the voice of God in nature, but that god who speaks through the landscape and weather of the Pacific Coast is notoriously nonspecific. Such a god is usually simply "the universe," a deity some Californians talk about with a flatness that would make even Spinoza yearn for something more specific. The problem perhaps lies in the very category of "general revelation," which presupposes that whenever created things testify of God, that testimony is to be understood as God's own indirect speech, that is, revelation. Perhaps Christian theology in Californian categories would have incentive to call into question some of the received opinions about general revelation, and permit the emphasis to fall once again on special revelation, God's word in Scripture. Materials for a Californian treatment of special revelation would call on many disciplines, but what would be especially interesting is a history of Bible interpretation in California, including how Scripture has been taken to support or challenge imperialism, Manifest Destiny, and westward expansion.[15]

---

[15]   Working on the doctrine of revelation also includes a number of methodological decisions. On these, see Chapter 2 of this present volume discussing theological localism and

The Doctrine of God

The aspect of the doctrine of God that matters most for a localist project is the idea of naming toward God analogically from experience. All cultures do this, and all cultures tend toward diffuseness and idolatry in doing so. Yet the basic movement of thought is perhaps unobjectionable and certainly unavoidable. Liberal theological method is already fully employed in speaking of a God of California culture, or in "naming toward the transcendent mystery" from this particular place. Such theologies will find the god they seek, as they always have. For Christian theologians who affirm that God can only be known where he has revealed himself authoritatively in Christ through the Scriptures, the whole project of theological localism is admittedly less urgent. But as California continues to develop as a self-conscious regional entity, theologians working here will increasingly speak and write as Californians, with or without self-awareness.

The Doctrine of Creation

Kevin Starr has noted how a certain awareness of the natural world is a constant theme in California intellectual, artistic, and cultural life:

> A streak of nature worship—sometimes mawkish and sentimental, sometimes neopagan in its intensity, and, toward the millennium, frequently Zen-like in its clarity and repose—runs through the imaginative, intellectual, and moral history of California as a fixed reference point of social identity. A society that had consumed nature so wantonly, so ferociously, was, paradoxically, nature's most ardent advocate.[16]

The respect for the natural world sits uneasily with a sense of the human role in shaping and using natural resources. In a state that has manipulated its water supply more impressively and productively than Rome or Holland, a theology of stewardship is crucial. Indeed, the point is that one or more such theologies are already operating unacknowledged. Probably every time the word "paradise" is invoked to describe the place, something eschatological is being conjured. California is usually called a paradise because of its great natural beauty, and its literature and culture are marked by an ecological awareness that runs from

---

the choice between the method of correlation on the one hand and kerygmatic theology on the other.

[16]   Kevin Starr, *California: A History* (New York: Random House, 2005), xiii.

John Muir's early conservationism (which he developed with constant use of religious metaphor, in gorgeous latter day King James English) to the host of recent Buddhist and New Age spiritualities. A theological account of creation developed in Californian terms is an obvious desideratum.

The Doctrine of Providence

The State of California came into being, as part of the US, under the influence of the strange doctrine of Manifest Destiny, as the dream of westward expansion and the vision of an empire "from sea to shining sea" pressed for realization. California's self-understanding has always been involved with a secularized doctrine of providence, and the conviction that God or the gods wanted this very development to happen. That secularized providence is indistinguishable from a latent cultural eschatology, whether developed in terms of "Continent's End" (the title of a Jeffers poem) or an acceleration toward the end of history.

The Doctrine of Anthropology

"What is California man, that thou art mindful of him?" the provincial theologian may ask God. For some observers, the human project seems to be particularly on display and at stake in California. If California is "America, only more so," and America is a focusing and radicalizing of most Western traditions and many Eastern ones, then the proper study of Californian mankind is man. As Josiah Royce pointed out in his "Pacific Coast" essay, a particular mindset is formed in California: "intimacy with nature means a certain change in your relations to your fellowmen. You get a sense of power from these wide views, a habit of personal independence from the contemplation of a world that the eye seems to own."[17] This habit of personal independence is often manifested in an acute self-consciousness that what humans secrete is culture, and that they do it in order to further their purposes. If the modern project can be thought of as a self-fashioning enterprise, then it has entered a self-aware state in California, where selves fashion themselves on purpose to carry out their work. Some philosophers (for instance, Jaspers) have argued that the sort of self-transcendence that generates the urge toward self-fashioning is not in fact a modern trait, but goes back to that global meta-event known as the axial age. If so, the axial age may be thought to be taking a final turn at the leftmost edge of America.

---

[17]   Royce, *Race Questions, Provincialism, and Other American Problems*, 202.

The Doctrine of Sin

Polish-Lithuanian poet Czeslaw Milosz has hinted at a demonology of California, attempting to name the malevolent territorial spirits that have operated here from ages past. We do not need to embrace Milosz's demonology in order to develop a distinctly Californian doctrine of sin. Outsiders viewing California could easily fill in the elements of our hamartiology, and often do so. Joan Didion, without calling it sin, has explored this territory at some length, and has linked it to an equally anonymous notion of salvation. Josiah Royce, in the first truly critical history of California, considered the state to have developed its own unique original sin as a province: seizing political control of the land in an act of violence and sham legitimacy, when ownership and consolidation of the territory was all but inevitable anyway.

The Doctrine of Salvation

Several factors enter into the complex doctrine called soteriology. First there is a vision of the good life, an account of what properly flourishing human life should look like. Then after an account of how it is jeopardized or lost, there must be an account of the cost of its retrieval. For California, this story may take several forms, from the ecological to the political. When considered as a political question, the cost of restoring the good life can be seen in classic fictional discussions of justice like The Oxbow Incident, or in the news stories of Rodney King attempting to stop the Los Angeles riots with the hapless question of cheap atonement: "Can't we all just get along?" California's urban areas have given the clearest proofs since Aeschylus that the furies of a grieved and victimized people must be recognized rather than shrugged aside.

The Doctrine of Church

Has California actually evolved new forms of religious life? Does the old-world parish model of church ministry work here? What was the pattern of missions settlements and frontier settlements? Christianity was brought here with a definite intention for it to exert a civilizing influence; how has it done so? The *Christian* religion has enjoyed less official establishment in California than it has in most other parts of the US, being less integrated into city centers, educational institutions, and public life. What has been the effect?

The Doctrine of Eschatology

In the doctrine of the final things, it is clearer than elsewhere that California has generated disparate and contradictory materials for theological construction. There is on the one hand a paradisiacal vision of final blessing indistinguishable from the boosterism built into California's self-understanding, and on the other hand a persistent dystopianism and sense that this is where everything comes to die. From Robinson Jeffers's vision of "Continent's End"[18] to Nathanael West's apocalyptic mob scenes in *Day of the Locust*,[19] visions from the book of Revelation seem already to have made themselves at home on California's soil.

Theologies of the Californias?

What Royce graspingly called individuality we now know as diversity, and we have more of it than he could have imagined. Our radical diversity makes "a theology of California" pretty ambiguous. Some might say that, whereas Royce thought that America had so much national unity that we needed to cultivate provincialism, the situation a century later is reversed. We may have worn out our unifying structures. But about the benefits of a higher provincialism, an awareness of the blessings of the region, he was surely right. Framing a theology of California presupposes that there is such a thing as a single California, and it may be more reasonable to apply the tools of localism and the strategies of regionalism to the whole range of overlapping, irreducible, and finally diverse Californias: what we seek and find may be theologies of the Californias.

---

[18] "Continent's End," in Robinson Jeffers, *Selected Poems* (New York: Vintage Books, 1964), 4.

[19] Nathanael West, *Miss Lonelyhearts and The Day of the Locust* (New York: Modern Library, 1998).

Chapter 11

Is There a Theology of California?
A Sociologist's Response

Richard Flory

Asking a sociologist to respond to contributions on theological engagements with place—in this case California—is a potentially dangerous invitation. Although I am interested in theology and think that theology is an important endeavor, my own view is somewhere between those of Jeff Tweedy (founder and leader of the rock band Wilco) and theologian Alister McGrath, who have each written about theologians. Tweedy sings, "Theologians, they don't know nothing about my soul,"[1] while McGrath has argued for the importance of "organic theologians," who are deeply connected with their religious communities, not "well-intentioned yet tunnel-visioned students of Richard Hooker or Thomas Aquinas, who know their ideas backwards, yet can neither critique nor apply them."[2] While I will admit that theologians may know something about my, or anyone's soul, theology that is divorced from the life of the religious communities it is intended to serve seems rather like a rudder without a ship.

A further danger lies in the relationship between sociology and religion. From the proto-beginnings of the sociological enterprise, the discipline was intent on supplanting theology and installing itself as the "scientific" moral voice for society. That goal was quickly dropped, and not all of the so-called founding theorists would have agreed with such an attempt. Max Weber comes most immediately to mind, who in his introduction to *The Protestant Ethic and the Spirit of Capitalism*,[3] makes the explicit point that if the reader was looking for moral judgments about religion, they needed to go to the "conventicle," as his task was to provide an explanation of the relationship between religion and the rise of modern capitalism, not to provide a judgment about the relative worth

---

[1]   Jeff Tweedy, Mikael Jorgensen, and Chris Girard, "Theologians," Nonesuch Records, Inc. (2004).

[2]   Alister E. McGrath, *The Future of Christianity* (Oxford: Blackwell, 2002), 153.

[3]   Max Weber, *The Protestant Ethic and the Spirit of Capitalism* (New York: Routledge, 1992).

of different religions. Yet, at least from the early days of the discipline, there were either explicit efforts to undermine religion and its role in society,[4] or those that predicted its demise and the gradual emergence of a religion-less, rationally and scientifically ordered secular society.[5] In the latter, as humans and societies evolved, they would inevitably outgrow the need for religion—and by extension its theological content—leaving it behind as a relic of more primitive times.

Of course, this hasn't happened. Instead, even the casual observer can see that religion hasn't gone anywhere, rather, it is everywhere and it drives the actions— for good and bad—of both individuals and groups the world around. One prominent example is modern Pentecostalism, having emerged as an identifiable movement in the early twentieth century, and now comprising (depending on the source) upwards of 500–600 million adherents (this number would include charismatic Catholics, and all other charismatic Christian groups). One estimate predicts that Pentecostalism will account for 800 million people by the year 2025.[6] What is truly remarkable about this growth is that as recently as 1970, the number of Pentecostal believers was estimated to be only 67 million around the world. Further, the vast majority of this growth is taking place in the global South, usually as those societies are modernizing and becoming enveloped in the global capitalist system. This, then, is the opposite of what secularization theories predicted. Instead, as these societies become more "rational" and "scientific," they are embracing a religious perspective—a theology—that is strikingly non-rational, and experiential.

Thus as a sociologist, I would suggest that my starting point in thinking about theology is somewhat different than that of the other authors in this volume. My "causal" arrow goes from society and culture to theology and the Bible (or other sacred text), and is largely dependent on empirical observations. That is, while I have certain basic theoretical assumptions about how things work in the social world, I take what is often referred to as a "grounded theory"[7] approach,

---

    4   See for example, Christian Smith, *The Secular Revolution: Power, Interests, and Conflict in the Secularization of American Public Life* (Berkeley: University of California Press, 2003).

    5   Perhaps most famously seen in Peter Berger, *The Sacred Canopy* (New York: Doubleday, 1967) and most recently Steve Bruce, *Secularization: In Defence of an Unfashionable Theory* (Oxford: Oxford University Press, 2011).

    6   Todd M. Johnson, "Global Pentecostal Demographics," in *Spirit and Power: The Growth and Global Impact of Pentecostalism*, Donald E. Miller, Kimon H. Sargeant and Richard Flory (eds), (New York: Oxford University Press, 2013), 319–28.

    7   For the classic, founding statement on grounded theory, see Barney G. Glaser and Anselm L. Strauss, *The Discovery of Grounded Theory: Strategies for Qualitative Research* (New Brunswick: AldineTransaction, [1967] 1995).

letting the empirical evidence help direct the theoretical explanations that are developed. At the same time, I work from an interpretive theoretical frame that takes seriously the particular religious practices, institutions, and theologies that religious communities have developed, and that assumes that religious beliefs have real power in the world. Max Weber's famous metaphor for this was the railroad "switchman" who pulled the switch that directed the train from one track to another, so religious ideas act to direct social action onto one or another "track," leading to different sorts of results for societies.

With all of that as preamble, in what follows I want to accomplish three tasks with this short response chapter. First, I want to lay out some empirical groundwork about what religion looks like in California. This is admittedly a very general framing of the state of religion in California, but it will provide some basic understanding of what the religious landscape looks like, and hopefully allow for further questions to be raised about a theological engagement with California. Next, I will engage with what Fred Sanders (Chapter 10) has laid out as some of the possibilities of a project dealing with a theology of California. Finally, I will raise a few questions and issues that I hope can inform the future theological reflection about California culture.

Religion in California

California is a paradox. While it is known as one of the most progressive states in the US, home to the entertainment industry and various innovative technology companies, it has also produced conservative—even reactionary—counter-movements. For example, California's Proposition 13 ignited the property tax revolt of the 1970s and the nativist sentiments of the early 1990s resulted in Proposition 187, which aimed to restrict immigrant access to public resources such as education and health care. And, in 2008, Californians passed Proposition 8, which created a state constitutional amendment that effectively outlawed gay marriage.[8]

---

[8]   Prop 8 was ruled as unconstitutional in 2010, an overturn that was maintained on appeal in 2013 by the US Supreme Court. It is important to note in the context of this volume that the primary religious proponents of Prop 8 were the Catholic Church, the Church of Jesus Christ of Latter Day Saints, and a collection of other conservative religious groups, mostly evangelical and fundamentalist Protestant. In my view this signals the powerful role that religious organizations can still play in public life (whether one likes their positions or not), even in a state that is as avowedly liberal and supposedly secular as California.

This paradoxical identity is mirrored in the religious landscape of the state. Given its reputation as the center for the "secular" pursuits provided by the entertainment and recreational industries, most people might be surprised to know that California has a vigorous religious presence that has actually *increased* over the last 30 years. According to the decennial Religious Congregations and Membership Study (RCMS),[9] there are currently 23,558 religious congregations in the state, which claim a total of 16,765,751 adherents, or 45 percent of the population. Since 1980, the number of religious congregations has grown by 3,416 congregations and 5,874,853 adherents, an increase of religious adherents of approximately 10 percent, from 34.5 to 45 percent. Further, while California lags behind the national numbers of religious adherents (as a percentage of total population) by almost four percent, the national trend in adherents has been declining since 1980. Californians are also busy putting their faith and values to work through faith-based nonprofit organizations. According to the National Center for Charitable Statistics,[10] California has 29,579 "religion-related" nonprofits, accounting for 20 percent of all registered nonprofits in the state.

Yet, likely due to its independent nature, California has much less of a religious establishment than any other state in the West, and less than all other regions of the US. This may be one reason why there is so much religious experimentation in California; more freedom from institutional hierarchies allows for independence and creativity in religious expression and belief. Of course there are more traditional religious expressions in churches, synagogues, temples, and mosques, but these are often independent or minimally associated with some larger religious governing body. Thus, for example, according to the Pew Religious Landscape survey,[11] Californians are more likely to belong to independent "nondenominational evangelical" congregations than any other region of the country. And, despite the number of religious congregations and adherents in California, the Pew survey also shows that as compared to other parts of the US, Californians are less likely to believe in a God who is a personal being, less likely to believe in either heaven or hell as real places, and is generally ahead of the trend of "religious nones," that is, those who have no institutional religious affiliation, having a greater percentage of its population identify as having "no religion in particular."[12]

---

[9]   Available at http://thearda.com/RCMS2010/ (accessed December 14, 2013).

[10] http://nccs.urban.org/index.cfm (accessed December 14, 2013).

[11] http://religions.pewforum.org/ (accessed December 14, 2013).

[12] Bruce Phillips, "Past Meets Present: The Religious Landscape of California," unpublished paper presented at the annual meeting of the Society for the Scientific Study of Religion, November 7–10, 2013, Boston, Massachusetts.

The idea that California is a paradox also extends to how we think about California. From outside of the state, most people think of California as having some sort of unified identity, not unlike the old joke about California and granola (both are full of fruits, nuts, and flakes). But, to anyone who has lived in California for any amount of time, although there is one California, there are many ideas held about California by its residents. First, the sheer size of the state makes any sort of unified identity problematic. People who live in one part of the state often dislike, and seldom visit other parts of the state. Most obviously we see this in the "northern California vs southern California" competition, and in some cases conflict such as over scarce resources like water. But that framing leaves out geographic areas like San Diego, the Central Valley, the "north state" (north of Sacramento), the Eastern Sierras, the Central Coast, and other areas. Each of these has its own perspective on California and the other regions in the state, with some hoping to eliminate some parts of the state, and others pushing for their own secession from the state.[13]

These regional differences show up in religious institutions and expressions as well. According to the RCMS and only looking at four counties (Los Angeles, Orange, Riverside and San Francisco), in each county the trend since 1980 has been toward an increasing number of religious adherents. The RCMS reveals some surprises, most notably that by this measure at least, in each year, LA County has more religious adherents as a percent of its total population than does largely politically conservative Orange County. Thus in 1980 the percentage of religious adherents in Los Angeles County was 39 percent, while in Orange County it was 31 percent. This gap grew significantly by 2010 with religious adherents at 53 percent in Los Angeles County and 35 percent in Orange County.

Another way to understand the relative presence of religion in different regions of California is to look at the number of religious congregations. The RCMS shows that evangelical Protestants by far have the most congregations of any religious group in these four counties. Yet there are some differences between these counties that beg interpretation. For example, as a percentage of all religious congregations in each county, evangelicals make up 47 percent of the congregations in Los Angeles County, 59 percent in Orange County, 65 percent in Riverside County and 38 percent in San Francisco. We see similar kinds of differences between geographic areas in the number of megachurches and the number of religion-related nonprofit organizations. What accounts for

---

[13]   Note the recent effort by a Riverside County politician to organize "South California" and secede from the larger state of California: Jennifer Medina, "California Counties Talk of Cutting Ties to State," *New York Times,* July 12, 2011, http://www.nytimes.com/2011/07/13/us/13secession.html?pagewanted=all&_r=0 (accessed December 14, 2013).

these differences between different regions? One explanation for why some areas have few or no megachurches is the lack of population to support them, but in most areas across the state, there are significant numbers of religion-related nonprofits, which to me indicates some form of religion, and the attendant theologies that drive this kind of activity, that is active in the public sphere.

Theology(ies) of/from California(s)

Where does this leave us, and what relation could all of those numbers possibly have to developing a "theology of California," or indeed whether a theology of California is even possible? This volume includes several initial efforts at bringing theological reflection to different elements of California culture, from Hollywood (of course!), megachurches, the inner city, historic California missions, surfing (naturally), and Silicon Valley, suggesting that theological reflection about California is possible. However, Fred Sanders (Chapter 10) raises what in my view are actually the necessary and important framing questions in terms of how we might think about the relationship between theology and California. First, in his discussion of the relationship between theology and a particular locale, he suggests that "the task is perhaps best thought of as somewhere between 'A Theology of California,' and 'Theology from California.'" Second, in the final paragraph of his chapter, he raises the possibility that owing to the diversity of the state, there need to be "theologies" of California(s).

Thus Sanders has articulated the important point that "theology of" and "theology from" are different although related tasks. Indeed, my reading of the other chapters in this volume is that they are each operating in some way out of the "theology of" California framework. From my perspective there is not much to add about theology of or from, other than that sociologically it makes more sense to think about the "theology from" end of the spectrum. That said, for me, the bigger issue, and more difficult task is to think about what either a "theology of" or "theology from" could look like, given the diversity of *everything* in California.

Thinking about the basic theological categories that Sanders notes (revelation, God, creation, providence, anthropology, sin, salvation, church, and eschatology) in the context of just the religious diversity noted above, let alone the larger diversity that is characteristic of California, makes me think that *theologies of (or from) Californias* (note the multiple plurals) is the only possibility. That is, it seems that any effort to build theology(ies) of/from California(s) needs to allow for a pluralistic approach in order to take into account all of the different understandings of California and Christianity (let alone other religious traditions) that are represented in the state. And although this volume demonstrates some of the diversity within California, it remains remarkably univocal in its basic evangelical Christian perspective, and mono-cultural as represented by its authors (myself included). In the latter, all of the authors except one are white/anglo, and all of the authors except one are male. My point is not to denigrate either the authors or their contributions to this volume. Rather, it is to point out the basic sociological insight that things like race, ethnicity, social class, religious tradition and socialization, and a host of other things, matter in the way that the world is experienced and how one understands how the world "works." I would posit that this extends to the kind of theology that is produced as well.

This then leads me to ask, what might theological engagement with California, even restricting the categories to those noted above from Sanders, look like from, for example, an African American or Latino perspective? What theological dialogue would ensue with more diverse perspectives in conversation with each other? Future efforts to theologically engage with California culture (and I would hope politics, economics, and social structures) need to include a much more diverse set of voices in order to create a more robust discussion about how theological reflection can help us to understand not only California, but also American society more generally, and wherever around the world that California culture has gone.[14]

Finally, I want to consider two forms of diversity that have not been addressed in this volume (with the exception Metzger in Chapter 9), each of which is closely related to different theologies, and that need to be taken into account in any theology, whether of or from California, or anywhere else. Historically, California has been the land of opportunity. The history of the state is full of stories of entrepreneurial people who moved here because of the freedom and opportunity to pursue whatever their dreams were. Many of these people, including many successful religious innovators, failed in their first, second, or even third attempts, but ultimately managed to become successful, largely because of "something" that California afforded them. Yet, according to a recent analysis by University of Southern California sociologist Manuel Pastor,

---

[14]   On a recent trip to London and Paris, I observed the global reach of the surf and skate culture whose origins are in southern California. The juxtaposition of several young men skateboarding on makeshift ramps and jumps in the shadow of the Eiffel Tower was instructive about the global reach of such trends.

California now ranks sixth in the US in income inequality.[15] Where has the opportunity gone, and will it ever return? How might this level of inequality find an adequate response in a theology of or from California?

Second, focusing on opportunity through the lens of race and ethnicity yields a similar result. Pastor shows that across a 20-year timeframe (1989–2009), the African American and Latino populations in California have consistently lagged behind the economic gains of whites and Asian/Pacific Islanders, suggesting that there is something in California that works against advancing economic opportunities of African Americans and Latinos. It is important to add here that we can disaggregate race and class and say that the evidence shows that race matters in determining people's life chances (that is, the actual and potential quality of their lives, the ability to support themselves and their families, and the like), independently from social class. To be completely blunt about it, the entire US socioeconomic system favors whites, and to a certain degree Asian/Pacific Islanders, with African Americans and Latinos generally being shut out or tracked into more subservient roles.[16] As applied to theological reflection, differences based on socioeconomic class and race/ethnicity suggest that the assumptions that theologians bring to their task, based on their differential social positions, will influence the kind of theological reflections they are able to make. Thus, what can a theology of/from California say about these forms of systemic inequality? How can an effort such as exemplified in this volume work to remedy more limited (dare I say privileged?) theological reflection on California culture, politics, economics and social structures? In my view, any theology that ignores or supports this sort of inequality has an insufficient anthropological component, and fails to adequately engage texts and traditions that call for a prophetic role for theology and theologians.

In the end, I think one way to think about California and theology is not to focus on the unique or unusual characteristics of California, or theology of/from here, or to argue for some sort of California theological exceptionalism. Rather, perhaps one goal might be to create a prophetic role within and for the theology that results from this project that is rooted in the experiences and realities of California that then might serve as a model for thinking about theology more broadly. As my USC colleague Manuel Pastor likes to say, "California is America, only sooner." Thus perhaps a theology of/from California(s) can make a contribution to theological discourse that while rooted in the California

---

[15] Manuel Pastor, "Facing the Future: California Trends and Transformations," presentation at the University of Southern California, September 12, 2012.

[16] Brad Christerson, Korie Edwards, and Richard Flory, *Growing Up in America: The Power of Race in the Lives of Teens* (Palo Alto: Stanford University Press, 2010).

experience, transcends that experience. In this, specific theological/religious claims need to be made despite, or better, because of California's diversity, and that are linked to issues related to diversity, inequality, and opportunity.

The potential peril attached to this project is that Jeff Tweedy's words will indeed be proved true, or that theology and theologians remain insulated within the academy with little or no influence on local congregations and communities. The promise however is that greater theological engagement with one of the most important culture generating regions in the world will result in awareness that not only help to further develop more robust and insightful understandings of the human soul, but that are brought to bear in both religious communities and the public square, contributing to a social environment that favors true human development and flourishing.

Chapter 12

Is There a Theology of California? An Historian's Response

Richard Pointer

As the title of my short chapter indicates, I have been asked to respond as an historian to the project or idea of a Theology of California, particularly as Fred Sanders has outlined it. I am happy to do so and in the process, reflect on behalf not only of myself as an historian but the community of historians in general. Though doing the latter is tricky business, my hope is that what I propose here would find general acceptance within my guild. I need to define that guild as somewhat broader than just historians of California since I myself am not one of them. Though I have taught California's history on a number of occasions, I do not consider myself an expert since my own research and writing focuses elsewhere on the North American continent. So I come to this task not as a specialist in California but as a teacher and scholar who has lived and worked in California for the past 20 years.

Perhaps it is fitting to start with where Sanders begins—that is, with Josiah Royce. As his chapter indicates, Royce wrote a history of the early years of the American phase of California's story, dealing with the dramatic events of the 1840s and 1850s. In the midst of that effort in the 1880s, Royce wrote to his friend Henry Oak and pronounced that writing history was a far tougher task than writing philosophy because historians were constrained by empirical facts.[1] Whether Royce would have lumped writing theology in the same camp with writing philosophy, I will let others decide. My point is simply that Royce recognized that historians operate under certain types of constraints different from other disciplines and those naturally affect the way they interact with the past and for that matter, the present as well. Royce himself tested the limits of those constraints in his historical writing, particularly in his repeated bent towards offering moral judgments. That propensity leaves some twenty-first century

---

[1] Ronald A. Wells, "Josiah Royce: Constructing the History of California," *Fides et Historia* 33 (2001), 31.

historians feeling more than a bit queasy, but more about that later. For now, I want to identify more positively a number of ways or places where historians might resonate with a Theology of California project.

Early in Sanders's chapter, he poses the question, how might a thinker be formed by regional loyalties? At its heart, that is an historian's question because it involves contextualizing, and that is what historians do. In this case, I see Sanders at least implicitly asking that question in two ways. Looking backwards, he asks, "how have Californians been shaped in their thinking about everything and anything by their California context?" Looking forward, he asks, "how might Californians and other thinkers use the stuff of California, physical and metaphysical, to shape or develop their thought?" To pursue either of those queries will engage us in fundamentally historical enterprises. Historians will naturally welcome any project that promises such historical engagement.

Historians will also welcome Fred's emphasis on the value of the local or the value of a regional sensibility. Paying attention to the significance of the particular is crucial for good historical work. In following Royce's championing of the value of provincialism, Sanders challenges us to identify anew the distinctiveness of California as province, as place. I think he wants us to mine the particularities of its history, culture, genius, geography, mythology, self-identity and much more so that we can ultimately both describe and contribute to a "Californian theological imagination." Whether there has been or can be such a thing are questions this whole volume seeks to address. For now I simply want to say that Sanders's call for localizing our study, perhaps including our theologizing, rings true as a worthy endeavor for me as an historian. It promises both to enhance our local self-understanding and to reveal important things about even larger entities. In California's case, that might be the American West, the experience of peoples of color, or the US as a whole. Certainly that is what Josiah Royce had in mind for his history of California; after all, its subtitle was "A Study of American Character."

A third way that some, though not all, historians will resonate with Sanders's project has to do with his call for a "Theology *of* California" (my emphasis) which he defines as "bringing theological reflection to bear on this entity which is California, to offer a theological account of its existence and character." By that I take him to mean he wants us to engage in theological analysis, critique, and evaluation of California, including both its lived reality and its life as an idea. Such scrutiny will resonate with the sensibilities of most historians. The historian's task is to say something more about the past than simply what is obvious. It is to point up the hard truths, the ironies, the paradoxes, the contradictions, and the contingencies in the human record. Historians are forever looking for all the help they can get from other disciplines in doing that demanding work. There is no reason to think that theologians could not be of some vital use to us in this endeavor alongside what poets, novelists, visual artists, playwrights, philosophers, sociologists, and many others have already offered. More specifically, theological reflection on California would likely offer some valuable moral reflections upon the state of California, past and present. Some of the best students of California's past have been willing to include moral evaluations in their analyses, including Royce, as mentioned above, and Kevin Starr. For example, in Starr's 1998 article entitled "The Gold Rush and the California Dream," he forthrightly labeled as "sins" the egregious acts of some of that event's participants and made clear that the legacy of "the sins of the fathers" were still with us today.[2] Seasoned historians, in my view, only permit themselves to make such evaluations at the far end of their efforts to understand and explain the complexities of a particular past. The quest to make a moral point can never be the starting place or guiding principle of historical inquiry. Conversely, though, the failure in certain cases to offer some moral insight or reflection at the end of the narrative may also represent a kind of moral failing on the part of the historian, and perhaps especially so for those with serious religious convictions.

One final place of resonance for historians regarding Sanders's proposal is the theological construction work that he names a "Theology *from* California" (my emphasis). He defines that effort as "theological reflection about the usual subjects in this particular location, intentionally cultivating resources that are Californian." One might call it "theology through a California lens." Here historians, or at least Christian historians, will be on board if that work is rooted in very good history. In each of his brief descriptions of the various loci of systematic theology, he alludes quickly to intellectual tendencies or strains of thought and belief that have marked the history of the California mind and imagination. If theologians want to draw on those streams and explicitly label them as "Californian," historians will likely have few objections as long as the theologians have done their historical homework well. One of the challenges, however, that theologians would face in prospecting among the raw material of California history and culture is the fact that for nearly every impulse, trend, or way of thinking that Californians have manifested, one is able to find a countervailing impulse, trend, or way of thinking that complicates any too easy or too quick conclusion that something is quintessentially Californian. So, for

---

[2]   Kevin Starr, "The Gold Rush and the California Dream," *California History* 77 (1998), 60–1, 66–7.

example, I would argue that California is the land of innovation but it is also the land of imitation; in a similar vein, it is plausible to see California as both leader and follower, California as environmental destroyer and environmental protector, California as Eden and East of Eden, and California as the beginning of the continent and the end of the continent. Those sorts of dialectics in the state's ethos and essence can be multiplied many times over. Sanders asserts this very point in relation to the doctrine of eschatology when he writes "California has generated disparate and contradictory materials for theological construction" about final things. With a little spade work, would the theologian find the same thing to be true across the other theological topics as well? That obstacle to a Theology from California is not insurmountable. But it should give theologians pause when they seek to build their work upon the foundation of the California experience.

Such a caveat is a convenient bridge to further reflection on where historians might get nervous or leery about a Theology of California project. One such place involves the cultivation of resources from California that was just described as being at the heart of the Theology from California enterprise. Historians will worry that that approach may foster too shallow searches of California's history for a usable past to serve some theological ends. Quests for a usable past are not inherently dubious; all individuals, communities, and institutions engage in them and they can serve vital purposes, especially in providing stories that help define the identity of peoples and organizations. They become dubious, however, when they deal fast and loose with the historical record, when they ignore more than they reveal, when they condense to the point of reductionism, when they paint the past in stark black and white tones rather than in full color, or when they portray history as a simple morality tale. As historian Tracy McKenzie has recently stated, "we must beware of the temptation to go to the past for ammunition rather than illumination—more determined to prove points than to gain understanding."[3] Conscientious theologians can be trusted not to abuse the past consciously in these types of ways. Their training should help them to resist the temptation to proof text from California's past or present. But historians will nevertheless worry that when looking for resources in California soil to help them build a theology, those same folk may unwittingly do injustices to the past through ignorance or incompleteness. They may still be able to produce what appears to be good theology. But if it is based on bad history, historians will see it more as a loss than a gain.

---

3   Robert Tracy McKenzie, *The First Thanksgiving: What the Real Story Tells Us About Loving God and Learning From History* (Downers Grove: InterVarsity Press, 2013), 16.

A second concern for historians entails something akin to what I alluded to earlier regarding criticisms of Josiah Royce's history of California as overly moralistic. One recent historian, for instance, dismisses Royce's moralizing this way: "He [that is, Royce] lectured the young state of California about its moral shortcomings in the tone of an understanding but disappointed father. The lecture over, Royce returned once more to the study of philosophy."[4] I suspect that some historians will fear that theological analysts of past or current California culture as part of a Theology of California project could commit some similar sins. That is, taking theological stock of the existence and character of California might easily lend itself to moral conclusions that are overly broad or too thinly based on the historical or sociological record. The results would once again be a type of abuse of the past. Naturally not all of the theological work that Sanders has in mind for his Theology of California project would fit into a moral theology category. But some would and at this point historians would want to see special care taken to write with appropriate nuance, balance, and understatement.

Those same qualities should mark efforts to assess the significance and distinctiveness of California. At least I think they should. But in engaging in a project that by design champions the importance and uniqueness of California, we run the risk of inflating both. And that possibility will make historians nervous as well. Royce claimed that the early history of California was of "divinely moral significance."[5] It may be but might not we be able to say the same thing about the early history of any of the other 49 states? If we say no, are we really prepared to make a case for some form of California exceptionalism? At a time when the majority of American historians are finding claims for American exceptionalism decreasingly persuasive, are we confident that a convincing argument can be formulated for some version of California's uniqueness? Intuitively, we may have the sense that comparable volumes to this one will not be discussing a "Theology of Montana" or a "Theology of Arkansas." But claims for California's importance and uniqueness cannot be presented simply as self-evident truths. Instead, they will need to be defended through careful historical and sociological work and presented once again with appropriate nuance, balance, and understatement.

A related concern and one which has no doubt occurred to all of this volume's contributors is which California does Sanders have in mind. If we are going to focus on this province, are we sufficiently confident that we can speak of a single

---

[4]   Malcolm Rohrbough, *Days of Gold: The California Gold Rush and the American Nation* (Berkeley: University of California Press, 1997), 298.

[5]   Ronald A. Wells, "Revising the Sesquicentennial Narrative: The Importance of Josiah Royce's 'California' for Our Time," *California History* 80 (2001), 141.

California? Evidence surrounds us that there are many Californias with their own cultural, economic, demographic, religious, and political identities. Are all of those distinct Californias sufficiently integrated to allow us to conceptualize the whole as a single entity in the twenty-first century? Is there really a California identity? Given its enormous size geographically and demographically, should we be giving more attention to the growing localism and regionalism *within* California rather than treating California as a whole as the *local* or the *province*? In other words, have we chosen the right unit to measure?

Those, then, are some of the concerns as well as some of the appealing dimensions from a historian's perspective of a Theology of California, especially as Fred Sanders has portrayed it. I must confess that as a non-theologian, it has been challenging to get my head around the concept of a Theology of California. The chapters in this volume have certainly shed important light on what it might be and reduced some of my confusion. But enough ambiguity remains for me about the endeavor, even after writing this response that my list of questions continues to be much longer than my supply of answers. Are we asking whether there has been or could be a "California Theology"? I imagine most of my fellow contributors would be quick to say "I'm not sure" or to argue for making that plural given the long history of diversity in the colony and then the state. So we would need to speak of California Theologies. Exploring the *historical* dimensions of that phenomenon seems far more straightforward for this scholar of American religious history. I suppose we might call that endeavor "Theology *in* California." Reading some of the other chapters in this book makes it clear that the TECC Project also wants to pursue what might be labeled a "Theology *for* California." By that I mean work that will be of direct service to the church and Christian activity in California. Crafting such a theology or theologies will naturally fall primarily to the theologians. But they will do well to keep inviting the sociologists, historians, and other students of the Golden State to the table. Finally, I wonder if we might also want to ponder a "Theology *about* California." In the vein of the biblical prophets or Jonathan Edwards, might we want to consider the place of California in the entire history of redemption?[6] We could certainly consider that question historically and investigate how Californians and other Americans have situated California within God's cosmic scheme. Or more modestly, we could follow Kevin Starr's lead and think in terms of California's place within the American dream, a cosmic scheme of its own. But since theologians may be more ambitious and less cautious than us historians,

---

6   I am indebted to my Westmont colleague Telford Work, a theologian, for this suggestion.

why not ask where does this province, to return to Royce, fit within God's salvific work in the world? Has it, does it, or will it have a particular or unique role to play? Do Californians believe that their place holds special theological significance or meaning? Is that an important part of California identity, as old as the Franciscan missions and as young as what brought new immigrants across the California border this morning? Those are big enough questions to keep us occupied well into California's future.

Selected Bibliography

Abrahamson, Eric John. *Building Home: Howard F. Ahmanson and the Politics of the American Dream.* Berkeley: University of California Press, 2013.

Barth, Karl. *Church Dogmatics.* G.W. Bromiley (trans.). London: T&T Clark, 1936–1977.

Bartholomew, Craig G. *Where Mortals Dwell: A Christian View of Place for Today.* Grand Rapids: Baker, 2011.

Bellah, Robert N. *Habits of the Heart: Individualism and Commitment in American Life.* Berkeley: University of California Press, 1985.

Bevans, Stephen B. and Katalina Tahaafe-Williams (eds). *Contextual Theology for the Twenty-First Century.* Eugene, OR.: Wipf and Stock, 2011.

Blumhofer, Edith L. *Restoring the Faith: The Assemblies of God, Pentecostalism, and American Culture.* Champaign, IL.: University of Illinois Press, 1993.

Bollier, David. *The Promise and Peril of Big Data.* Washington, DC: Aspen Institute, 2010.

Bracher, Frederick. "California's Literary Regionalism," *American Quarterly* 7/3 (Autumn 1955), 275–84.

Brands, H.W. *The Age of Gold: The California Gold Rush and the New American Dream.* New York: Doubleday, 2002.

Bretherton, Luke. *Resurrecting Democracy: Faith, Cities and the Politics of the Common Good.* Cambridge, UK: Cambridge University Press, forthcoming.

Brown, Delwin, Sheila Greeve Davaney, and Kathryn Tanner (eds). *Converging on Culture: Theologians in Dialogue with Cultural Analysis and Criticism.* New York: Oxford University Press, 2001.

Calvin, John. *Institutes of the Christian Religion.* John T. McNeill (ed.) and Ford Lewis Battles (trans.). Philadelphia: Westminster Press, 1960.

Carroll, Bret E. "Worlds in Space: American Religious Pluralism in Geographic Perspective." *Journal of the American Academy of Religion* 80/2 (June 2012), 304–64.

Chaves, Mark. *American Religion: Contemporary Trends.* Princeton: Princeton University Press, 2011.

Christerson, Brad, Korie L. Edwards, and Richard Flory. *Growing Up in America: The Power of Race in the Lives of Teens*. Palo Alto: Stanford University Press, 2010.

Chytry, Josef. *Mountain of Paradise: Reflections on the Emergence of Greater California as a World Civilization*. New York: Peter Lang, 2013.

Crouch, Andy. *Culture Making: Recovering Our Creative Calling*. Downers Grove, IL.: InterVarsity Press, 2008.

Davis, Mike. *City of Quartz: Excavating the Future in Los Angeles*. New York: Verso, 1990.

Deverell, William and David Igler (eds). *A Companion to California History*. Malden, MA: Blackwell, 2008.

Didion, Joan. *Slouching Towards Bethlehem*. Reprint, New York: Penguin, 1974.

Didion, Joan. *Where I Was From*. New York: Vintage Books, 2003.

Dochuk, Darren. *From Bible Belt to Sunbelt: Plain-Folk Religion, Grassroots Politics, and the Rise of Evangelical Conservatism*. New York: W. W. Norton, 2010.

Douglass, John Aubrey. *The California Idea and American Higher Education: 1850 to the 1960 Master Plan*. Palo Alto: Stanford University Press, 2000.

Dyrness, William. *Poetic Theology: God and the Poetics of Everyday Life*. Grand Rapids: Eerdmans, 2010.

Eliot, T. S. *Notes Towards the Definition of Culture*. London: Faber, 1948.

Emerson, Michael O. and Christian Smith. *Divided by Faith: Evangelical Religion and the Problem of Race in America*. New York: Oxford University Press, 2000.

Ernst, Eldon G. "Religion in California." *Pacific Theological Review* 19 (Winter 1986), 32–53.

Ernst, Eldon G. "The Emergence of California in American Religious Historiography." *Religion and American Culture* 11/1 (Winter 2001), 31–52.

Ernst, Eldon G. *Without Help or Hindrance: Religious Identity in American Culture*. 2 ed. Lanham, MD: University Press of America, 1987.

Farmer, Jared. *Trees in Paradise: A California History*. New York: W.W. Norton, 2013.

Flory, Richard and Donald E. Miller. *Finding Faith: The Spiritual Quest of the Post-Boomer Generation*. New Brunswick, NJ: Rutgers University Press, 2008.

Ford, Nick and David Brown. *Surfing and Social Theory: Experience, Embodiment and Narrative of the Dream Glide*. New York: Routledge, 2006.

Fradkin, Philip L. *Wallace Stegner and the American West*. Berkeley: University of California Press, 2008.

Ganas, Monica. *Under the Influence: California's Intoxicating Spiritual and Cultural Impact on America*. Grand Rapids: Brazos, 2010.

Garcia, Matthew. *From the Jaws of Victory: The Triumph and Tragedy of Cesar Chavez and the Farm Worker Movement*. Berkeley: University of California Press, 2012.

Gendzel, Glen. "Not Just a Golden State: Three Anglo 'Rushes' in the Making of Southern California, 1880–1920." *Southern California Quarterly* 90/4 (2008–2009), 349–78.

Gill, Robin. *Society Shaped by Theology*. Sociological Theology, vol. 3. Burlington, VT: Ashgate, 2013.

Gill, Robin. *Theology in a Social Context*. Sociological Theology, vol. 1. Burlington, VT: Ashgate, 2012.

Gill, Robin. *Theology Shaped by Society*. Sociological Theology, vol. 2. Burlington, VT: Ashgate, 2012.

Goff, Philip. "Religion and the American West." In *A Companion to the American West*. William Francis Deverell (ed.). Malden, MA: Wiley-Blackwell, 2003.

Gordon, Larry. "Students sample the large shelf of California literature." *Los Angeles Times,* January 1, 2012.

Hackel, Steven W. *Junípero Serra: California's Founding Father*. New York: Hill and Wang, 2013.

Hanson, Victor Davis. "Life with the Vandals." *City Journal*, 22/3 (Summer 2012), http://www.city-journal.org/2012/22_3_diarist-selma-ca-vandalism.html, (accessed December 15, 2013).

Hecht, Richard D. and Vincent F. Biondo, III (eds). *Religion and Culture: Contemporary Practices and Perspectives*. Minneapolis, MN: Fortress Press, 2012.

Holmes, Stephen R. (ed.). *Public Theology in Cultural Engagement*. Milton Keynes, UK: Paternoster, 2008.

Jacobsen, Eric. *The Space Between: A Christian Engagement with the Built Environment*. Grand Rapids; Baker, 2012.

Jeffers, Robinson. *Selected Poems*. New York: Vintage Books, 1964.

Jenson, Robert W. *Essays in Theology of Culture*. Grand Rapids: Eerdmans, 1995.

Kenney, Martin (ed.). *Understanding Silicon Valley: The Anatomy of an Entrepreneurial Region*. Stanford: Stanford University Press, 2000.

Kim, Sebastian. *Theology in the Public Sphere: Public Theology as a Catalyst for Open Debate*. London: SCM, 2011.

Kirk, J. Andrew and Kevin J. Vanhoozer (eds). *To Stake a Claim: Mission and the Western Crisis of Knowledge*. Maryknoll, NY: Orbis, 1999.

Kirkpatrick, David. *The Facebook Effect: The Inside Story of the Company that is Connecting the World*. New York: Simon and Schuster, 2010.

Kotler, Steven. *West of Jesus: Surfing, Science and the Origins of Belief*. New York: Bloomsbury, 2006.

Krattenmaker, Tom. *The Evangelicals You Don't Know: Introducing the Next Generation of Christians*. Lanham, MD: Rowman and Littlefield, 2013.

Lorentzen, Lois Ann, Joaquin Jay Gonzalez, Kevin M. Chun, and Hien Duc Do (eds). *Religion at the Corner of Bliss and Nirvana: Politics, Identity, and Faith in New Migrant Communities*. Durham, NC: Duke University Press, 2009.

Lynch, Gordon. *Understanding Theology and Popular Culture*. Blackwell, 2005.

Maffly-Kipp, Laurie F. *Religion and Society in Frontier California*. Newhaven, CT: Yale University Press, 1994.

Malone, Michael S. *Betting It All: The Entrepreneurs of Technology*. New York: Wiley, 2002.

Malone, Michael S. *The Valley of Heart's Delight: A Silicon Valley Notebook, 1963–2001*. New York: John Wiley & Sons, 2002.

Mathews, Joe and Mark Paul. *California Crackup: How Reform Broke the Golden State and How We Can Fix It*. Berkeley: University of California Press, 2010.

Mayo, Morrow. *Los Angeles*. New York: Alfred A. Knopf, 1933.

McLaughlin, David J. *The California Missions Source Book*. Scottsdale: Pentacle Press, 2012.

McNamara, Kevin R. (ed.). *The Cambridge Companion to the Literature of Los Angeles*. Cambridge, UK: Cambridge University Press, 2010.

McWilliams, Carey. *California: The Great Exception*. Berkeley: University of California Press, 1999.

Metzger, Paul Louis. *Connecting Christ: How to Discuss Jesus in a World of Diverse Paths*. Nashville: Thomas Nelson, 2012.

Metzger, Paul Louis. *New Wine Tastings: Theological Essays of Cultural Engagement*. Eugene, OR: Wipf & Stock, 2011.

Miller, Donald E., Kimon H. Sargeant and Richard Flory (eds). *Spirit and Power: The Growth and Global Impact of Pentecostalism*. New York: Oxford University Press, 2013.

Milosz, Czeslaw. *New and Collected Poems, 1931–2001*. New York: Ecco, 2003.

Milosz, Czeslaw. *The Witness of Poetry: The Charles Eliot Norton Lectures*. Cambridge: Harvard University Press, 1983.

Milosz, Czeslaw. *Visions from San Francisco Bay*. New York: Farrar, Straus, Giroux, 1982

Milosz, Czeslaw. *The Captive Mind*. New York: Penguin Popular Classics, 1953.

Moe-Lobeda, Cynthia D. *Healing a Broken World: Globalization and God*. Minneapolis: Fortress Press, 2002.

Newbigin, Lesslie. *The Gospel in a Pluralist Society*. Grand Rapids: Eerdmans, 1989.

Niehbur, H. Richard. *Christ and Culture*. New York: Harper & Row, 1956.

Osio, Antonio María. *The History of Alta California: A Memoir of Mexican California*. Rose Marie Beebe and Robert M. Senkewicz (trans.). Madison, WI: The University of Wisconsin Press, 1996.

Paddison, Joshua. *American Heathens: Religion, Race, and Reconstruction in California*. Berkeley: University of California Press, 2012.

Perkins, John M. *Let Justice Roll Down*. Ventura, CA: Gospel Light, 2006.

Perkins, John M. *Beyond Charity: The Call to Christian Community Development*. Grand Rapids: Baker, 1993.

Polk, Dora Beale. *The Island of California: A History of the Myth*. Lincoln: University of Nebraska Press, 1995.

Reid, Daniel G. (ed.). *Dictionary of Christianity in America*. Downers Grove: InterVarsity Press, 1990.

Rios, Victor M. *Punished: Policing the Lives of Black and Latino Boys*. New Perspectives in Crime, Deviance, and Law. New York: New York University Press, 2011.

Rogers, Everett M. and Judith K. Larsen. *Silicon Valley Fever: Growth of High-Technology Culture*. New York: Basic Books, 1984.

Rohrbough, Malcolm. *Days of Gold: The California Gold Rush and the American Nation*. Berkeley: University of California Press, 1997.

Roof, Wade Clark and Mark Silk (eds). *Religion and Public Life in the Pacific Region: Fluid Identities*. Lanham, MD: Rowman and Littlefield, 2005.

Roof, Wade Clark. "Pluralism as a Culture: Religion and Civility in Southern California." *The Annals of the American Academy of Political and Social Science* 612 (July 2007), 92–99.

Roth, John K. (ed.). *The Philosophy of Josiah Royce*. New York: Crowell, 1971.

Royce, Josiah. *California, from the Conquest in 1846 to the Second Vigilance Committee in San Francisco: A Study of American Character*. Boston: Houghton Mifflin, 1886.

Royce, Josiah. *Race Questions, Provincialism, and Other American Problems*. New York: Macmillan, 1908.

Sandos, James A. *Converting California: Indians and Franciscans in the Missions*. New Haven, CT: Yale University Press, 2004.

Saxenian, AnnaLee. *The New Argonauts: Regional Advantage in a Global Economy*. Cambridge: Harvard University Press, 2006.

Saxenian, AnnaLee. *Regional Advantage: Culture and Competition in Silicon Valley and Route 128*. Cambridge: Harvard University Press, 1994.

Scharen, Christian B. (ed.). *Explorations in Ecclesiology and Ethnography*. Grand Rapids: Eerdmans, 2012.

Schrag, Peter. *California: America's High-Stakes Experiment*. Berkeley: University of California Press, 2008.

Schrag, Peter. *Paradise Lost: California's Experience, America's Future*. Rev. ed. Berkeley: University of California Press, 2004.

Schultz, Quentin. *Televangelism and American Culture: The Business of Popular Religion*. Grand Rapids: Baker, 1991.

Silver, Marisa. "Oh, California." *New York Times*, March 18, 2013.

Smith, Christian. *The Secular Revolution: Power, Interests, and Conflict in the Secularization of American Public Life*. Berkeley: University of California Press, 2003.

Smith, James K.A. *Desiring the Kingdom: Worship, Worldview, and Cultural Formation*. Grand Rapids: Baker Academic, 2009.

Starr, Kevin. *Golden Gate: The Life and Times of America's Greatest Bridge*. New York: Bloomsbury, 2010.

Starr, Kevin. *California: A History*. New York: Modern Library, 2005.

Starr, Kevin. *Coast of Dreams: California on the Edge, 1990–2003*. New York: Alfred A. Knopf, 2004.

Starr, Kevin. *Americans and the California Dream, 1850–1915*. New York: Oxford University Press, 1973.

Sutton, Matthew Avery. *Aimee Semple McPherson and the Resurrection of Christian America*. Cambridge: Harvard University Press, 2007.

Szasz, Ferenc Morton. *Religion in the Modern American West*. Tucson, AZ: University of Arizona Press, 2000.

Taylor, Bron. *Dark Green Religion: Nature, Spirituality and the Planetary Future*. Berkeley: University of California Press, 2010.

Taylor, Charles. *A Secular Age*. Cambridge: Harvard University Press, 2008.

Tillich, Paul. *Systematic Theology*, vols. 1–3. Chicago: University of Chicago Press, 1951–1963.

Vanhoozer, Kevin J., Charles A. Anderson, and Matthew J. Sleasman (eds). *Everyday Theology: How to Read Cultural Texts and Interpret Trends*. Grand Rapids: Baker, 2007.

Ward, Pete (ed.). *Perspectives on Ecclesiology and Ethnography*. Grand Rapids: Eerdmans, 2012.

Warshaw, Matt. *The History of Surfing*. San Francisco: Chronicle Books, 2010.

Warshaw, Matt. *The Encyclopedia of Surfing*. New York: Harcourt, 2005.

Warshaw, Matt (ed.). *Zero Break: An Illustrated Collection of Surf Writing 1777–2004*. New York: Harcourt Books, 2004.

Webster, John, Kathryn Tanner, and Iain Torrance (eds). *The Oxford Handbook of Systematic Theology*. Oxford: Oxford University Press, 2007.

Wells, Ronald A. "Josiah Royce: Constructing the History of California." *Fides et Historia* 33 (2001), 29–38.

Wells, Ronald A. "Revising the Sesquicentennial Narrative: The Importance of Josiah Royce's 'California' for Our Time." *California History* 80 (2001), 124–41.

Wilford, Justin G. *Sacred Subdivisions: The Postsuburban Transformation of American Evangelicalism*. New York: New York University Press, 2012.

Williams, Harry Louis. *Straight Outta East Oakland*. Oakland, CA: Soul Shaker Publishing, 2008.

Williams, Harry Louis. *No Easy Walk: The Dramatic Journey of African-Americans*. Downers Grove: InterVarsity Press, 1999.

Wuthnow, Robert. *Sharing the Journey: Support Groups and the Quest for a New Community*. New York: The Free Press, 1996.

Index

A Secular Age 145n15, 145; *see also* Taylor, Charles

Abrahamson, Eric John 39n12

achievement 177, 182, 186

Alter, Hobie 141

AMD (Advanced Micro Devices, company) 163, 183

apocalyptic (theology) 47, 92, 227

Apple (company) 85, 99, 163, 185–6; *see also* Steve Jobs

aqueduct 97, 113n2

Aquinas, Thomas 229

architecture 39, 78, 80–81, 91, 97, 178

atemporal 40; *see also* temporal/temporality

Atonement 226

Augustine, St. 12, 58, 72, 145, 146, 147, 151

Babel, the Tower of 184–6

Baker, Bruce (contributor) 2, 5, 16n18, 163

Balthasar, Hans Urs von 5, 132, 133, 135, 136n67

Barth, Karl x, 21, 37, 38n10, 46n27, 114, 119, 147, 171

Bartholomew, Craig 46n27

Bavinck, Herman 148n24

Beach Boys, The 141–2

Begbie, Jeremy S. 54n50

Blumhofer, Edith 101, 102n9–14

Bollier, David 186n53

Bonhoeffer, Dietrich 37

Borgmann, Albert 13

Bracher, Federick 24–8

Brands, H.W. 114n3

Bretherton, Luke xv, 45n26, 63

Brown, Bud 141

Brown, Cedric 197n18

Brown, David 139n1, 148n25, 152n34

Brown, Edmund G. "Pat" 42

Brown, Jerry 52

Brueggemann, Walter 14, 16, 100

Buddha 139n1, 142n7

Buddhist 33, 139n1, 176, 225

California

culture *passim*

literature 1, 3, 19n2, 24–8, 87

Calvin, John 100, 101n5, 148n24, 151–3

Calvinism 12, 140

Calvinist 12, 139–40, 161, 184

Cameron, Kirk 108

Carroll, Bret E. 50n40

Catholic/Roman Catholic 5, 13, 41, 77, 79–80, 84n40, 85n43, 88n51, 92n58, 93, 97, 107, 111, 140n5, 149, 191n6, 201, 205n33, 231n8

Catholicism 76n8

Catholicized 83

charismatic Catholic 230

Cavanaugh, William 131

celebrity 87n47, 90, 105, 110–11

culture 4, 71, 99, 109

evangelist 101, 103

model of church 4, 99–112

Central Valley xv, 96n76, 233

Christ and Culture 12n9

Christianity 45, 49n36, 63n73, 64–5, 82–3, 84n37, 88, 102n10, 105, 124n33, 126, 142, 153,162, 200, 226, 229n2, 235; *see also* Evangelical, Protestant, Catholic

American Christianity 106, 201

consumer Christianity 116

global Christianity 4

Liberal Christianity 203–4n30

pop-Christianity 118
truth claims of 22
Christianity Today (magazine) 108, 35n42,
110, 191, 206
Christology, Christological 38n10, 51n45
Chytry, Josef 2n1, 46n28, 60n66
Cisco (company) 163
community 1, 14, 45, 82, 102, 114, 116,
117n11, 119–20, 124, 127, 130–33,
135, 166, 169, 174–6, 178–9, 181,
189–215, 220n5, 221–2, 239
believing community 108
Christian community 109, 210–11
community development 6, 189,
196n14
covenantal community 170–71, 175,
183, 187; *see also* Covenant
of faith 113, 158
of gathered believers 80
gay community 56
human community 60
of irresponsible strangers 11
(pseudo) community 130
surf community 157
Covenant/covenantal 39, 59, 170, 171,
174–5, 181, 183, 187; *see also*
community
Covolo, Robert S. (contributor) 2, 3, 139
creation (theology) 18, 23, 33, 40, 50,
51n45, 54, 97, 114, 127, 128,
144n11, 146, 148n24, 151, 153–6,
171–3, 222–5, 234
Crouch, Andy 85
Crystal Cathedral 52, 80, 107

Dale, Dick 141
death 15, 27–8, 37, 56, 58, 64n76, 71, 86,
89n54, 91, 94, 113, 114n2, 119,
155, 182n43, 204n32, 212
Derrida, Jacques 56–7
Deverell, William 1, 50n42
Didion, Joan 4, 9, 10, 18, 32, 35, 52, 53,
67, 226
Disney, Walt 60, 185
Disneyland 60, 66, 85, 107

Dochuk, Darren 58n60, 103n15
doctrine 21, 32–3, 37, 53, 92, 148, 151, 223–7
of creation 148n24, 224–5
of revelation 223
of sin 226
Douglass, John Aubrey 41n17, 42n19
Dyrness, William 148n25, 151
dystopia 227

Eastwood, Clint 214–5
education 95, 105, 175, 180, 192–6, 202,
226, 231
higher 15n15, 40–42, 62, 64, 66, 95, 105
of native Californians/Indians 85–6,
88, 93–4
religious 93–4, 118
Eliot, T.S. 29, 48–9, 55–6
Emerson, Michael 192n9
entertainment 14, 52, 57, 58, 60, 99, 105,
126, 231–2
entrepreneur, entrepreneurial 2, 113,
163–87, 235
entrepreneurialism 103
entrepreneurship 171–2, 176, 182
eschatology (theology) 23, 45n26, 47n31,
222, 227, 234, 242
cultural eschatology 33, 225
eternal/eternity 14, 36n6, 47, 99, 131,
134–5, 145–6
work of Christ 101
Evangelical/Evangelicalism 3–5, 15, 46n27,
48, 58n60, 59n64, 62n68, 80,
82, 85n42, 99–103, 105–9, 111,
115n6, 116–17, 129, 132, 134, 140,
192n9, 200–203, 231, 233, 235
"nondenominational evangelical" 232
postdenominational (PDE) 119–21,
123, 125, 128, 129, 130
evangélicos 92
Evangelical Theological Society 2
evangelism/evangelist/evangelistic/
evangelize 6, 63, 90, 93, 97n77, 101,
103, 105, 117, 120, 124, 125n35,
129, 139, 161, 163, 183, 189, 196
drive-by 189–215

Facebook (company) 116, 125n37, 186
Farmer, Jared 66n80
Farlow, Matthew (contributor) 2, 5, 113
farming 97, 166
film, filming 14, 17, 60, 76, 85, 88, 104,
    108, 111–12, 144, 149, 209n41
    Bottle Shock 96
    Citizen Kane 86
    Crash 190n3
    industry 16
    Gran Torino 214n50
    The Mission 83
    The Passion of the Christ 108
    producer 141
    technology 58
Finney, Charles 109–10
Flory, Richard (contributor) 2, 6, 47n30,
    65, 115n5, 116, 117, 118n14–17,
    120, 123n28, 126n39, 130n51,
    134n62, 229, 230n6, 236n16
Ford, Nick 139n1, 148n25, 152n34
Foucault, Michel 56
Fradkin, Philip L. 19n1
Frost, Robert 25

Ganas, Monica (contributor) 2, 4, 13–18, 99
Gendzel, Glen 104n22
geography 51, 114n3, 131n54, 166, 240
Gibson, Mel 108, 112
Gill, Robin 38n11
global 2, 4, 10n3, 15, 65n78, 82, 97n77,
    131, 194, 163n2, 167, 225, 235n14
    markets 181
    South 230
    capitalist system 230
globalize/globalization 82, 203n30
Gold Rush, 11–12, 15–16, 53n49, 63,
    104n22, 114n3, 241, 243n4
Golden Gate Bridge 78
Golden Gate International Exposition of
    1939 86
Golden State *see* California
Google (company) 163, 176
    Googleplex 176
Gordon, Larry 19n2

Gordon, Lyndall 55, 56n52
government 15n15, 73, 75–6, 83, 94n68,
    189n2, 191n6, 204
Grenz, Stanley J. xii, 46n27, 59n64, 65, 127

Hackel, Steven W. 75n6, 79n18, 88n49
Hauerwas, Stanley 36, 40n15, 42n18
heaven/heavenly 11–12, 14, 45, 58, 61–2,
    101–2, 120, 131, 146, 206, 209, 232
hedonism 141, 153, 207
hell 11–12, 14, 139, 232
Hewlett-Packard (company) 163, 167–8
    Hewlett, William and David Packard
    164n3, 167, 178–9, 185
Higher Proventialism 6, 62, 219–22, 227
hippies 61
Holmes, Steven R. 45n26, 50, 51n44,
    58n61–62, 59n64
homosexual 61
Hooker, Richard 229

imago Dei 50, 65n79, 127, 168–9, 171–4,
    181, 186–7
individualism 66, 103, 127, 199
Institutes of the Christian Religion 101n5,
    151; *see also* Calvin, John
Intel (company) 163, 176–9, 185
interpreter 48, 222
interpretation 65n79, 101n5, 140n5, 170,
    220, 233
    Bible 223
    cultural 177
    theological 164, 169

Jackson, Jesse 106
Jacobsen, Eric O. 50n41
Jackson, Helen Hunt 87
Jeffers, Robinson 11n5, 25, 32–3, 225, 227
Jefferson, Thomas 103
Jesus 4, 5, 33, 38, 39, 43, 45–6, 51, 53n48,
    58, 62–4, 66, 80, 89, 91, 92, 93n65,
    101, 103, 105, 106, 107, 110, 111,
    113–15, 119–24, 126–36, 130,
    136, 142, 150, 154, 157–9, 161,
    164, 191n5, 195, 210n43, 213, 224

body of 85n43, 130–131, 135, 190, 199, 206, 212
as a celebrity figure 110
as image 110
Jesus Christ Superstar 110
Jesus Movement 85n42
people 142
as word 110
words of 124
work of 101, 111
Jesus Christ of Latter Day Saints, Church of 231n8
Jobs, Steve 164n3, 185–6
Johnson, Todd M. 230n6
judgment (theology) 61, 100, 102, 106, 155, 160, 184,
moral judgments 229, 239
justice, injustice 10n4, 14, 40, 57, 59, 60n6, 151, 173n19, 191n6 198n19, 200n23, 201, 204n31, 209n41, 211n45, 213, 226, 242

Kant, Immanuel
post-Kantian 160, 161
Katin, Walter 141
Kenney, Martin 163n2, 180n39, 181n41, 182n44
Kim, Sebastian 47n29
King, Martin Luther, Jr 111, 190, 222
Kirkpatrick, David 186n53
Knoll, Greg 141
Kotler, Steven 150–51, 153
Krattenmaker, Tom 201, 202n27
Krötke, Wolf 171
Kuyper, Abraham xi, 18
Kuyperian 12; *see also* Calvin, John

Lindbeck, George 153
literature 10, 23–4, 33, 72, 83, 86, 161
about the missions 86
California 1, 19n2, 24–8, 36, 87, 224
sociological literature on spirituality 130

localism 6, 19–20, 22–3, 33, 103, 153, 219, 223, 240, 243–4
Los Angeles 26, 49n39, 58, 76, 78n15, 79, 80, 102–5, 113n2, 205, 206n36
Luther, Martin 100, 101n5, 128

Mclaughlin, David J. 73n3, 74n4, 75n5, 79n15, 81n27, 82n29, 83n36, 96n74
Malone, Michael S. 164n3, 167n10, 168n12, 177, 178, 183n39
martyr, martyrdom, martyriological 48, 134n65; *see also* Vanhoozer, Kevin
Maslow, Abraham 148, 149n25
Mayo, Morrow 104
megachurch 5, 80, 113–20, 123–6, 128, 130, 134, 136, 200, 233–4; *see also* Saddleback Community Church
Metzger, Paul Louis (contributor) 2, 5, 128n42, 189, 201n24–26, 235
Microsoft (company) 99
Miller, Donald E. 115n5, 116–17, 118n14–17, 120, 123n28, 126n39, 130n51, 134n62, 230n6
Milosz, Czeslaw 3, 28–32, 226
mission, missions 62n69, 71–98, 102, 119, 125n35, 131–2, 134–5, 166, 174, 178, 226
California 4, 71–98, 234
Christian 66
of the church, church's xiv, 53–4, 121
corporate 177
of Facebook 186
Franciscan 4, 71–98, 245
Spanish 71–98
missional 47n31, 71–2, 174, 200
missionary, missionaries 4, 48, 139–40, 183, 187
Calvinist 161
missiology, missiological, missiologist 2, 4, 14, 71, 84, 91, 92, 97
of California 74, 76, 80, 97, 98
Moe-Lobeda, Cynthia 203
Mouw, Richard (contributor) 2–3, 9, 12

movies *see* film, filming
Muir, John 33, 225
music, musician, musicology 23, 36n6, 54, 58, 85, 124, 147n23, 168
    MTV Music Award 109
    musical style 126
    surf music 141
myth 3, 27, 32, 60, 63, 66–7, 88, 140, 149, 155, 160, 182, 240

narcissism 153
New Age 33, 225
Newbigin, Lesslie 64, 194
novel, novelist 26–7, 42, 87, 221, 241
Noyce, Robert N. 167, 175–9

O'Neil, Jack 141
Osio, Antonio Maria 84n38, 87n46

Pannenberg, Wolfhart 43n22
Passion of the Christ, The 108
Pastor, Manuel 235–6
Pentecostal, Pentecostalism 31, 61, 101–2, 230
Perkins, John M. 10n4, 60n65, 198n14, 200n23, 210, 211n45
Phelps, Edmund 173
poem, poetry 11n5, 28–9, 32–3. 81, 168, 187n54, 225, 227n18
poet, poetic, poetically 3, 27, 29–32, 35, 55, 65, 86, 147–8, 149n25, 151–2, 175, 226, 241
Pointer, Richard (contributor) 2, 6, 65, 239
politics 15n15, 39, 45n36, 58n60, 72, 78, 101, 103, 140, 180, 203, 235–6
    politician 18, 35, 52, 63, 65
    political 19, 37–8, 46–7, 49, 75, 109, 140, 192, 195–6, 197, 201–2, 223, 244
    California 26, 28, 60, 87, 143
Polk, Dora Beale 66n80
pornography 58, 59n63
Postdenominational Evangelical (PDE) 120–30; *see also* Evangelical/ Evangelicalism, postdenominational

prison/prisons 10n4, 52, 59–60
    camps 10n4, 213n49
Protestant/Protestantism 140n5, 191, 201
    conservative Protestantism 104
    dissenting Protestantism 175–6
    evangelical Protestant 80, 202n27, 231, 233
    fundamentalist Protestant 231
    Protestant Calvinists 184
    Protestant Evangelicalism 58n60
    Protestant model of work 145
    Protestant Reformation 95
    The Protestant Ethic and the Spirit of Capitalism 184n48, 229
providence (theology) 23, 32–3, 155, 157n43, 222, 225, 234

reconciliation (theology) 66, 115, 122, 133, 135–6
redemption (theology) 6, 23, 66, 133, 184, 222, 244
religion/s 6, 14, 17–18, 31, 41, 42, 44, 47n30, 52, 57, 58n60, 62, 65, 78, 84, 101–5, 116, 129, 140, 148n25, 149–51, 153n36, 192n9, 198n19, 201, 202n27, 205n33, 226, 229–34; *see also* secular/secularism
    Eastern 142
    history of 159
    sociology of 43n21
Revelation (Book of the Bible) 15, 92, 227
Revelation (theology) 23, 37, 39, 45, 47, 51, 115, 123, 135, 153, 160, 164, 223, 234
Rios, Victor M. 60n65
Rogers, Everett M. 164n3, 167n9, 168, 180n38, 182, 183n46
Rorty, Richard 57
Royce, Josiah 6, 9, 11–12, 16, 24, 53n49, 62–3, 219–22, 225–7, 239–41, 243–4

Sabbath 146
Saddleback Community Church 5, 80, 114–22, 125–6, 129–32, 134n63

San Francisco 2, 6, 11n6, 25–6, 29,
    30n37–8, 32, 41, 57, 74–8,
    91,189–90, 192, 194, 198, 207,
    230, 215, 220n4, 249
  Bay Area 5, 32, 204, 211, 212
  earthquake 102
  San Francisco Chronicle 209n41
  Theological Seminary 37
Sanders, Fred (contributor) 2–3, 6, 19, 36,
    46n27, 62, 65, 219, 231, 234–5,
    239–44
Sandos, James A 76n9, 78n17, 79n18,
    82n30–31, 85n43, 92n59–60,
    92n63, 93n64–6, 94n68–72,
    96n73, 97, 98n78
Saxenian, AnnaLee 163n2, 166n7, 168n14,
    174n32, 178n31–2, 179, 180n37
Schuller, Robert 106, 107
Schultz, Quentin 105
Scripture/Scriptures/Holy Scriptures 33,
    38–9, 47, 53, 59, 61, 65, 100, 102,
    105, 119–20, 137n24, 150n30,
    151, 153–5, 159, 161, 168, 201,
    202, 223–4
secular/secularism/secularization 36, 42n19,
    64, 78, 79n19, 83, 85, 88, 94n68,
    103, 120n22, 145n15, 149, 153,
    164, 226, 225, 230, 231n8, 232
secularized doctrine of providence 32–3
sex/sexual/sexuality 56, 58–9, 66, 76, 140
Sexton, Jason S. (contributor) 1–2, 4, 35,
    59n64, 65n79
Shaw, David 107
Silicon Valley 5, 13, 80, 163–87, 234
Sin (theology) 23, 32, 58, 66, 92, 101n6,
    106, 128, 181, 187, 226, 234
Smith, Christian 192n9, 230n4
Smith, James K. A. 16n18
Smith, Ted A. 109, 110n46–7
sociology 23, 51, 140n5, 152n34, 229
Spirit, Holy Spirit 45, 47, 51, 66, 113,
    115, 120, 122, 125, 127, 129,
    133–5, 144n11, 151–2, 154, 164,
    167n11, 168–9; *see also* Pentecostal,
    Pentecostalism

spirit, spirits 31, 41, 76n8, 143, 155, 164,
    178, 182, 230n6
  of California 26
  of Capitalism 140n5, 184n48, 229:
    see also Weber, Max
  of collaboration 211
  entrepreneurial 173, 179, 182–3
  human 186
  of innovation, innovative 163, 172–4,
    181n41, 182, 187
  of the people of San Francisco 91
  pioneer 114
  of a place 25
  of Silicon Valley 5, 164, 168–9, 171,
    173, 175, 181, 183–4, 186; *see also*
    Silicon Valley
  territorial 28–9, 32, 226
spiritual 11, 13, 14n13, 17, 23, 29, 31,
    47, 92–3, 96n73, 99n1, 100, 102,
    107, 111, 118, 122, 126, 131, 142,
    149–50, 152, 163, 171, 176–7, 181,
    183–5, 187, 207–8, 212, 220
spirituality 33, 104, 106, 130, 142, 149,
    149n26, 171, 173–4, 184, 198n19,
    225 *see also* Buddhist, New Age
sport 17, 39, 52, 109, 140n3, 151, 152,
    156
Starr, Kevin 11n5, 37n9, 42n19, 53n49,
    57n58, 62n69–70, 78n16, 81n23,
    163n1, 174, 180n40, 214n49, 224,
    241n2, 244
Stegner, Wallace 19 236
Steinbeck, John 25–7
Stringfellow, William 15
subculture 154, 161
  Christian subculture 115
Sun Microsystems (company) 163
surf/surfing 139–62, 180, 234, 235n14
  culture 5, 13, 139–62
surfer 71, 139–62
Sutton, Matthew Avery 58n60, 101n8,
    103n19, 104

Taylor, Bron 142n7, 149
Taylor, Charles 24, 145n15, 149–50

TECC (Theological Engagement with
California's Culture) Project 2–6,
10n3, 32, 37, 42n19, 82n32, 244
technology 39, 52, 60, 80, 82, 100, 104,
163–7, 169, 174, 176n27, 180–81,
183–4, 231
filming 58
Spanish 84
temporal/temporality 17, 40, 54n50, 78,
131, 145–7
Tillich, Paul 20–22, 46n27
Torrance, Iain 44n23
Torrance, Thomas F. 61
Trinitarian 119, 127n42, 170, 201n26
Trinity 148n24, 201n26

Universal Studios 104
utopia 56, 97

Vanhoozer, Kevin 46n27, 47, 48n33, 49,
66, 154

Ward, Graham 147n23
Ward, Pete 165n6
Warren, Rick 117, 123, 125–9, 133–4
Warshaw, Matt 139n2, 140, 145n13, 147n20

Waters, Alice 10n3
Weber, Max 140n5, 149n27, 184n48, 229,
231
Webster, John B. 21n6, 44n23, 171n18
Wilde, Oscar 57
Wilford, Justin G. 115n6, 117–8,
119n19–20, 120–21, 123, 124n31,
125n34, 128–32, 134
Williams, Harry Louis 210n43
Williams, Jack S. 92n57
Williams, Jane 51
Williams, Jeri 200n23
Williams, Rowan 132, 195n13
Wilson, Edmund 27, 28n25
wisdom 25, 44, 62, 139, 151, 164–5,
183–4, 210–11, 214, 222
Christian wisdom 48
God's wisdom 43, 157
wisdom of the Creator 156
Wolfe, Tom 175–6, 178n29, 179
Wuthnow, Robert 199n20

Yeh, Allen (contributor) 2, 4, 71

Zuckerberg, Mark 186; *see also*
Facebook